The Industrial Revolution

THE INDUSTRIAL REVOLUTION

Key Themes and Documents

James S. Olson with Shannon L. Kenny

Unlocking American History

Santa Barbara, California • Denver, Colorado • Oxford, England

Library of Congress Cataloging-in-Publication Data

Olson, James Stuart, 1946–
 The industrial revolution: key themes and documents / James S. Olson with Shannon L. Kenny.
  pages cm
 "Unlocking American history."
 Includes bibliographical references and index.
 ISBN 978-1-61069-975-4 (hard copy : alk. paper) —
ISBN 978-1-61069-976-1 (ebook) 1. Industrial revolution—United States.
2. Industries—United States—History. 3. Industrialization—United
States. 4. Technological innovations—Social aspects—
United States—History. I. Kenny, Shannon L. II. Title.
 HC105.O452 2015
 330.9'0340973—dc23   2014026577

ISBN: 978-1-61069-975-4
EISBN: 978-1-61069-976-1

19 18 17 16 15   1 2 3 4 5

This book is also available on the World Wide Web as an eBook.
Visit www.abc-clio.com for details.

ABC-CLIO, LLC
130 Cremona Drive, P.O. Box 1911
Santa Barbara, California 93116-1911

This book is printed on acid-free paper ∞

Manufactured in the United States of America

CONTENTS

PREFACE

This book presents the story of how and why the Industrial Revolution occurred from the mid-eighteenth century to the early twentieth century in the United States through the lens of the most prevalent themes fueling the watershed developments of the era. In the mid-eighteenth century, 98 percent of the people of the world lived in rural settings and functioned in subsistence economies. Geographic horizons were limited because poor transportation systems impeded efficient travel. Most people were born, lived, and died in confined locales. Society revolved around extended families, the cycles of the moon, and the seasons of the year, and except for a tiny urban minority, people's lives did not differ dramatically from those of ancestors who had lived centuries, or even millennia, before. But the Industrial Revolution changed everything. Rural villages gave way to cities, and home production gave way to factories. The subsistence economy gradually became commercial, barter was replaced by money, and local markets merged into national and international markets. Extended families disintegrated into nuclear families, political and economic institutions of every variety grew larger, and social life became more impersonal. Economic competition intensified, and geometric increases in industrial and agricultural production created unprecedented economic growth and prosperity. Power flowed to the industrializing countries because they could afford to invest large volumes of resources into the military. The industrialized nations eventually dominated global politics and set the course of world affairs.

The content of this book was designed for an advanced high school and beginning undergraduate readership. It will support teachers and students in Advanced Placement U.S. History courses as well as being a valuable supplement to any Common Core history curriculum related to the Industrial Revolution. In particular, the book's organizational themes have been carefully selected to align with primary- and secondary-source material, with a view to stimulating analysis and understanding of historical events and figures in connection to the macro change occurring during this relatively short period. The Advanced Placement curriculum framework for the period which encompasses the Industrial Revolution (Period 6: 1865–1898) centers on key concepts such as the rise of big business, technological change, internal mass migration and urbanization, and popular movements as well as government led initiatives to reshape U.S. economic policies. The A to Z encyclopedic entries in this book provide the requisite background information for students to become fluent in thinking and writing about these concepts. Finally, the AP Exam and the Common Core Standards for History and Social Studies for grades 11–12 focus on the incorporation of primary sources into analysis and presentation of course content along thematic lines.

How to Use This Book

The Industrial Revolution is designed to provide students a ready reference for studying the course and impact of the Industrial Revolution in the United States. Although imposing chronological and thematic parameters on an event of such magnitude and such diverse ramifications is impossible, we have focused generally on the period from the 1750s to the 1920s and categorized the volume's entries according to ten conceptual thematic categories: Agriculture and Food Industry, Business and Finance, Economics, Environment and Natural Resources, Industrialism, Labor, Politics, Social Change, Technology, and Transportation. The Introduction provides a summary of the history of the Industrial Revolution in the United States during the late nineteenth century and an analysis of how changes in the American economy affected society and politics in general. The body of the book consists of alphabetically arranged entries on important individuals, events, technologies, ideas, and movements. Cross-references to other entries are indicated by boldface type. The book also includes a chronology of significant events, a range of primary-source documents from the era, a sample Document-Based Essay Question (DBQ) similar to those found on the Advanced Placement (AP) U.S. History Exam, together with a list of top tips for successfully answering DBQs, and a bibliography of suggested further readings. Additionally, provided in the appendix of the book is a list of specific learning objectives students can use to gauge their working knowledge and understanding of the period. These objectives are similar to the thematic learning objectives presented in the AP U.S. History curriculum framework.

KEY THEMES

Agriculture and Food Industry—Throughout the nineteenth century, new technologies in agriculture dramatically increased productivity, but in the process, many small farmers found it increasingly difficult to compete, just as small manufacturers could not compete with big business. By the 1880s, overproduction washed away farmers' income and expenses escalated. Railroads charged more to haul crops, and grain elevators held farmers hostage. Buying land, seed, and equipment meant borrowing at exorbitant interest rates.

Business and Finance—Entrepreneurs produced more and more goods for sale in ever-expanding markets, while smaller enterprises disappeared, swallowed up in the corporate feeding frenzies of the late 1800s. Small companies gave way to big companies, and big companies to still bigger ones. Some businessmen aimed at nothing less than the domination of an industry and succeeded beyond their imagination.

Economics—Throughout the nineteenth century, developments in the management and distribution of capital in the areas of banking, currency exchange, and a series of new legislation and Supreme Court decisions came to form the basis of our national economy as it exists today.

Environment and Natural Resources—Exploitation of the country's huge deposits of natural resources, such as iron ore and coal, and the ability to move large volumes of these commodities very efficiently by railroad or Great Lakes barges, fuelled the Industrial Revolution. Exploitation of natural resources also began to have a negative effect on the natural environment.

Industrialism—In the United States, the first factories began appearing in the 1790s and early 1800s in the New England textile industry. Factory conditions soon appeared in anthracite and bituminous coal mines, iron foundries, meat-packing plants, smelters, and textile industries. The dark side of industrialism inspired a cadre of intellectuals to dispute laissez-faire doctrine.

Labor—The Industrial Revolution changed forever the relationship between employers and workers. In the preindustrial economy, workers usually enjoyed highly personal relationships with their employers. The Industrial Revolution changed all that. Since labor was a key component of business overhead, employers had little compunction about cutting wages and many workers could easily find themselves facing untenable economic situations, with wages falling and prices rising. Many workers felt that their only recourse was to organize into labor unions and bargain collectively with employers.

 Politics—An activist federal government had its origins in the post–Civil War era when discontent with the downside of the Industrial Revolution—the wide income gap between the rich and the poor; low pay, long hours, and unsafe factories for workers; and increasing environmental problems—increased. Out of such discontent emerged the Populist movement of the 1890s and the Progressive movement of the first two decades of the 1900s.

 Social Change—The old rural, agricultural economy gave way to an economy of factories and mass production and a society in which most people lived in larger towns and cities. The Industrial Revolution also produced a large, visible working class and a new upper class of fabulously wealthy individuals. A new generation of social workers insisted that something needed to be done to improve the lives of America's most vulnerable citizens—the poor, immigrants, working women, and children.

 Technology—Because of new technologies and new sources of power, factory and agricultural productivity grew by leaps and bounds during the nineteenth century.

 Transportation—The Industrial Revolution could not have occurred without rapidly expanding markets. A transportation infrastructure had to be developed to allow the economy to expand beyond the limits of rivers and deep-water ports. In the 1820s, the so-called canal era emerged in the United States. Railroad construction, which began in the late 1820s, accelerated in the 1840s, and exploded in the 1850s, gradually linked the North and East into a huge single market.

INTRODUCTION

This section presents an overview of the Industrial Revolution in the United States from the mid-eighteenth century to the 1920s according to the most central historical topics of inquiry from the era as follows: economic change, immigration and population growth, transportation, the growth of the economy as a national market developed, how mass production and technology affected workers and the workplace, how corporate consolidation led to the rise of big business, how immigration and migration led to urbanization and the social and economic change that came with it as more people moved to cities, labor and labor unions, the influence of corporations on national politics, and the emergence of a reform movement. We have designed this section thematically in order to contextualize the volume's entries against the backdrop of these overarching themes in particular because this is how students will be expected to demonstrate their understanding of the material they have learned in Advanced Placement and Common Core courses.

The Industrial Revolution

By the late 1700s in England and the early 1800s the United States and much of Western Europe experienced a radical change in the way people lived their lives, resulting from the technological innovations and new methods of producing goods that gave rise to the Industrial Revolution and equally pivotal shifts in the organization of the economy and human society. The Industrial Revolution altered every aspect of American life, precipitating the rise of big business, depopulating the countryside, stimulating development of the labor movement, and giving rise to big government.

Economic Change

The Industrial Revolution was precipitated by several developments necessary for the scale of economic revolution that took place. First, the Industrial Revolution needed an elite group of successful merchant capitalists to launch and direct it. In the major cities of Europe and the United States the age of exploration had produced a class of highly successful global merchants who had developed the financial resources that funded the Industrial Revolution. In turn, the expansion of the economy over the next century resulted in the rise of the middle class and an increase in income and standard of living that revolutionized the structure of American society. Throughout the nineteenth century, developments in the management and distribution of this capital in the form of contract law, banking, currency exchange, and a series of legislation and Supreme Court decisions came to form the basis of our national economy as it exists today.

Immigration and Population Growth

After centuries of a nearly stagnant growth rate, during the mid-eighteenth century, the world's population grew by around 57 percent, and by the early twentieth century, the world's population had doubled in size from the onset of the Industrial Revolution 100 years before, a growth that was highly concentrated in the United States and Europe. This rapid population growth provided the workers and the consumers upon whom the Industrial Revolution depended. Death rates declined because widespread adoption of the potato as a staple crop improved the diets of poor people, the invention and use of the smallpox vaccine gradually reduced deaths from epidemic disease, Europe did not experience a major war during those years, and improved urban sanitation that came as a result of separating water supplies from sewage and removing garbage from city streets. In the United States, population boomed even more due to the arrival of tens of millions of immigrants during the nineteenth century.

Transportation

The Industrial Revolution could not have occurred without rapidly expanding markets. A transportation infrastructure had to be developed to allow the economy to expand beyond the limits of rivers and deepwater ports. Only then could commercial values penetrate subsistence economies and provide new opportunities for consumption. Better transportation systems stimulated unprecedented expansion in markets, which in turn provided new opportunities for merchant capitalists to produce and distribute goods.

In the United States, tremendous energies were invested in transportation systems during the nineteenth century. In the 1790s, private entrepreneurs, sometimes with federal and state subsidies, began constructing toll roads between major cities. Contractors cleared forests and constructed roads with a paved, all-weather base that greatly facilitated wagon traffic between major towns and cities. Historians have dubbed this the "turnpike era," and by the 1840s, all of the major towns and cities of the Northeast and the Atlantic coast had been linked up in the network of toll roads. As a result, the shipment of goods became more efficient, and larger volumes of products could be moved in shorter periods of time, reducing freight costs and the unit cost of each product.

In the 1820s, the so-called canal era emerged in the United States, in which state governments helped finance the construction of canals linking major cities. The most influential of the dozens of canals constructed during the 1820s–1840s was the Erie Canal, an immense project in upstate New York that linked the cities of Albany and Buffalo. Once the Erie Canal was in operation, goods could be shipped by barge from New York City to Albany via the Hudson River, from Albany to Buffalo via the Erie Canal, and from Buffalo to Cleveland and eventually to Chicago along the Great Lakes. The entire hinterland of upstate New York, northern Ohio, northern Indiana, and northern Illinois became linked up with New England and the Atlantic coast in a huge market. Once the Erie Canal was completed, freight costs dropped from more than $100 a ton to just $15. Total canal mileage in the United States increased from 1,270 in 1830 to 3,700 in 1850.

But there were limits to just how much of America could be accessed by canal construction. Geography and the availability of water determined canal construction, and a new technology was needed to penetrate other areas of the country. Railroad construction, which began in the late 1820s, accelerated in the 1840s, and exploded in the 1850s, gradually linked the North and East into a huge single market. Railroad construction lagged in the South because the plantation economy had for years relied on the South's abundant river system to get cotton, hemp, sugar, and tobacco to ports along the Gulf and Atlantic coasts. After the Civil War, construction of the transcontinental railroads brought the Pacific Coast, Southwest, and intermountain West into the railroad nexus. Between 1850 and 1920, the number of miles of railroad track in operation jumped from approximately 10,000 to 263,821. By then, more than 80 million Americans had become consumers in a single national market.

Economy: A National Market

Because of turnpikes, canals, and railroads, it became possible for merchant capitalists anywhere in the country to ship manufactured products efficiently. A manufacturer in Boston, Massachusetts, for example, could compete with a manufacturer in Buffalo, New York, because freight costs no longer priced him out of distant markets. Such an idea—driving local manufacturers out of business in distant markets—had been unthinkable before because the poor transportation system had made it prohibitively expensive to market products beyond the confines of a limited geographic region. But as markets expanded, so did demand for manufactured goods, and to satisfy that demand and profit from it, merchant capitalists needed increased volumes of manufactured goods. They embarked on a search for new ways of organizing workers and new technologies to produce goods in greater volumes.

Industrialism: Mass Production and the Effects of Technology on Workers and the Workplace

Prior to industrialization, manufactured goods had been produced in small shops or in homes by artisans who fashioned them with hand tools. Merchants had developed the so-called putting-out system in which they traveled from home to home and shop to shop delivering raw materials to the artisans and picking up finished products for sale. But because of the rise of a national market, the merchants soon learned that the putting-out system was inadequate, that it could never provide the volume of goods necessary to meet demand. The solution was obvious: have workers travel daily to the same location to work under the same roof. The merchant would see that raw materials were delivered there and that finished goods were picked up for shipment and distribution. These single locations became known as factories.

In the United States, the first factories began appearing in the 1790s and early 1800s in the New England textile industry. Factory conditions soon appeared as well in anthracite and bituminous coal mines, iron foundries, meat-packing plants, smelters, and textile industries. For all intents and purposes, however, the workers in the new factories still fashioned goods by hand from scratch. Each worker, equipped with a full set of tools, worked at an individual workbench and manufactured products.

The merchant capitalists soon identified inefficiencies in the process. With each worker fashioning goods from scratch, most tools lay idle during much of the day, and it soon became obvious that some workers were better, or more efficient, at certain tasks than at others. Labor specialization, known as the "division of labor," in which workers performed specific tasks all day long, became the answer for such inefficiencies. Instead of distributing complete sets of tools to all workers and allowing them to perform every task in the production process, the merchant capitalist, now more commonly known as a factory owner or businessman, provided only the tools necessary to perform a specific task, and workers were assigned the tasks they were most efficient at performing. They were also told to remain at their worktables all day long and that the goods they were to work on would be brought to them. Such a process became known as an assembly line. Goods were brought to workers who performed one task on them, and the product was then delivered to another worker who would complete the next step in the assembly or production process.

The concept of interchangeable parts also helped revolutionize the manufacturing process. Until the system of interchangeable parts made its appearance in the United States in the early 1800s, manufactured goods were hand tooled, with each part having to be individually fitted during the assembly process. Each product, when finished, was by necessity unique, with tolerances and specifications that might be quite different from the next product coming off the line. Eli Whitney was one of the early pioneers of interchangeable parts in the United States. He had received a contract from the federal government to manufacture 10,000 muskets, and to fulfill the contract, he mass-produced parts with rigid specifications and extremely narrow tolerances, so that any single part could be used in any completed musket. In the next stage of productivity gains, entrepreneurs looked for new technologies to make workers more efficient. The English textile industry led the way. A series of inventions to speed up the spinning of cotton thread—James Hargreaves's spinning jenny (1764), Richard Arkwright's rotating-flyer spinning wheel (1769), and Samuel Crompton's spinning mule (1779)—made textile workers 250 times more efficient than when they had worked individual spinning wheels. The new technologies stimulated steadily increasing demand for cotton, which grew exponentially. In 1760, the British imported 2.5 million pounds of cotton. That number jumped to 22 million pounds in 1787. On the other side of the Atlantic, Eli Whitney's invention of the cotton gin (1793), which separated seeds from cotton fiber without using teams of hand-picking workers, led to huge increases in the size of the South's cotton crop. In 1837, Great Britain imported 366 million pounds of cotton, and finished British cotton cloth soon flooded the world. These new cotton-processing technologies were soon transferred to the United States, where a thriving textile industry developed in New England.

Changes in heavy industry occurred soon after. Because of abundant supplies of coal in Great Britain and the United States, iron manufacturing became more efficient. Traditionally, iron forges had used wood for heat, but wood could not generate enough heat to burn sufficient volumes of carbon from the iron. The result was iron products that were somewhat weak. But coal-fired forges generated higher temperatures, which burned off more carbon and made stronger iron products. In the middle of the nineteenth century, the use of coke and iron gave birth to the steel industry in Great Britain and the United States, and steel became the building block of the Industrial Revolution.

To secure even greater productivity gains, entrepreneurs began adopting new forms of power. For much of human history, machinery had been powered simply by human movement, and at the beginning stages of the Industrial Revolution, waterpower had been harnessed to limited degrees. Waterwheels placed in rapidly moving rivers and streams provided the energy to run some machines. But it was James Watt's invention of the steam engine in Great Britain in 1765, which he patented in 1769, that provided a new source of power for the Industrial Revolution. The coal-fired steam engines were soon adapted to an almost infinite variety of machines, which then increased worker productivity even more. Late in the nineteenth century, electric power began to come on line in industrial factories, generating even greater productivity gains.

Because of new technologies and new sources of power, factory productivity grew by leaps and bounds during the nineteenth century, giving rise to what historians and economists called mass production. Factories that had once produced goods by the dozens or the hundreds each day now saw themselves producing them by the thousands or even tens of thousands. Between 1889 and 1919, gross manufacturing production in the United States increased geometrically, from $9.37 billion to $62.4 billion. The United States ranked fourth in industrial outputs behind the United Kingdom, France, and Germany in 1865, yet by 1900 had grown to rank first in industrial outputs, to remain the world's largest domestic economy to this day.

Business: Corporate Consolidation Prompted the Rise of Big Business

Until the Industrial Revolution, most manufacturing enterprises were small family affairs, doing business primarily in local or regional markets because poor transportation systems did not allow a more expansive vision. The development of a national market, however, provided opportunities for successful entrepreneurs to sell products everywhere. A few proved more competitively adept than others, and their businesses thrived, growing by leaps and bounds, garnering more and more market share and larger proportions of profits. The successful companies swallowed up less competitive rivals, driving them out of business or combining with them.

The late-nineteenth-century American economy nurtured immense concentrations of wealth and power. The appearance of the super-rich galvanized reformers. Entrepreneurs produced more and more goods for sale in ever-expanding markets, while smaller enterprises disappeared, swallowed up in the corporate feeding frenzies of the late 1800s. Small companies gave way to big companies, and big companies to still bigger ones. Some businessmen aimed at nothing less than domination of an industry and succeeded beyond their imagination.

At just five feet two inches, Andrew Carnegie seemed an unlikely titan. Emigrating from Scotland when he was thirteen, he worked in a cotton textile factory for $1.20 a week. He worked as a telegrapher before joining the Pennsylvania Railroad. At the age of twenty-four, he was named manager of the railroad's Pittsburgh division. He lived frugally, saved pennies, and invested wisely. By the time of his resignation in 1865, his investments produced $50,000 a year, and he thought briefly about retiring. After a trip to England in 1873, he decided that the future rested on girders of steel. In 1875, he erected a steel mill in Homestead, Pennsylvania, and by 1901, when he sold out to J. P. Morgan, Carnegie had built the world's largest corporation. He bought out rivals, a process known as horizontal integration, and in purchasing coal mines, iron ore, and railroads—operations contributing to the main enterprise—he achieved what is termed *vertical integration*. Integration guaranteed a steady flow of supplies into the mill and a steady flow of finished products out. In 1901, when J. P. Morgan handed him a check for $480 million, he told the steel magnate, "Mr. Carnegie, I want to congratulate you on just having become the richest man in the world."

John D. Rockefeller was soon even richer. A devout Baptist committed to God and money, he did for oil what Carnegie did for steel. Oil was used for lighting lamps and for lubricants, and the Industrial Revolution created huge demand. Rockefeller expanded horizontally, purchasing facilities of other oil refiners or driving them out of business. Acquiring oil supplies, constructing barrel factories and storage tanks, and building pipelines, he achieved a vertical integration that cut his costs. In 1870, Rockefeller formed the Standard Oil Company.

In 1882, Rockefeller developed the trust, a legal device creating essentially a monopoly. Several companies surrendered voting rights to a trust board, which made important decisions. The trust limited competition by setting prices or allocating specific markets out to single companies, which charged whatever the market could endure. In return, companies received trust certificates entitling them to a share of profits. Within a few years,

Standard Oil controlled the industry, crushing rivals, fixing prices, and earning millions, chiefly from the world's demand for kerosene. When the internal-combustion engine created huge demand for gasoline, Rockefeller was positioned to become a billionaire. Trusts proliferated.

Urbanization: Immigration and Migration as Factors in Social and Economic Change

The Industrial Revolution also triggered rapid growth in city populations. Throughout the nineteenth century, new technologies in agriculture dramatically increased production and productivity, but in the process, many small farmers found it increasingly difficult to compete, just as small manufacturers could not compete with big business.

After the Civil War, farmers swarmed over the Great Plains. Between 1870 and 1900, Minnesota's population jumped from 439,000 to 1.751 million. Kansas's population grew even more sharply, from 364,000 people to 1.47 million. The population of Nebraska rose from 123,000 to 1.012 million. Farm acreage nearly doubled, from 493 million to 839 million. There were 2.66 million family farms in 1866 and 5.377 million in 1900.

New technologies made each acre more productive. Farmers did not need to push wooden or iron plows through hard prairie soil and harvest wheat or corn by hand. Cyrus McCormick had invented the reaper in 1831, John Deere patented the steel plow a few years later, and dozens of other invention throughout the late nineteenth century improved agricultural production. The South produced 2 million bales of cotton on 6.3 million acres in 1866 and 11 million bales on 25 million acres in 1898. In 1866, wheat farmers harvested 152 million bushels from 15 million acres; in 1900, they gathered 675 million bushels from 44 million acres.

But the success of American agriculture brought trouble. By the 1880s, farmers felt poor and exploited and wanted culprits to blame. A bushel of wheat commanding $1.53 in 1866 brought 58 cents in 1898. Between 1865 and 1900, the commodity price index fell by half. Farmers worked more and more for less and less. While overproduction washed away income, expenses escalated. Railroads charged more to haul crops, and grain elevators held farmers hostage. Buying land, seed, and equipment meant borrowing at exorbitant interest rates. The actual number of small farms increased during the era because of mass immigration and the sale of public-domain land, but most of the new small farms were not economically viable. Bad weather complicated matters. The hot summer of 1887 blistered Kansas wheat and Nebraska corn, and the harsh winter of 1888 froze tens of thousands of cattle. The family farm entered a long decline. Small operations, unable to outproduce or undersell large commercial farms with the latest machinery, suffered badly. In the late 1880s and 1890s, 90 percent of American farms changed hands as bankrupt farmers sold out. Untenable small farms disappeared into larger farms, and small farmers, with their wives and children, vanished into big cities. Between 1887 and 1891, thousands of families in western Kansas pulled up stakes, their eastward-bound wagons bearing such placards as "In God we Trusted, in Kansas we Busted."

Farmers with large amounts of land could afford the new technologies, negotiate lower interest rates on land purchases, and buy supplies in bulk from wholesalers. Smaller farmers could not, and they found themselves being squeezed out of business, unable to sell commodities at competitive prices because their costs were simply too high. Many went bankrupt; others simply sold out and went looking for work. That search brought most to the towns and cities, where they went to work in the burgeoning industrial economy.

The increase in jobs in manufacturing sectors fueled rapid urbanization in U.S. cities. This one shift in labor patterns set off a domino effect of social and economic change—lower production costs made goods more affordable to consumers, who now had more expendable income on leisure, entertainment, or nonessential items, which in turn fueled the growth of retail, service, and leisure industries in the cities. Agricultural advancements and the growth of a national market provided a more readily available and less expensive food supply. Urbanization tied to an increase in wage labor affected the transition from largely extended family living to a nuclear family structure, and contributed to the rise of the middle class in the United States. Concentration in urban areas influenced an increase in political involvement among middle- and lower-class citizens tied to the Populist movement and the rise of machine party politics. Urbanization at this level also produced lasting negative effects that continue to plague U.S. cities today, such as class and racial segregation, devaluation of women's work based on the doctrine of separate spheres in which women are limited to the private sphere of the home and men's domain consists of the public sphere related to work and politics, taxing child labor, unhealthy living and working conditions due to poor environmental management on the part of the government, and neglectful safety policies in factories.

Labor and Labor Unions

By the 1830s, unions were appearing by the dozens, but they tended to be local and transitory. After the Civil War, the National Labor Union (NLU) tried to organize all unions into an umbrella group and demand an eight-hour workday, but in 1872, its leaders miscalculated, opting for political action and endorsing a labor party in the elections. The strategy flopped, and when the economy collapsed in 1873, the NLU disintegrated. For a time, the Knights of Labor was a powerful organization. Formed in 1869, the Knights thrived under the leadership of Terence Powderly, who invited skilled and unskilled workers and women to join. He wanted equal pay for women, an income tax, and worker cooperatives. But late in the 1880s, when several strikes failed, the union collapsed.

Samuel Gompers, British-born head of the cigarmakers' union, filled the vacuum in 1886 with the American Federation of Labor (AFL), a national body committed to organizing skilled workers in craft unions. Gompers ignored child workers, women, and the unskilled. A gifted tactician, he realized that the NLU and the Knights of Labor had self-destructed by organizing the unskilled, whose work stoppages could be easily crushed by strikebreakers. The AFL included only skilled workers. By 1900, the American labor movement claimed a membership of more than 1 million workers; three out of five held AFL union cards.

A former socialist, Gompers understood that capitalism's roots reached deep into American soil. Few workers wanted to destroy the political economy; they simply wanted a more humane capitalism. Gompers promoted a new vision of individual rights. Americans had long defined civil rights in legal terms—the right to vote and hold public office, freedom of expression, and protection from such government abuses as cruel and unusual punishment, kangaroo courts, double jeopardy, and unreasonable searches. Gompers proffered an economic vision of individual rights—the right to a living wage, a safe workplace, reasonable hours, and freedom to join unions. During his tenure with the AFL, which lasted into the 1920s, Gompers never saw government as the primary agent for protecting workers, but he did redefine rights and set in motion a movement that eventually made the federal government the ultimate arbiter of worker rights.

Among episodes of violence that punctuated the struggle for worker rights, events in Pennsylvania won national attention. Influenced, as fact or legend would have it, by the Molly Maguires, miners rebelled against repression and low wages, not in any organized uprising but in acts of murder, mugging, and other disruptions of the system. In 1873, miners struck the Philadelphia and Reading Railroad, which owned several anthracite coal mines. The mines hired private detectives and strikebreakers. The strike lasted five months and produced riots, arson, and murder. Police charged dozens of activists with murder and mayhem. On slim evidence, juries convicted twenty-four, and ten were executed.

In 1877, when the Baltimore & Ohio Railroad issued a 10 percent wage cut, workers went on strike. Management persuaded Maryland's governor to call out the state militia and keep the trains running. The strike spread from coast to coast, shutting down rail traffic in fourteen states. Workers torched railroad cars, removed rails, sabotaged bridges, and assaulted company officials. State troops treated striking workers like an enemy army. When the great railroad strike of 1877 ended, more than 100 people had been killed. President Rutherford B. Hayes had to call in federal troops to reopen the lines in West Virginia. Scottish-born Allan Pinkerton, president of a detective company hired by railroad executives to break the strike, blamed the unrest on a "spirit spread through the ranks of railroad employees by communistic leaders and their teachings."

Similar fears greeted a strike at McCormick International Harvester in 1886. Chicago police, bent on assisting management, killed four participants. In support of the strikers, anarchists staged a rally at Haymarket Square. Suddenly, a homemade bomb exploded in the middle of the rally, killing seven policemen and wounding twenty-seven others. Angry police killed four demonstrators, and a wave of antiradicalism swept through the Midwest. On trumped-up charges and little evidence, Chicago police arrested eight known anarchists. All eight were convicted; four were executed, and the others drew long prison sentences.

One of the bloodiest strikes took place in 1892 at the Carnegie Steel Works in Homestead, Pennsylvania, and the confrontation took on all the dimensions of civil war. The Amalgamated Association of Iron, Steel, and Tin Workers struck the mill, and Carnegie decided to break the union. He then cut wages 20 percent, repudiated the union, and hired strikebreakers to work the plant and 300 Pinkerton guards to protect them. On July 6, 1892, a pitched battle between striking workers and Pinkertons erupted, armed workers attacked, and by late afternoon, nine workers and three Pinkertons lay dead. A week later, the governor of Pennsylvania mobilized the state militia. Carnegie accused the workers of radicalism, an exaggeration that gained credibility on July 23 when Alexander Berkman, a Russian émigré anarchist, shot and stabbed H. C. Frick, Carnegie's assistant. Frick survived, but the strike did not. Berkman single-handedly had broken the back of the strike, convincing much of the public that the Amalgamated Association of Iron and Steel Workers shared his penchant for revolutionary violence. After five months, the union caved in, formally ending the strike on November 20, 1892. The remaining workers faced twelve-hour workdays and debilitating wage cuts.

Corporate Influence on National Politics and the Emergence of Reform Movements

The dark side of industrialism inspired a cadre of intellectuals to dispute laissez-faire doctrine. That required attacking the idea that private property rights rested on absolute principles. Opposition to the excesses of capitalism thus involved an inquiry into the nature of truth, which over the course of the Industrial Revolution would be translated into reform movements such as Populism and Progressivism that called for government regulation of big business to rectify the social and economic inequities industrialization had quickly produced.

An important contributor to philosophical inquiries into essential truths as they pertained to wealth and power was Harvard professor William James. James rejected metaphysical speculation in favor of rational conclusions drawn from experience. In his famous essay "The Will to Believe" (1897), James argued that an idea can be held to be true insofar as it sits well within the tangle of concrete personal experience, thus implying that human beings need not abide by doctrines out of the past. The term *pragmatism* became attached to James. In its conviction that "truth" could change over time, as the tangible experience changes within which ideas must find their uneasy lodging, pragmatism undermined abstract, absolutist, and fixed philosophical notions.

Pragmatists confronted a wall of dogma and tradition. Adam Smith's Wealth of Nations, which had appeared in 1776, still dominated economics. Smith had described a world of fixed economic laws. Unfettered capitalism, modified by public assistance to the indigent, leaves human beings free to compete as producers and consumers; prices rise and fall according to demand, and at any given moment, economic conditions—prices, production, and employment—balance evenly. It makes no more sense for government to interfere with natural economic laws than it does to tinker with gravity. Laissez-faire—leaving the economy to its own devices—is the course of truth, Smith believed.

Prevailing assumptions about society were just as rigid. Such sociologists as William Graham Sumner of Yale spawned "social Darwinism," lifting Charles Darwin's theory of natural selection, or survival of the fittest, out of biology and superimposing it on human society. Survival of the fittest explained not only the diversity of animal life but extremes of human wealth and poverty. Occupants of the upper class reside there because of intelligence and ambition, and just as surely, the poor are poor for their stupidity, sloth, and physical disability. Society must "minimize to the utmost the relations of the state to industry," because government tends to steal incentive from society's most productive people. "We cannot go outside this alternative: liberty, inequality, survival of the fittest; not liberty, equality, and survival of the unfittest. The former carries society forward, and favors all its best members; the latter carries society downwards and favors all its worst members." Government programs to ameliorate "the suffering of the poor are folly," Sumner argued. But Smith and Sumner did not go unchallenged. Critics accused them of flawed logic.

Teaching at Chicago, Stanford, and Missouri, Thorstein Veblen transformed economic thought. In *The Theory of the Leisure Class,* which he published in 1899, he defined ostentation as the ruling objective among the wealthy. "In order to gain and hold the esteem of men," he wrote, "it is not sufficient merely to possess wealth or power. The wealth or power must be put in evidence, for esteem is awarded only on evidence." The wealthy engage in "conspicuous consumption" to display their success. Elsewhere Veblen argued that modern business classes seek their advantage not in efficient production but in the gain that comes from disrupting the flow of production. The technicians and skilled workers of modern industry, to the contrary, are motivated by what Veblen called the instinct of workmanship, which new technology sharpens. The economy is not a self-regulating mechanism operating according to natural law. It is rooted in human experience, bad and good. People can influence economic institutions and determine the future.

Less sophisticated was Henry George, a journalist whose 1879 book *Progress and Poverty* traced poverty to private property in land and natural resources and to government policies encouraging transfers of land to the wealthy. "Poverty deepens as wealth increases, and wages are forced down while productive power grows, because land, which is the source of all wealth, and the field of labor, is monopolized." Growth in population drives up land values. The rich get richer by doing little. George's solution was the "single tax"—that is, a tax on the "unearned increment" in all land values created by population growth. That would allow productive work to express itself. The single tax never got far, but before obscurity engulfed Henry George, he convinced millions that poverty was man-made, not the outcome of natural law. Others, such as Lester Ward, a proponent of reform Darwinism, argued that man has the agency to transform his environment, and therefore has the capacity to reform economy and society to alleviate poverty.

The first move toward government regulation of private business occurred in the Midwest. In 1867, Oliver Kelley, a government clerk in the Bureau of Agriculture, formed the Patrons of Husbandry, or Grange, primarily to relieve the loneliness of farm life, but when farmers gathered for picnics, talk drifted to economics. They blamed railroads and bankers for their plight, and the more they talked, the angrier they became. Grangers lobbied state legislatures. In 1873, Illinois set maximum rates that grain-storage facilities could charge. The grain-storage operators filed suit, and *Munn v. Illinois* wound its way to the Supreme Court. The Court, rejecting the idea that private property is immune to governmental regulation, upheld the state's right to regulate grain-storage rates, holding that it fell within the authority of the state to act for the welfare of its inhabitants.

But companies fought back. They based their argument on a particular reading of the Fourteenth Amendment. Adopted in the era of Reconstruction and designed to protect the rights of the former slaves, this amendment contained a provision declaring that no state shall "deprive any person of life, liberty, or property, without due process of law." Opponents of the Illinois law claimed that the Fourteenth Amendment extended such protections to corporations as well as individuals. The Illinois law, they argued, was an unconstitutional interference with private property.

In the following decade, the Court came to agree. In 1886, it wrapped corporate rights in a warm constitutional blanket, ruling in *Santa Clara County v. Southern Pacific Railroad* that the word "person" in the Fourteenth Amendment included businesses, and that certain kinds of regulation of business amounted to violations of due process. The decision awarded civil rights to corporations, making it more difficult for state legislatures to regulate them. Later in that year, in *Wabash, St. Louis & Pacific Railroad Co. v. Illinois,* the Court reversed *Munn* and overturned an Illinois law regulating railroads. The Court in this instance made as its main argument not that the Illinois statute ran counter to the Fourteenth Amendment but that in interfering with a railroad that crossed state lines, Illinois was intruding on the authority of Congress to regulate interstate commerce. Wabash eroded the foundation on which the Granger cases rested. In 1890, the extent of the erosion became clear in *Chicago, Milwaukee & St. Paul Railroad Co. v. Minnesota.* Minnesota had established a state commission to set railroad freight rates and grain-storage rates, but the Supreme Court ruled that the law deprived corporations of due process and violated their property rights. By declaring state laws unconstitutional, the Supreme Court guaranteed that disgruntled Americans would look to Congress for assistance.

Railroads felt the heat first. In the South and West, farmers complained about freight rates, and eastern merchants concurred. California novelist and journalist Frank Norris captured the discontent, comparing railroads to "the leviathan, with tentacles of steel clutching into the soil, the soulless Force, the iron-hearted power, the master, the Colossus, the Octopus." Some railroad magnates and investment bankers weighed in as well. Between 1880 and 1893, railroads had assumed huge debts to construct 80,000 miles of track. They built track faster than the economy could absorb it. Cutthroat competition, falling revenues, and bankruptcy ensued. Perhaps the government could set rates and keep the roads from undercutting one another.

In the Interstate Commerce Act of 1887, Congress assumed responsibility for managing a sector of the economy. It was a modest beginning. The law prohibited rebates, in which railroads kicked back portions of freight payments to wealthy customers; prevented roads from charging more money per ton mile for short hauls than for long hauls on the same line; and banned the formation of railroad pools, in which several roads conspired to set minimum rates. Congress insisted that the railroads levy "reasonable and just" charges. A five-member Interstate Commerce Commission would enforce the law by investigating complaints.

Three years later, in 1890, under similar pressures from Americans convinced that the Carnegies and the Rockefellers of the world destroyed competition and kept prices high, Congress passed the Sherman Antitrust Act, which declared that "every contract, combination in the form of trust or otherwise, or conspiracy, in restraint of trade or commerce among the several States or with foreign nations is hereby . . . illegal." Corporate monopolies could now be held in violation of the law. Then a rider to the Wilson-Gorman Tariff of 1894 imposed the first peacetime federal income tax. A reason was that since Wilson-Gorman reduced tariff schedules, an alternate source of revenue might be needed. Another was the view that the wealthy ought to pay a larger share of government expenses. The income tax was modest—2 percent on incomes in excess of $4,000—but the rich protested, and the Supreme Court in 1895 declared the income tax unconstitutional.

An activist federal government had its origins in the post–Civil War era when discontent with the downside of the Industrial Revolution—the wide income gap between the rich and the poor; low pay, long hours, and unsafe factories for workers; and increasing environmental problems—increased. Out of such discontent emerged the Populist movement of the 1890s, the Progressive movement of the first two decades of the 1900s, and the New Deal of the 1930s. Since then, Americans have engaged in a vigorous public-policy debate over the merits of government regulation at the federal level, a debate that is certain to continue into the distant future.

ALPHABETICAL LIST OF ENTRIES

TOPICAL LIST OF ENTRIES

Agriculture and Food Industry

Agricultural Revolution
Armour, Philip Danforth
*Chicago, Milwaukee &
    St. Paul Railroad Company
    v. Minnesota* (1890)
Deere, John
Donnelly, Ignatius
Granger Laws
McCormick, Cyrus Hall
Meat Inspection Act of 1906
Meat-Packing Industry
Ocala Platform
Populists
Pure Food and Drug Act of 1906
Sinclair, Upton Beall
Swift, Gustavus Franklin
Tractor

Business and Finance

Antitrust
Bailey v. Drexel Furniture Co.
    (1922)
Bank of the United States
Carnegie, Andrew
Chrysler, Walter Percy
Clayton Antitrust Act of 1914

Commerce Clause
Contracts Clause
Corporation
Du Pont, Pierre
Durant, William Crapo
Federal Trade Commission
    Act of 1914
Ford, Henry
Ford Motor Company
Frick, Henry Clay
General Electric Corporation
General Motors Corporation
Gibbons v. Ogden (1824)
Granger Laws
Great Atlantic and Pacific Tea
    Company
Gould, Jay
Hammer v. Dagenhart (1918)
Holding Company
Horizontal Integration
Infrastructure
Intellectual Property Rights
Interlocking Directorate
Interstate Commerce Commission
Lochner v. New York (1905)
Monopoly
Morgan, John Pierpont
Munn v. Illinois (1877)

Environment and Natural Resources

Industrialism

Economics

Labor

Transportation

LIST OF PRIMARY DOCUMENTS

Engineer Horatio Allen's Description of the First Run (1851)
Andrew Carnegie's "Gospel of Wealth," *North American Review* (1889)
Carnegie's Letters to Frick during Homestead Strike (1892)
McClure's Magazine Muckraking Expose on Standard Oil and
    Rockefellers by Ida Tarbell
Atlantic Monthly Article on Telegraph Technology (1860)
Harper's Weekly Report on Construction of the Transcontinental
    Railroad (July 27, 1867)
Chicago Tribune's Coverage of the 1871 Great Fire
Chicago Tribune Article on the Haymarket Riot of 1886
Jacob Riis's *How the Other Half Lives* (1890)
Booker T. Washington's Atlanta Compromise Speech (1895)
Political Cartoon, *"The Little Boy and the Big Boys"* (1901)
Political Cartoon from *Puck, "The Kind of Anti-Trust Legislation That Is
    Needed"* (1902)
Frederick Jackson Turner's "The Significance of the Frontier in American
    History" (1893)
Charles Eliot Norton's "True Patriotism" (1898)
Upton Sinclair's *The Jungle* (1906)

A

A&P. *See* Great Atlantic and Pacific Tea Company

Agricultural Revolution

Closely associated with the Industrial Revolution was a concomitant revolution in agricultural production. Both of the so-called revolutions had far-reaching consequences for the United States and the world. Both also had their origins in **infrastructure** and technological changes that swept across the United States in the nineteenth century. The rapid improvements in infrastructure, primarily the changes wrought by **turnpikes**, **canals**, and **railroads**, created a national economic marketplace in the United States in which goods, including farm commodities, could be cheaply shipped anywhere.

The improved transportation system provided farmers with new opportunities to transcend a local, subsistence economy and produce commercially for distant markets. Farmers became keenly interested in techniques to maximize land use and improve their yields per acre. During the nineteenth century, dramatic improvements in technology improved farm productivity. **Eli Whitney**'s cotton gin, which he invented in 1793, led to unprecedented increases in cotton production. In 1801, the United States produced approximately 100,000 bales of cotton, but that number rose to 171,000 bales in 1810, then leaped to 731,000 bales in 1830, 2.133 million bales in 1850, and more than 5.5 million bales in 1860. New technologies increased productivity in other commodities, although not so dramatically. Beginning in the 1820s, the cradle replaced the sickle for harvesting grain, and during the late 1820s and early 1830s, the cast-iron plow replaced the old wooden plow. By the mid-1840s, **John Deere**'s **steel** plow was in wide use. Hiram and John Pitts developed the thresher fanning mill late in the 1830s, and **Cyrus Hall McCormick**'s reaper revolutionized grain production. As a result of these technologies, farmers were able to farm more land than ever before.

There was also far more land available. Government policies helped promote land settlement. The Louisiana Purchase of 1803 doubled the territory

Settlers in front of their sod home in 1887. During this period, agriculture meant a livelihood for half of the American population. (AP Photo)

of the United States, while the Adams-Onís Treaty of 1819 secured Florida from Spain. In 1845, the United States annexed Texas, and in 1846, an Anglo-American treaty delivered much of the Oregon Territory to the United States. As a result of the Mexican-American War, the United States acquired from Mexico what is today the states of California, Arizona, New Mexico, Utah, Nevada, and part of Colorado. All of these territorial acquisitions opened up vast tracts of land for settlement. To encourage settlement and to promote productivity on the land, Congress passed two pieces of legislation in the early 1860s: the Homestead Act and the Morrill Act. In 1862, the Homestead Act provided 160 acres of public domain land free to any individual prepared to live on the land and to improve it over a period of several years. Once that period had been completed, the homesteader received fee simple title to the land. As a result of the Homestead Act, settlers swarmed across the American West. Between 1865 and 1900, the number of acres in wheat production in the United States jumped from 22 million to 47 million, while corn went from 40 million to 91 million, oats from 11 million to 30 million, cotton from 9 million to 24 million, and hay from 20 million to 42 million acres. Between 1865 and 1900, the number of farms in the United States increased from 2.66 million to 5.377 million, and the number of acres of land in production went from 493 million to 839 million.

In addition to the availability of more land and less labor needed to work it, yields per acre improved because of scientific agriculture. By the late 1700s, the need for crop rotation, cultivation of legumes, the employment of fertilizers, and control of soil erosion were known among educated people, but it took decades for these practices to be widely adopted by American farmers. Agricultural societies, where farmers shared information, began forming in the 1780s, and the county fair movement, which started in the early 1800s, had a similar impact. Such farm journals as *The American Farmer* and *Cultivator* became national in their circulation by the 1840s. Government policies encouraged scientific agriculture. In 1862, Congress passed the Morrill Act, which granted public domain land to state governments willing to establish agricultural colleges to promote scientific agriculture. The Morrill Act led to the establishment of government agricultural agents in counties throughout the country, where farmers had access to the latest information on how to increase productivity. By the end of the nineteenth century, the United States had become the breadbasket of the world.

Amalgamated Association of Iron, Steel, and Tin Workers of the United States

This union was one of the nation's first successful unions. Before the Industrial Revolution, workers labored in small business enterprises for employers who often treated them paternalistically. Workers interested in pay raises or burdened with complaints or frustrations could approach the owner and express their needs and opinions personally. Also, most pre–Industrial Revolution manufacturing enterprises tended to function in local markets, where competition was confined to nearby businesses. Most workers felt no need to organize and bargain collectively because they had access to their employers.

The Industrial Revolution fundamentally changed the relationship between workers and owners. As business enterprises grew in size during the nineteenth century, relationships became less and less personal. Layers of management grew between workers and business owners, and negotiations over wages and working conditions became more institutionalized. Also, as the American economy became more national in scope, with a market vastly expanded by **railroad** construction, competition became fiercer. Workers often found themselves squeezed by external competition and unable to gain access to employers to express their grievances.

The labor movement emerged from these economic realities. In 1858, ironworkers in Pittsburgh, Pennsylvania, established the Sons of Vulcan, an incipient union. The union was very successful because membership was confined to iron puddlers, a highly skilled occupation. Similar unions sprouted in the Pittsburgh area, and in 1872, several of them merged into the Associated Brotherhood of Iron and Steel Heaters, Rollers, and Roughers. Employers opposed the organization of workers, but because the brotherhood consisted largely of skilled workers, employers had little leverage. They could not afford to fire them because the cost of retraining new workers was too high.

In 1873, a rival union appeared—the National Union of Rollers, Roughers, Catchers, and Hookers of the United States. For several years, the two unions competed with each other to organize workers, but in 1876, they suppressed their differences and merged into the Amalgamated Association of Iron, Steel, and Tin Workers of the United States. By 1891, with a membership of more than 25,000, the union had become one of the most influential in the United States.

But in 1892, union leaders made a disastrous decision. They struck the Carnegie Steel Works at Homestead, Pennsylvania, and the so-called **Homestead Strike** all but destroyed the union. A virtual war erupted around the plant between union workers and goons hired by **Andrew Carnegie**. The strike was ruthlessly crushed, and membership declined. Although the union's membership recovered somewhat in the early 1900s, the **United States Steel Corporation**, successor to Carnegie Steel Works, refused to bargain with the union until the 1930s. By that time, the Amalgamated Association's membership stood at only 10,000 members.

American Federation of Labor

The first successful national American labor union was the American Federation of Labor. The Industrial Revolution changed forever the relationship between employers and workers. In the preindustrial economy, workers usually enjoyed highly personal relationships with their employers. The apprenticeship system often found boys leaving their own families to live with the families of their employers, and a paternalistic culture often governed relationships there. That paternalism usually affected other workers as well. Shops tended to be small, with few businesses employing more than a handful of workers. Grievances could be handled one-on-one, as could negotiations about wages and working conditions. In addition, in the preindustrial world, workers were usually craftsmen who fashioned products from scratch and saw them to their finished state. Workers identified with the product and took great pride in their work.

The Industrial Revolution changed all that. As the size of companies grew, so did the number of employees, and the rise of large **corporations**, with hundreds and even thousands of employees, of necessity required several layers of management between workers and their employers. Relationships became more and more impersonal, and workers found it increasingly difficult, and then impossible, to work out grievances with their employers. Also, the Industrial Revolution inaugurated rapid technological changes in the production process, most of which devalued unskilled labor and undermined wage levels. Finally, successful entrepreneurs like **Andrew Carnegie** and **John Davison Rockefeller** realized that the key to long-term financial success was cutting costs, which they did at every opportunity. Since labor was a key component of business overhead, employers had few compunctions about cutting wages whenever the opportunity presented itself. Many workers found themselves facing untenable economic situations, with wages falling and prices rising.

Many workers felt that their only recourse was to organize into labor unions and bargain collectively with employers. Small local unions appeared in a number of northeastern cities in the 1820s, 1830s, and 1840s, but their reach was quite limited geographically. Also, employers unwilling to negotiate with a union in one city could easily relocate the business to another city where workers were unorganized. The answer to that dilemma was a national labor union that organized workers across the country. Several national unions had fitful and ultimately unsuccessful beginnings in the 1860s and 1870s, most notably the **National Labor Union** and the **Knights of Labor**, but they failed because they tried to organize unskilled as well as skilled workers and because they too often tried to dabble in politics.

The first successful national labor union was the American Federation of Labor (AFL), organized in 1886 when thirteen craft unions, composed exclusively of skilled workers, came together under the leadership of **Samuel Gompers**, who served as the AFL president. More than anything else, Gompers's refusal to organize unskilled workers explained the success of the AFL. He knew that the AFL's predecessors—the National Labor Union and the Knights of Labor—had failed in part because they had tried to bring unskilled workers into the union fold. But during work stoppages, management could easily replace unskilled workers with strikebreakers, which reduced union's leverage. Skilled workers, on the other hand, who could not easily be replaced, forced management to take potential work stoppages seriously. Gompers also approached strikes tactically, refusing to implement a work stoppage unless he was certain that management would cave in to his demands. Only then would he have and retain credibility among rank-and-file members.

Gompers also decided to forge the AFL into a lobbying organization, not a third political party. Rather than challenge the Democratic and Republican parties for control of the government, the AFL would try to bring voter pressure on all politicians. Finally, to make sure that the individual craft union leaders did not worry about losing their prerogatives to the AFL leadership, Gompers extended full autonomy to them. The AFL was simply an umbrella organization.

In terms of its objectives, the AFL under Gompers accepted the foundation of capitalism, eschewed all socialist and radical notions, and concentrated on bread-and-butter issues—better working conditions, higher wages, and shorter workdays and workweeks. At every opportunity, Gompers pilloried socialism and communism as inconsistent with American values. And his vision worked. In 1924, when he stepped down as head of the AFL, the union had a membership of 2.865 million people and was the most powerful labor organization in the country.

Gompers also set the tone for future labor leaders in the United States. A confirmed capitalist who believed that the best interests of workers would be achieved in a privately owned economy, Gompers was a vocal critic of **socialism**, which he knew that the vast majority of Americans opposed and which would only stifle economic growth. Instead, he worked through political lobbying and the careful use of well-timed labor strikes to exact from management higher pay, shorter workdays, and better working conditions. These limited economic objectives for the most part still govern labor relations in the United States today.

American Railway Union

The American Railway Union (ARU) was an industrial labor union for skilled and unskilled workers. The Industrial Revolution created huge, powerful business **corporations** that operated in a national marketplace, and industrial workers, who experienced dramatic changes in the quality of their lives, felt the need for labor organizations to represent them in negotiations with corporate management. But labor unions faced real disadvantages as well. Unions operating only in a local region eventually found themselves without leverage in negotiating with management, which had the ability to relocate business operations to other regions. Labor unions also faced internal competition between more elitist skilled or craft workers and unskilled, **mass production** workers. Skilled workers always had more leverage with management because their strikes could dramatically affect business operations. Unskilled workers had substantially less leverage since they could be easily replaced by strikebreakers. By the late nineteenth century, the drive to organize all workers on a national scale had begun to permeate the labor movement.

A leader in the campaign to organize all workers on a national level was **Eugene Victor Debs**, a former head of the Brotherhood of Locomotive

Firemen, a union of skilled craft workers. Debs resigned from the brotherhood in 1892, and in 1893, established the ARU for skilled and unskilled workers. Headquartered in Chicago, the ARU established the following as its economic objectives: higher wages, shorter workdays, safer working conditions, and better insurance policies. Debs's goals were consistent with those of other mainstream labor unions. Within a year, ARU's membership was approaching 150,000.

But Debs then made a huge tactical error. In 1894, he called a nationwide strike against the Pullman Palace Car Company, a manufacturer of luxury **railroad** cars. At the time, the Pullman Company, based in Chicago, had earned a well-deserved reputation for crass exploitation of workers in its company town. Pullman workers lived in Pullman-owned housing, shopped in Pullman-owned stores, sent their children to Pullman-owned schools, and received their weekly pay in Pullman scrip. When the **Depression of 1893** struck the economy, **George Pullman**, owner of the Pullman Company, slashed wages, prompting Debs to launch the strike. Across the country, ARU workers refused to handle any train equipped with a Pullman car.

But the Pullman Company was also committed to breaking the strike. The ARU's refusal to handle trains with Pullman cars created unprecedented traffic jams and interruptions in shipments. Pullman appealed to the Grover Cleveland administration for assistance, arguing that the strike had become a federal matter because the railroads shipped in interstate commerce and carried the federal mail. Attorney general of the United States Richard Olney, a corporate attorney before he joined the cabinet of President Grover Cleveland, took management's side in the strike. He obtained a federal court injunction that went against the union and ordered Debs to halt the strike. Debs defied the court order, and the strike continued. To enforce the court order, Olney deployed thousands of federal troops all along railroad lines, and pitched battles soon raged between workers and soldiers. The troops soon crushed the strike, and federal marshals arrested Debs. He was tried, convicted of criminal conspiracy, and sentenced to six months in a federal prison. The ARU did not survive the strike. Upon his release from prison, Debs announced his conversion to socialism. Only then, he was convinced, would workers stand a chance of securing fair treatment from their own government.

American System

With the end of the War of 1812, a burst of nationalism spread throughout the United States. It found its public policy expression in what Senator **Henry Clay** of Kentucky called his "American System." Like Secretary of the

Treasury **Alexander Hamilton** a few decades before, Clay was convinced that the United States would never be able to assume its rightful place among the powers of the world without a modern industrial economy. He was also convinced that the federal government had a key role to play in the development of such an economy. By establishing a national bank, the federal government could exercise some control over the monetary system and stabilize prices, which would encourage a positive climate for capital investment. By passing high tariffs on imported manufactured goods, Congress would protect American industry from unnecessary competition. By using federal funds to finance **internal improvements**—that is, construction of **turnpikes**, **canals**, and **railroads**—Congress would help create a national market. All of these proposals were described by Clay as the "American System."

The American System became wrapped up in political debates of the era. For such people as Clay or President John Quincy Adams, who represented the National Republican Party and then the Whig Party, the federal government had a responsibility to pass high tariffs, sponsor a national bank, and finance internal improvements. Most Americans in the Northeast supported the idea, since high tariffs would protect Northern industries, new internal improvements would link them with the western interior, and a national bank would provide capital to Northern **factories**. But southerners generally opposed the American System. Since the South had few factories, tariffs would only raise the prices they had to pay for manufactured goods without providing them any benefits. As for federally financed internal improvements, the South's river system made it relatively easy to ship goods to Gulf and Atlantic ports. Southerners worried that they would be taxed to pay for government projects that would only benefit northerners. Throughout the 1810s, 1820s, 1830s, and 1840s, the debate reverberated throughout the halls of Congress, generally with Democrats opposing the American System and National Republicans and then Whigs favoring it.

In the end, the **Civil War** resolved the issue. Congress passed the Morrill Tariff in 1862, which raised rates on imported manufactured goods; the **National Banking Acts of** 1863 and **1864**, which established a national banking system; and the Pacific Railway Act of 1863, which provided for federal government subsidies to construct a **transcontinental railroad**. The American System had essentially become a national policy.

Antitrust

The issue of antitrust has been part of the fabric of American public policy since the 1880s. The term *antitrust* refers to the federal government's effort to prevent **monopoly** and preserve a competitive economy by forcing the breakup of companies that have come to control the market for a particular product or service, especially when those companies exercise their power to limit access to that market by a potential competitor.

In the preindustrial economy, antitrust was largely a moot question because the exercise of a national monopoly, in the absence of national markets and **factories** capable of filling such extensive demand, was all but impossible. But after the **Civil War**, as **railroad** and **telegraph** construction made the rapid, efficient shipment of goods and information possible, business enterprises grew larger and larger until such firms as **United States Steel Corporation**, **Standard Oil Company** of New Jersey, or the Northern Securities Company had established effective monopolies. Critics charged that monopolistic companies damaged the economy by eliminating competition and driving up prices. The only way to protect consumers and small businesses, they argued, was to employ the power of the federal government to break up the monopolies into smaller, less dominating enterprises. In antitrust action, **Populist** and **Progressive** reformers saw the restoration of economic justice to America.

During the era of the Industrial Revolution, Congress passed two pieces of antitrust legislation, the **Sherman Antitrust Act of 1890** and the **Clayton Antitrust Act of 1914**. At first, antitrust advocates encountered serious and almost fatal opposition from the U.S. Supreme Court. The Court employed a very restrictive interpretation of the **commerce clause** of the U.S. Constitution in a case involving the merger of the country's major sugar refiners. In 1895, *United States v. E.C. Knight Company* provided the first test case of the Sherman Antitrust Act, and the reformers lost. The arguments revolved around the question of congressional authority over interstate commerce and whether a manufacturing monopoly fell under the jurisdiction of the Sherman Antitrust Act. The real issue in the decision concerned the extent to which a manufacturing entity functioned within the context of interstate commerce. In its decision, the U.S. Supreme Court agreed with the lower court's dismissal of the government's case, making a sharp distinction between manufacturing and commerce and insisting that a manufacturing entity's intention to distribute its products across state lines did not open its activities to federal regulation. Otherwise, the Court concluded, Congress would enjoy regulatory jurisdiction over every element of a modern economy. *United States v. E.C. Knight Company* had a dampening effect on the ability of the federal government to preserve a competitive economy.

But in the early 1900s, a new wave of business consolidations escalated public concern about the survival of a free market and generated more antitrust activity from the federal government. Two 1911 cases in particular revealed a shift in the Supreme Court's position. In *Standard Oil Company v. United States* and *United States v. American Tobacco Company*, the Supreme Court upheld orders accusing the companies of restraint of trade and dissolving them.

Armour, Philip Danforth

During the Industrial Revolution, the meatpacking industry went through a process of **mass production** and corporate consolidation that brought about a near **monopoly** by the end of the nineteenth century. The leading entrepreneur and businessman in the industry was Philip Danforth Armour. Armour was born in Stockbridge, Wisconsin, on May 16, 1832. During the **Civil War**, with demand for beef at a peak because of the consumption needs of Union soldiers, Armour and his brothers went into the meat-packing business. The fact that more than 1 million Americans in the North were in the military provided the Armours an unprecedented opportunity. The demand for canned meat was especially huge because the troops needed to be able to eat in the field.

The business thrived, and in 1870, the Armours founded the Armour Meat Packing Company and relocated to Chicago, where rail traffic was now delivering millions of head of cattle annually. Chicago became the meat-processing capital of the world, and the Armours built the biggest business in the city's stockyards. The Armour plant was soon characterized by the latest mass-production technologies. Live cattle were delivered by rail to the Armour stockyards, where giant feedlots fattened them up for slaughter. Each head of cattle destined for slaughter was forced into a chute, where a worker bludgeoned it to death with a sledgehammer blow to the head. Chains that were wrapped around the carcass's feet and linked to an assembly line then lifted the body up, where it was quickly quartered. Workers then harvested every product possible from the carcass—hides, hooves, horns, and entrails, in addition to the meat products. By the late 1870s, thousands of cattle per day were being processed through Armour's Chicago facilities.

With the advent of **refrigeration** in boxcars, the Armours were able to deliver quarter sections of beef anywhere in the country, and they did so. By the mid-1890s, Armour sales exceeded $200 million per year, and the company had become the heart of what some critics called the "Meat Trust"—a monopoly that jacked up prices and delivered poor-quality meat to customers. During the Spanish-American War, Armour delivered millions of cans of beef to U.S. soldiers, but critics accused the company of selling tainted, rotten beef to the troops. The nickname "embalmed beef" was widely employed to describe the product. Philip Armour denied the accusations, but the controversy left him a broken man. He died in 1901. His son, J. Ogden Armour, then assumed control of the firm. During the next twenty years, he raised Armour's sales to more than $1 billion annually, and the company employed more than 40,000 workers.

Automobile

Except for the **railroad**, the automobile was the most important technology for the economics of the Industrial Revolution, and its social impact proved to be even greater than that of the railroad. In 1879, George Selden of Rochester, New York, applied for the first patent on a gasoline-driven automobile engine, but the patent was not awarded until 1895. By that time, the **Duryea brothers** of Springfield, Massachusetts—Charles E. Duryea and J. Frank Duryea—had already demonstrated the first successful gasoline-driven automobile. During the next several years, a series of inventions produced what we recognize today as a modern automobile—the pneumatic tire (1892), the clincher tire (1899), the sliding-gear transmission (1902), the steering knuckle (1902), the standard, easily dismounted tire rim (1904), automatic lubrication systems (1904), front bumpers (1906), the V-8 engine (1907), the electric self-starter (1911), the all-**steel** automobile (1912), and hydraulic brakes (1918).

But it was **Henry Ford** who created the modern automobile industry in the United States. With the advent of his Model T, first introduced in 1908, the car became more and more affordable. As Ford implemented every

An automobile enthusiast in his 1921 Ford Model T. (Library of Congress)

conceivable production technology, the price of the Model T fell steadily, from $450 in 1908 to $250 in 1920. Suddenly millions of Americans could afford an automobile, and millions purchased one. The sales of new cars jumped from 4,100 in 1900 to 63,500 in 1908, 461,500 in 1913, 1.951 million in 1920, and 4.5 million in 1929. Similar increases occurred in the number of automobiles registered in the United States, from 9.2 million in 1920 to 26.7 million in 1929.

The boom in automobile production brought concomitant increases in the production of steel, glass, rubber, paint, leather, and **petroleum**. Demand for better-quality roads led to a boom in construction, engineering, and architecture, and satellite businesses sprouted—service stations, roadside hotels and fast-food restaurants, engine repair and body shops, and vacation resorts. By 1925, the automobile industry had surpassed steel and petroleum, in terms of the annual gross value of its products, as the dominant sector of the economy.

Its social impact was equally, if not more, revolutionary. The sale of millions of automobiles created a "car culture" in the United States. Dating patterns changed because young couples were no longer confined to home, church, or the downtown soda shop. Real estate developers produced satellite communities known as "suburbs" far from downtown centers, and workers began commuting by car to their jobs. In rural areas, the automobile permitted school-district consolidation and allowed farmers to do their banking and shopping in larger towns. Finally, the automobile redefined the meaning of the term *freedom*. Until the advent of the automobile as a mass consumption item, Americans defined *freedom* in political and economic terms—the right to vote and hold public office; freedom of religion, speech, and press; and the right to a decent job and safe working conditions. After the advent of automobile, *freedom* acquired additional meaning—the right of an individual to travel wherever and whenever he or she pleased. The automobile, within a matter of decades, introduced fundamental changes into American social, political, and cultural life.

B

Bailey v. Drexel Furniture Co. (1922)

By the early 1920s, after the conclusion of World War I and the revival of progressive reform sentiments in some sections of the country, debate over the proper role of the federal government in the private economy resumed. In the 1918 case of *Hammer v. Dagenhart,* the U.S. Supreme Court invalidated the Keating-Owen Child Labor Act of 1916, which prohibited from interstate commerce manufactured goods made by children. Congress passed the measure with large majorities by virtue of its authority under the Constitution to regulate interstate commerce. But the Court held that the Keating-Owen Child Labor Act interfered with the police powers of the states. Congress reacted to the decision by passing the Child Labor Tax Act of 1919, which imposed confiscatory excise taxes on products manufactured by child labor. The owners of the Drexel Furniture Company sued on the grounds that Congress was actually using its taxing power to regulate what should be a state matter. The case was argued before the Supreme Court on March 7–8, 1922, and decided by an 8–1 vote on May 15, 1922.

In its decision, the Court essentially upheld its earlier decision in *Hammer v. Dagenhart,* concluding that the so-called regulatory nature of the provision was actually prohibitory and that Congress had exceeded its constitutional authority and invaded the rightful, sovereign domain of state and local governments. Progressives howled in protest, claiming that **child labor** was an evil that undermined families and social cohesiveness. In the end, however, such decisions were doomed. During the New Deal, which was little more than a decade away, the federal government would dramatically expand its economic role and scope, eclipsing the role of state and local governments in regulating the workplace. *Bailey v. Drexel Furniture Co.* would soon be relegated to the scrap heap of American legal history when the New Deal outlawed child labor.

Baltimore & Ohio Railroad

The Baltimore & Ohio Railroad (B&O) was one of the first **railroads** in the United States and perhaps the most important, particularly for the boost it provided to the Industrial Revolution. The B&O was chartered in 1827 to connect the city of Baltimore, Maryland, with the settlements of the Ohio River valley on the other side of the Allegheny Mountains. During the next sixty years, construction of the B&O took the railroad first to Wheeling, West Virginia, and then on to Ohio, Indiana, Illinois, and Virginia. During the **Civil War**, the B&O was critically important in moving Union soldiers and matériel back and forth between the various theaters of conflict.

After the Civil War, under the management of John W. Garrett, the B&O became central to the burgeoning transportation **infrastructure**. Before the Industrial Revolution could really take off, the U.S. economy needed to be functioning as a national market, which would allow the most cost-efficient industrial manufacturers to sell their mass-produced goods everywhere. The B&O linked Virginia, Maryland, Kentucky, Ohio, Indiana, and Illinois and such major cities as Baltimore, Cleveland, and Chicago into a single marketplace. A host of raw materials—including iron ore, **coal**, and beef—and finished goods plied their way back and forth along the B&O tracks. Along with the **Pennsylvania Railroad** and the **New York Central Railroad**, the B&O was a key element in the northeastern and Midwestern rail network.

Bank of the United States

The Bank of the United States was the first national bank in the country. Critical to the launching and success of the Industrial Revolution in the United States was the existence of a stable monetary system. Economists recognize the importance of a sound monetary system as an essential part of a nation's financial **infrastructure**. When money—or the medium of exchange—is stable and retains value, economic transactions are encouraged. On the other hand, when money is unstable, with rapid inflation or rapid deflation, economic transactions are stalled and economic growth is retarded.

The foundation of a sound monetary system was laid in 1791 when Congress, at the behest of Secretary of the Treasury Alexander Hamilton, established the Bank of the United States. Hamilton viewed the bank as a critical financial institution in the new republic. The bank could serve as a repository for government funds, a source of capital for fledgling American manufacturing enterprises, and a vehicle for issuing a reliable currency, which would dampen inflationary pressures and encourage investors to put capital at risk.

Establishment of the bank was controversial. The Federalist Party, led by President George Washington and Hamilton, represented northeastern business and banking interests and backed the idea of a national bank. The Democratic Republicans, led by Thomas Jefferson and James Madison, opposed the bank. The Democratic Republicans, whose constituency consisted largely of southerners, westerners, workers, and farmers, feared that the national bank would stack the economic deck in favor of the privileged and discriminate against the working classes. They also argued that the bank would be an unconstitutional extension of the authority of the federal government. Debtors, who often appreciated inflation because it reduced the value of the dollars they were paying back on long-term loans, feared that the national bank would stabilize prices. Nevertheless, the Federalists prevailed, and in 1791, the Bank of the United States was established with a twenty-year charter.

During the next two decades, the debate over the Bank of the United States continued, but as the Democratic Republicans replaced the Federalists as the dominant political party in the United States, the bank's days were numbered. When its charter expired in 1811 during the James Madison administration, Congress refused to renew it, and the bank disappeared.

The timing could not have been worse. One year later, the United States entered the War of 1812 with Great Britain, and the lack of a government central bank complicated financial operations necessary to the efficient conduct of the war. It became obvious to President Madison that eliminating the national bank had been a mistake, and in 1816, at his request, Congress established the Second Bank of the United States and gave it a mission very similar to that of its predecessor.

Controversy surrounding the Second Bank of the United States exploded into the public consciousness with the **panic of 1819**. The bank had intentionally pursued conservative monetary policies in order to stem the tide of land speculation and in doing so had inadvertently prompted a financial panic. Democrats, now led by Andrew Jackson, soon targeted the bank for destruction, while the National Republicans, led by John Quincy Adams and **Henry Clay**, defended the bank. When Jackson became president of the United States in 1829, the bank's days were numbered. In October 1833, after his successful reelection campaign, Jackson precipitously withdrew all government money from the Second Bank of the United States, essentially sending it careening toward bankruptcy. When the bank's charter expired in 1836, Congress refused to renew it, and the Second Bank of the United States joined the first in history. When its federal charter expired, the bank secured a state charter from Pennsylvania and changed its name to the Bank of the United States of Pennsylvania.

Most economic historians looking back upon early American history credit Alexander Hamilton, more than any other American, with being responsible for establishing a political climate conducive to economic growth, particularly industrial growth. He recognized that in the future, a nation's wealth and power would largely be a phenomenon of its industrial economy, and by urging federal tariffs, he intended to provide protection to America's fledgling manufacturing enterprises. He also realized the need for stability in the money markets to encourage economic investment, and his plans for a national bank, funding of the national debt, and the assumption of state debts were all aimed at providing that financial stability. It would take decades before Americans fully appreciated his wisdom. After the demise of the Second Bank of the United States during the Jackson administration, the U.S. money markets functioned without the benefit of a central bank. The National Banking Act of 1864 partially rectified the problem, but it was not until the Federal Reserve Act of 1913 that the United States finally had an effective mechanism for regulating the money markets.

Bell, Alexander Graham

A good communication system, which economists identify as part of a country's **infrastructure**, was a necessary prerequisite to sustain the Industrial Revolution of the nineteenth and early twentieth centuries. Alexander Graham Bell's invention of the **telephone** revolutionized communications in the United States, infinitely improving the efficiency of transmitting information. Bell was born in Edinburgh, Scotland, on March 3, 1847. After finishing his education at the McLauren Academy and the Royal High School in Edinburgh, Bell went to work for his father in London. The elder Bell was an inventor and elocution teacher specializing in speech issues, and his Visible Speech System became a popular method for teaching the deaf. The younger Bell's mother was hearing impaired. The family emigrated to Canada in 1870. In 1871, Alexander Bell moved to New England, where he began working with teachers of the deaf. In 1872, he opened a normal school in Boston for prospective teachers of the deaf. One year later, Bell joined the faculty of Boston University as a professor of vocal physiology.

At Boston University, Bell continued his research in deaf education and acoustics and began working on a process for converting electronic **telegraph** impulses into voice, which he called his electric speaking telegraph or telephone. In 1874, he developed the harmonic multiple telegraph and the telephonic telegraphic receiver, both of which were great advances in the electrical transmission of speech. Finally, on May 10, 1876, Bell demonstrated in Boston the first magnetoelectric telephone. Bell patented the invention and founded the Bell Telephone Company. The telephone soon became a ubiquitous consumer item in the United States and an essential vehicle for conducting business. Instead of waiting for the mail or having to translate Morse-code telegraph messages into written form, business-men could instantaneously transmit information by voice and thus could more readily market their products and solve problems. The company enjoyed sustained growth, and in 1885, Theodore Vail reorganized it into American Telephone & Telegraph (AT&T). AT&T was destined to become the world's largest communications firm.

Alexander Graham Bell spent the rest of his life in deaf education and inventing. Among his other patents were the photophone, which transmitted sound by light; the telephone probe, which helped locate metallic objects inside the body; the spectrophone; and the wax cylinder record to be used in phonographs. Bell died on August 2, 1922.

Alexander Graham Bell opens a long-distance telephone line from New York to Chicago in 1892. (Library of Congress)

Bellamy, Edward

Because the Industrial Revolution introduced vast changes into American life and generated much visible wealth for a few while most toiled at near-subsistence wages, a cohort of critics also appeared who asked difficult questions about the future of the country. One of them was Edward Bellamy. Born in Chicopee Falls, Massachusetts, on March 26, 1850, Bellamy grew up in a rural village near the city of Springfield. He came from a long line of Protestant evangelical ministers and attended Union College for a year, hoping to prepare himself for a legal career. He tried his hand at the law in Springfield for a year, but the work bored him. Bellamy then worked as a journalist, moving to New York City and writing for the *New*

York Evening Post. Writing suited him, and he returned to Springfield to work for several local papers.

In the early 1880s, Bellamy traded nonfiction journalistic writing for fiction, making more money writing short stories and romantic novels. He then scored a huge success with his 1888 novel *Looking Backward, 2000–1887,* which sold more than 500,000 copies. The novel took a harsh look at what the Industrial Revolution had done to the American economy and to American workers.

The novel's central character is Julian West, a proper, well-to-do Boston businessman who, instead of dying in an 1887 fire, slipped into a coma from which he emerged in the year 2000. Bellamy built romance into the story by having West fall in love with the great-granddaughter of his real fiancée. For science aficionados, *Looking Backward, 2000–1887* included descriptions of twenty-first-century technologies, including horseless carriages, airplanes, and music-playing machines.

But at the heart of the novel was a socialist critique of American society. In the year 2000, Julian West encounters an America in which the entire economy has been organized into a single enterprise. Each American citizen owns an equal share. All work is performed by an industrial army that each citizen joins at the age of twenty-one and in which he works until the age of forty-five. After completing that twenty-four-year "tour of duty," workers can retire. Work assignments are allocated on the basis of interest and ability. Wages have become obsolete because each American receives a perfectly equal share of the economy's production. All money and private business transactions are abolished. Private savings are strictly prohibited, and all excess capital reverts to the state.

Bellamy called this new economy *nationalism* to avoid the term **social- ism,** which he knew most Americans loathed. His own vision of the new economy seemed much more benign than the class warfare and revolutionary violence of Marxism. In the novel, socialism had come to the America of the year 2000 by the process of peaceful evolution. For Edward Bellamy, "The movement toward the conduct of business by larger and larger aggregations of capital, the tendency toward monopolies, which had been so desperately and vainly resisted, was recognized at last, in its true significance, as a process which only needed to complete its logical evolution to open a golden future to humanity. . . . industry and commerce, ceasing to be conducted by a set of irresponsible **corporations** and syndicates of private persons at their caprice and for their profit, were intrusted to a single syndicate representing the people, to be conducted in the common interest for the common profit" (Bellamy, 1888).

Bellamy's book was so popular that in 1889, a group of Boston readers formed a Nationalist Club to promote its vision of the American future. Within two years, more than 140 Nationalist Clubs had appeared in the

United States, all committed to fulfilling Edward Bellamy's dream. Between 1889 and 1891, Bellamy edited *The Nationalist*, a magazine devoted to his ideas, and from 1891 to 1894, he edited *The New Nation*. Bellamy tinkered with the idea of founding a Nationalist Party to compete with the Democrats and the Republicans, but the plan never had any real success, except in Rhode Island, where it managed to run a slate of candidates in 1891. Bellamy returned to writing and produced a sequel to *Looking Backward, 2000–1887* titled *Equality*, which was published in 1897. It was not nearly as successful as *Looking Backward*, and the next year, on May 28, 1898, Bellamy died of tuberculosis.

Although the vast majority of Americans had no interest in socialism because they perceived it as an ideology that would limit their opportunities to move up the economic ladder, Bellamy's ideas had a temporary popularity in the late nineteenth century. His ideas about the perfect economy were poorly conceived and would have been disastrous had any government tried to implement them, but more than any other American except **Eugene V. Debs**, Bellamy delivered a highly popular critique of **capitalism** and the Industrial Revolution. No other American ever enjoyed Bellamy's success in making socialism palatable, if only temporarily, to large numbers of people.

Bessemer Process

During the first half of the nineteenth century, as the Industrial Revolution got under way in the United States, the need for more durable metals for construction purposes increased dramatically. Buildings were constructed out of wood, but in urban areas, where property was at a premium, the need to build taller structures became more compelling. Wood could not be used, however, for constructing buildings more than four or five stories tall because of the inherent structural instabilities. In rural America, farmers searched for a new material for making implements, primarily because iron was too heavy and too brittle. Finally, **railroad** construction created a huge demand for rails, but because of iron's impurities, maintenance costs were very high.

Throughout the United States and Western Europe, inventors tinkered with the problem, and two men simultaneously came up with the answer. In 1851, William Kelly, an ironmaster in Kentucky, developed a process for converting pig iron into **steel**. He did so by blowing a concentrated current of air through the molten iron, which transformed it into hardened steel by decarbonizing it. Independently of Kelly, British inventor Henry Bessemer developed the technique and perfected it by 1856. The technique became known as the "Bessemer process." In the United States, the first Bessemer forge was constructed in 1864 in Troy, New York. The **mass production** of Bessemer steel, however, really began in 1873 with the formation of the Bethlehem Steel Company. That year, more than 800,000 tons of iron rails were manufactured, compared to 115,000 tons of Bessemer rails. The superiority of Bessemer steel, however, was abundantly clear, and it quickly overcame iron rails. Historians also credit the Bessemer process with making the construction of tall buildings—the so-called skyscrapers—structurally possible.

Bimetallism

Bimetallism is the use of two metals, usually gold and silver, jointly as a monetary standard at a set ratio of one to the other. During the second half of the nineteenth century, the Industrial Revolution created enormous increases in **factory** productivity, stimulating an unprecedented expansion in the economy. At the same time, however, the monetary system did not expand at a similar rate, and as a result deflationary pressures were put on prices. On farms throughout the country, gains in productivity produced great surpluses in corn, wheat, and rice, and in response, commodity prices fell. Most American farmers, especially in the South and the West, found themselves facing falling commodity prices and declining incomes while **railroad** freight rates and bank interest rates held steady. Many of them concluded that some means of inflating general price levels was the only way farming families could survive in the new economic world.

The bimetallist movement emerged from these concerns. It was based on the belief that if silver were reintroduced to the monetary system (the Coinage Act of 1873 had demonetized silver, leaving gold the only monetary unit in the United States), inflation would result, which would drive up commodity prices and farm income. Bimetallists gave little thought, however, to the fact that inflation would also drive up other costs. Nevertheless, bimetallists committed themselves to lobbying Congress for new legislation remonetizing silver. They found political support among silver-mining interests in such western states and territories as Colorado, Nevada, Utah, Idaho, and New Mexico.

Opponents of bimetallism took a completely different tack. They argued that silver inflation would ruin the economy by undermining business confidence and having a chilling effect on potential investors. It would raise the cost of food and clothing that workers had to buy, they claimed, and it would discourage investment, since lenders feared inflation. Rising prices would devalue the dollars they received over time as repayment of the loans they had extended.

The debate quickly assumed huge political proportions. Advocates of a single gold standard rallied to the Republican Party, which enjoyed considerable support within the business and banking communities. Democrats, on the other hand, backed the demands of bimetallists and worked in Congress to remonetize silver. When huge new silver discoveries in the late 1870s depressed silver prices, mining interests became even more vociferous in their support for remonetization, which would increase demand for their product and raise its price, while farmers felt that remonetization would stimulate price inflation and ease their income problems. The two interest groups became a potent political combination. In 1878, Congress passed the Bland-Allison Act, which required the federal government to purchase no less than $2 million and no more than $4 million worth of silver each month and to either mint the money into silver dollars or issue legal-tender paper currency backed by the silver. In 1890, Congress passed the Sherman Silver Purchase Act, which required the federal government to purchase 4.5 million ounces of silver every month at market prices and to issue in payment for it treasury notes that were legal tender and redeemable in gold or silver. The legislation however, had long-term economic consequences because it essentially overvalued silver and drove gold out of circulation. To keep from having to abandon the gold standard, Congress repealed the Sherman Silver Purchase Act in 1893.

The repeal only emboldened the bimetallists, who began calling for free coinage of silver. Best-selling books by William Harvey (*Coin's Financial School*, 1894) and **Ignatius Donnelly** (*The American People's Money*, 1895) further popularized the issue, and the new **Populist** Party endorsed free coinage of silver as well. In the presidential **election of 1896**, Republican candidate William McKinley lambasted the idea, while Democrats and Populists, and their candidate William Jennings Bryan, endorsed bimetallism. McKinley won the election handily, and the bimetallists declined rapidly in influence. Most economic historians today agree that free coinage of silver would have brought instability into the monetary system and retarded economic development, primarily by introducing uncertainty into the money markets, which would have discouraged capital investment. Declines in capital investment would have led to declines in industrial production and increased unemployment in the industrial sector. The likelihood that free coinage of silver would have produced the results silverites expected is extremely slim.

Bryan, William Jennings

William Jennings Bryan was born in Salem, Illinois, on March 19, 1860. He graduated from Illinois College in 1881 and then took a law degree from the Union College of Law in Jacksonville, Illinois, in 1883. Bryan practiced law in Jacksonville for four years before moving his practice to Lincoln, Nebraska. There Bryan became active in Democratic politics and won a seat in Congress in 1890. By that time, the economic life of Midwestern farmers was deteriorating under the pressure of massive overproduction and high railroad freight rates. Bryan was reelected to Congress in 1892 and associated himself with the silver bloc—a coalition of farmers and some industrial workers who believed silver inflation would cure the country's economic ills. He was unsuccessful in 1894 in his bid for a United States Senate seat. After leaving politics, Bryan became head of the editorial staff of the *Omaha World-Telegram* and an extremely popular speaker on the Chautauqua circuit. He toured the country advocating free coinage of silver.

Bryan rocketed to national prominence in 1896 at the Democratic National Convention in Chicago, where he delivered his famous "Cross of Gold" speech and won the party's presidential nomination. The Populist Party then nominated him as their candidate, and Bryan campaigned against the Republican nominee, William McKinley, on the free silver platform. Unable to put together a national coalition of workers and farmers, Bryan lost the election by 7,035,638 votes to 6,467,946. He sought the presidency again in 1900, using anti-imperialism as the issue against McKinley, but Bryan lost again, this time 7,219,530 votes to 6,358,071. Bryan ran again in 1908, but he lost to Republican William Howard Taft by 7,679,006 votes to 6,409,106.

In 1912 Bryan actively supported the presidential candidacy of Woodrow Wilson, and when Wilson won the election, Bryan was rewarded with the cabinet position of secretary of state. While at the State Department, Bryan negotiated thirty separate treaties with other nations providing for arbitration of international disputes, but he resigned from the cabinet in 1915 when he felt Wilson was reacting too aggressively to the sinking of the *Lusitania*. Bryan believed strictly in absolute neutrality, and he could not morally continue to serve under Wilson.

C

Canals

During the early nineteenth century, the greatest impediment to economic development in the United States was the lack of an adequate transportation **infrastructure**. The country abounded in land and open spaces, but linking different regions into an efficient economy required better, more effective ways of moving people and goods. The boom in canal construction in the 1820s, 1830s, and 1840s was a major attempt to fill that need. At its most fundamental level, canal construction was designed to connect interiors to river systems, or even river systems to river systems, to make sure that products could be shipped into regional, national, and international markets.

In 1817, the New York state legislature inaugurated the canal era by authorizing the construction of the **Erie Canal**, extending from Buffalo to Albany. After eight years of construction, the Erie Canal linked much of the Old Northwest and the New York hinterland with New York City, since products could now be shipped along Lake Erie to Buffalo, from Buffalo to Albany on the Erie Canal, and from Albany to New York City via the Hudson River. The Erie Canal's near-instant success inspired a boom of canal building throughout the United States, but especially in the Northeast and Midwest. In 1832, the Morris County Canal was completed, which crossed New Jersey and connected New York City with the Lehigh River. The James River and Kanawha Canal linked the cities of Richmond and Buchanan, Virginia. Another successful canal was the Chesapeake and Ohio, which connected Georgetown with Cumberland, Maryland. The **Ohio and Erie Canal** connected Portsmouth, Ohio, with Cleveland; the Miami Canal linked Cincinnati with Toledo, Ohio; the Wabash and Erie Canal tied together Toledo, Ohio, and Evansville, Indiana; and the Illinois and Michigan Canal connected Lake Michigan and the Illinois River and gave rise to the city of Chicago.

The great limiting factor for canals was geography. Canals could defy the law of gravity and go uphill only at great expense. By the 1840s, the advent of **railroads** all but rendered new canal construction irrelevant. Railroad construction and maintenance costs were cheaper, and there were no geographical limits. State and local governments and entrepreneurs quickly shifted their investment capital away from canals and into railroads.

Capitalism

Most economic historians are convinced that capitalism was a necessary prerequisite to the development of the Industrial Revolution in the United States. Defining capitalism is loaded with ideological implications, but most economists would be comfortable with the notion that capitalism is a form of political economy in which the vast majority of the assets of production and distribution are in private hands and are protected from capricious confiscation by the state. Within a capitalist economy, certain properties are owned by the state in order for it to carry out its police powers, but the bulk of economic activity is generated by private property owners.

Central to the successful functioning of capitalism is the legal sanctity of private property. In the early eighteenth century, philosopher John Locke in England laid the foundation for contemporary American views of private property. For Locke, private property was the key to individual rights because only men with assets of their own could protect themselves from capricious actions of government. Property endowed individuals with power and independence. The right to own and dispose of property, according to Locke, was a "natural right," given by God to all men and women. Without it, Locke argued, the economy would stagnate and society would disintegrate.

The U.S. Constitution clearly recognized the importance of private property, since the Founding Fathers generally endorsed Locke's philosophical notions and realized that only individuals with the right to keep what they had earned would possess the incentive to work hard and take economic risks. A political climate in which property could be randomly confiscated and redistributed to others would have a chilling effect on economic growth.

In the Fifth Amendment to the Constitution, the federal government was specifically prohibited from taking from individuals their "life, liberty, or property without due process of law," and the Sixth Amendment required that when government of necessity had to exercise eminent domain and seize private property for public purposes, the owner had to be awarded "just compensation," by which the Founding Fathers meant fair market value. In other words, individuals losing property to the state could not have their bottom-line financial position adversely affected by such actions.

After the **Civil War,** to protect recently emancipated slaves from discrimination at the hands of Southern state governments, the Fourteenth Amendment to the Constitution was ratified. It openly awarded citizenship and civil rights to former slaves and prohibited state governments from violating those rights. In subsequent federal court decisions, those "rights" were interpreted as those outlined in the Bill of Rights. In the case of *Santa Clara County v. Southern Pacific Railroad* (1886), the Supreme Court said as much, proclaiming that **corporations** enjoyed the same constitutional rights as individuals. Therefore, private property received the same protection from arbitrary state government action that it had enjoyed from arbitrary federal action.

During this period, a major public policy debate in the United States revolved around the question of whether state and federal regulation of private economic institutions, like business corporations, constituted a violation of their property rights. Businessmen anxious to avoid government interference employed **laissez-faire** rhetoric and private property claims to keep government at bay. Social reformers interested in maintaining competitive markets and eliminating the worst excesses of business irresponsibility, on the other hand, claimed that regulating companies for the sake of the general welfare did not substantively compromise property rights. Finally, socialists rejected the notion of private property altogether and claimed that only when government had seized the means of production and distribution would American society enjoy true equality.

Throughout the years of the Industrial Revolution in the nineteenth and early twentieth centuries, the federal courts found themselves evaluating, and usually limiting, interference in the marketplace by local, state, and federal governments. For the most part, the Supreme Court upheld the notion that the Founding Fathers had intended to leave most decisions about the allocation of goods and services to market forces. The greatest contribution the Supreme Court made to the protection of capitalism from arbitrary political interference was its interpretation of the **commerce clause** of the Constitution, which generally confined state government authority to the state's own territory and restricted federal authority to questions involving interstate commerce. In *Wabash, St. Louis & Pacific Railroad Co. v. Illinois* (1886), for example, the Court held that Illinois could not regulate railroad rates if any section of the railroad's route lay outside state lines. In *Gibbons v. Ogden* (1824), the court prohibited New York State from granting a monopoly on river traffic between New York and New Jersey.

As a result of the Supreme Court's interpretations, capitalism survived and thrived in the United States. Privately held corporations enjoyed a full array of constitutionally protected civil rights; governmental interference with private enterprise was carefully defined and limited; and capitalism was widely perceived as the most functional way of managing an economy.

 # Carnegie, Andrew

Andrew Carnegie—the greatest industrialist in U.S. history, the founder of the modern **steel** industry, and a symbol of all that was good and bad about the Industrial Revolution—was born in Dunfermline, Scotland, on November 25, 1835. His father was a handloom weaver. From his father, the younger Carnegie learned to hate unearned money and unnecessary labor, particularly when it appeared in the form of wealth and privilege based simply on what Carnegie called the "accident of birth."

The family immigrated to the United States in 1848 when the advent of power machinery in **textile** mills rendered hand labor inefficient and uneconomical. An economic depression that year also inspired the Carnegies to leave Great Britain. The family settled in Allegheny, Pennsylvania, where Andrew secured a work for $1.20 a week in a cotton factory. Carnegie quickly concluded that the job would get him nowhere in life, so he began attending night school, studying bookkeeping. His education soon earned him a job as a clerk.

He left the cotton factory in 1850 to work as a messenger boy in a Pittsburgh **telegraph** office. In what can be considered the classic route to success, he worked hard, earned a reputation for reliability, and wasted no opportunity to take on more responsibility. Continuing in night school, he studied telegraphy, Shakespeare, and debate. In 1853, Thomas Scott went to Pittsburgh as superintendent of the **Pennsylvania Railroad**, and he named Carnegie as his personal clerk and personal telegraph operator. Scott quickly came to depend on Carnegie and viewed him as a priceless asset. Carnegie was named superintendent of the Pittsburgh division of the Pennsylvania Railroad. With his own savings and money borrowed from friends and relatives, he also invested carefully in **railroads**, bridge-construction companies, and the infant **petroleum** industry.

In 1865, convinced that the economic future of America would be built on a foundation of steel, Carnegie resigned from the Pennsylvania Railroad. With an investment income in excess of $50,000 a year, he made even more money selling railroad securities in Europe, putting much of it into a Pittsburgh ironworks business. He did not immerse himself in the details of the business but instead traveled widely to pick up new technologies, generated capital to implement modern innovations, and made cutting costs a personal fetish. He aggressively marketed his products, and because of his low costs, his market share steadily increased as he left competitors behind.

Carnegie also committed himself to what economists would later call **vertical integration**—developing the ability to replace suppliers by assuming their duties. In 1870, Carnegie launched the process of vertical integration by producing the pig iron that his ironworks **factory** used. When the American economy collapsed, Carnegie was positioned to use his financial assets, which he had preserved through conservative management, and poured his resources into the iron and steel industry, buying up bankrupt properties at fire-sale prices. He erected a steel mill, incorporated every new technology, including the new **Bessemer process**, slashed prices, and by 1877 was producing 15 percent of all Bessemer steel in the United States. Railroads bought much of the Bessemer steel because its hard durability was far superior to softer steel and iron rails.

In 1882, Carnegie integrated further by purchasing a controlling interest in the H.C. Frick Coke Company, which supplied **coal** and coke to the steel factories. **Henry Frick**, a brilliant business manager, assumed supervision of the day-to-day operations of Carnegie's properties. He also identified other steel factories for Carnegie to purchase. In 1892, with Carnegie by far the largest steel producer in the country, the United States outproduced Great Britain in steel. It was an important moment in the history of the world because leadership of the Industrial Revolution had crossed the Atlantic from the Old World to the New.

But that year, Carnegie's public reputation was badly damaged by the strike at the Carnegie factory in Homestead, Pennsylvania. Frick badly mismanaged the strike, which erupted into a virtual civil war between workers and the goons and private detectives that Frick called in to break the strike. The strike broke the union and allowed Carnegie to cut costs and wages even more.

In 1896, Carnegie integrated further by leasing a huge interest in the iron-rich **Mesabi Range** of Minnesota. He also bought steamers to deliver iron ore and coal along the Great Lakes and railroads to bring the raw materials into his factories. The finished steel now coming out of Carnegie factories came from Carnegie-owned iron and coal mines, Carnegie-owned railroads and steamers, and Carnegie-owned pig-iron foundries. Because of the principle of vertical integration, which he had largely pioneered, and his constant focus on reducing costs, Carnegie came into virtual control of the entire steel industry in the United States. In 1899, the Carnegie Steel Company was incorporated with a capital of $320 million. In 1901, with financier **J. P. Morgan** engineering the financial transaction, Carnegie sold his interests for securities worth more than $400 million. When the final papers were signed, Morgan congratulated Carnegie for "just having become the richest man in the world."

Carnegie spent the rest of his life giving away the money. The lessons he had learned from his father back in Scotland had remained with him. In his 1889 treatise "The Gospel of Wealth," Carnegie expressed his belief that the rich should redistribute their wealth rather than simply pass it on to the next generation, where the money would foster idleness and consumption rather than useful pursuits. Through such foundations as the Carnegie Endowment for International Peace, the Hero Fund, the Carnegie Institute of Pittsburgh, and the Carnegie Corporation, he funded projects to encourage scientific research, library construction, higher education, and world peace. When Carnegie died in 1919, he was widely considered to be one of the most influential and contradictory men in the world, an exploiter of labor who gave money away and a ruthless businessman who played a central role in founding the modern steel industry and transforming the American economy into the most powerful in the world.

Central Pacific Railroad

The Central Pacific Railroad was one of the most important transportation improvements in the United States during the Industrial Revolution. During the **Civil War**, Congress passed the Pacific Railway Act, which provided federal funding for construction of a **transcontinental railroad**. In California, several prominent businessmen and railroad owners—Leland Stanford, Collis Huntington, **Charles Crocker**, and **Mark Hopkins**—formed a consortium to build the west-to-east link in the transcontinental railroad. Congress awarded them the contract in 1864 to build the road, which would link up with the **Union Pacific Railroad**, which was constructing the east-to-west line. The two roads met at Promontory Summit, Utah, on May 10, 1869. The transcontinental railroad changed the American economy. More than anything else, it created a national market, linking the people of the Pacific coast with the eastern settlements. American businessmen gained new access to Pacific and Asian markets, since goods could now be shipped efficiently across the continent and then around the world.

Chicago, Milwaukee & St. Paul Railroad Company v. Minnesota (1890)

During the 1880s, as farmers in the Midwest and South found themselves squeezed between falling income and rising prices, a political movement began to regulate the prices charged by railroads and grain-storage facilities. In Minnesota, the state's Railroad and Warehouse Commission was charged with regulating these rates, and the state legislature specifically prohibited any judicial appeals of the commission's decisions. The Chicago, Milwaukee & St. Paul Railway took exception to the legislation and sued in the federal courts, arguing that its constitutionally protected right to due process had been violated. The case was argued before the U.S. Supreme Court in January 1890, and the decision was rendered on March 24, 1890. The Supreme Court agreed with the railway that a denial of judicial review constituted a denial of due process. State legislatures could indeed regulate corporate activities under certain circumstances, but legislative decisions were also subject to judicial review. The *Chicago, Milwaukee & St. Paul Railway Company v. Minnesota* case was a landmark in American jurisprudence. It established a key tenet of administrative law—that judicial review of administrative-agency decisions is required in order to guarantee the preservation of constitutional rights. In reaching such a decision, the Court provided another protection to **corporations** and encouraged economic investment and growth.

Child Labor

The Industrial Revolution precipitated a vigorous, long-term debate in the United States over the merits and abuses of child labor. As **mass-production** techniques rendered certain skills obsolete, the employment of children became more and more common as a means of keeping wage costs down. Child labor became especially common in textile mills and mines. Reform movements calling for an end to child labor succeeded in several Northern states, resulting in anti–child-labor legislation. But when Southern states refused to pass a similar legislation, Southern **factory** owners soon enjoyed a competitive advantage over their Northern competitors, since their wage costs were lower. Many Northern factory owners then joined with the social-work community in calling for national legislation limiting child labor.

In 1904, the National Child Labor Committee was formed to lobby Congress for such legislation. Congress finally responded in 1916 with the Keating-Owen Child Labor Act, which prohibited in interstate commerce the shipment of any goods manufactured by child labor. The law defined such products as those made by any person under fourteen years of age. A number of Southern mill owners contested the legislation in federal court, and the case of ***Hammer v. Dagenhart*** reached the Supreme Court. In 1918, the Court decided the case, ruling the Keating-Owen Act unconstitutional. Congress then responded with a new legislation imposing a 10 percent

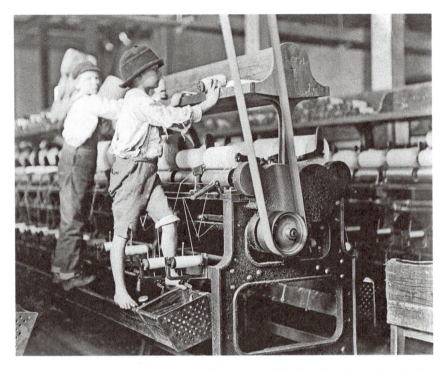

Two young boys climb on the spinning frame to mend broken threads and put back empty bobbins at a Macon, Georgia, textile mill in 1909. (Library of Congress)

federal tax on all goods entering interstate commerce that had been made by children. It too was appealed, and the case of **Bailey v. Drexel Furniture Co.** reached the Supreme Court. In 1922, the Court ruled this legislation also unconstitutional. It was not until the Great Depression that child-labor opponents finally prevailed, when the National Industrial Recovery Act, as well as other congressional laws, imposed restrictions on child labor.

Chrysler, Walter Percy

Along with the steamboat and the **railroad**, the **automobile** was the most important transportation innovation in the history of the Industrial Revolution, and Walter Percy Chrysler was one of the most important entrepreneurs in the history of the automobile industry. Chrysler was born in Wamego, Kansas, on April 2, 1875. Intellectually gifted, particularly in mathematics and mechanics, Chrysler after graduating from high school worked for several years in railroad machine shops. He apprenticed as a railroad machine mechanic and, after getting his certification as a master railroad mechanic, took a job with the Chicago & Great Western Railroad. By 1908, he occupied an executive position with the railroad supervising the work of more than 10,000 mechanics.

Chrysler left the Chicago & Great Western in 1912 to work for the American Locomotive Company, a change that required him to relocate to Pittsburgh, Pennsylvania. By that time, however, Chrysler's interests had shifted from railroads to automobiles, which he believed had the potential to introduce dramatic economic and social changes in American life. To pursue his dream, Chrysler left the American Locomotive Company for a much lower salary with **General Motors Corporation** (GM) in Detroit, Michigan. He was placed in the Buick division and soon had a dramatic impact on GM operations: slashing costs, introducing scientific management techniques, and implementing an assembly-line system in which automobile bodies were moved on a track down a line with workers. Production and profits boomed, and the GM management in 1916 named Chrysler president of Buick.

As Buick's president, Chrysler pushed the GM management to **vertically integrate** the company, and as part of that drive, GM purchased a controlling interest in the Fisher Body Corporation, the company that supplied GM with most of its bodies. By that time, however, Chrysler's days with GM were numbered, primarily because of a deteriorating personal relationship with **William Durant**, GM's president. Chrysler resigned in 1920 and spent the next two years with the Willys-Overland Company and later the Maxwell Motor Company. But he yearned to go out on his own and found a new automobile-manufacturing company. He had been developing the "Chrysler Six," a six-cylinder **internal-combustion engine**, and in 1922, he formed the Chrysler Motor Corporation to build it. In 1923, Chrysler manufactured and sold 32,000 models. In 1928, Chrysler purchased the Dodge Brothers Company, an automobile manufacturer with 20,000 employees, and introduced the Plymouth and DeSoto automobile lines. By the end of the decade, Chrysler had established more than 4,000 retail dealers throughout the country to sell Plymouths, Chryslers, Dodges, and DeSotos. Along with Ford and GM, Chrysler Motor Corporation had become one of the "Big Three" automobile manufacturers in the United States. Chrysler retired in 1935 and died on August 18, 1940.

Civil War

The Civil War in the United States was a landmark in the history of the Industrial Revolution. During the previous seventy years, American politics had revolved around a fairly consistent set of issues involving political economy. Beginning with Secretary of the Treasury Alexander

Hamilton's economic proposals in the 1790s and continuing through Senator **Henry Clay**'s "**American System**" in the 1810s, 1820s, and 1830s, Americans had debated the merits of protective tariffs, a national bank, and federally financed **internal improvements**. During these years, the Democratic Party tended to oppose protective tariffs, the national bank, and federally financed internal improvements, all because they were convinced that such policies would benefit well-to-do business and banking interests at the expense of workers and farmers. At the same time, the Federalist Party and its successors among the National Republicans, the Whigs, and then the Republicans supported all these three measures because together they would protect American industry, stabilize the monetary system and credit markets, and create a national market for the sale and distribution of manufactured goods. Debate over tariffs, the national bank, and internal improvements waxed and waned according to the political winds, depending on which party controlled Congress and the White House.

The secession of the Southern states in 1860 and 1861 all but ended the debate, for the next several decades at least. Without eleven Southern states, Democrats lost their control of Congress, and Republicans took charge, wasting no time in implementing their vision of political economy. In 1862, to satisfy Northern industrialists, Congress passed the Morrill Tariff, which increased rates enough to price many foreign producers out of the market. In 1863 and 1864, Congress passed and amended the **National Banking Act**, which required national banks to invest at least one-third of their capital assets in U.S. government securities. They could then issue national-bank notes on up to 10 percent of those investments. The law also imposed a 10 percent federal tax on state-issued banknotes, which essentially priced them out of existence. Finally, Congress passed the Pacific Railway Act of 1863 to finance the construction of a **transcontinental railroad**.

When the Civil War ended, the political economy of the United States finally resembled what Alexander Hamilton and Henry Clay had earlier envisioned. The federal government had become an active agent in creating a business-friendly political atmosphere and in encouraging economic growth. Critics soon claimed that the relationship between the federal government and big business had become too cozy, and **Populist** and then Progressive reformers demanded that the federal government reorient its exercise of power in order to eliminate the worst business abuses.

In addition to altering the relationship between the federal government and the business community, the Civil War helped accelerate the pace of the Industrial Revolution. Historians later debated whether or not the Civil War gave a boost to industrialization, but it seems clear now that the war stimulated wool **textiles**, shipbuilding, timber, food processing, shoe manufacturing, iron and **coal** extraction, and agricultural equipment. Only cotton textiles declined because the war interrupted the shipment of Southern cotton to Northern mills. Use of power-driven **sewing machines** to manufacture uniforms, boots, and shoes soon incorporated these industries into the **mass-production factory** system. Gail Borden's technology for canning milk gave rise to a new food-processing industry.

Clay, Henry

In the evolution of the American political economy during the years of the Industrial Revolution, Henry Clay played a central role in promoting the notion that the federal government bore a major responsibility for stimulating the industrial economy. Clay was born in Hanover County, Virginia, on April 12, 1777. After studying law privately, he was admitted to the Virginia bar in 1797. He did not, however, practice law in Virginia. Clay headed west in 1797, settling in Lexington, Kentucky. He practiced criminal law there and became active in politics, winning a seat as a Democratic Republican in the state legislature from 1803 to 1806. He was appointed to a brief term in the U.S. Senate from 1806 to 1807, returned and served in the state legislature from 1807 to 1809, and won a seat in Congress in 1811. Clay served in Congress from 1811 to 1814 and again from 1815 to 1821 and 1823 to 1825.

During his years in Congress, Clay grew more conservative as he pondered the economy and the American future. He became convinced that before the United States could assume a position of equality in the world, its industrial economy would have to mature. Clay proclaimed what he called his "**American System**"—high tariffs on imported manufactured goods to protect American industry and create jobs, a national bank to stabilize credit markets and the currency, and federally financed **internal improvements** to develop the nation's transportation system and create a national market. Such views alienated him from other Democrats, who preached **laissez-faire** and opposed federal intervention in economic affairs, and Clay soon threw his political lot in with the National Republicans and then the Whigs.

Clay ran for president in the elections of 1824, 1832, and 1844 and lost on each occasion. Between 1825 and 1829, he served as secretary of state in the cabinet of President John Quincy Adams, and he is credited as a congressman in 1819–1820 with engineering the Missouri Compromise. He served in the U.S. Senate again from 1831 to 1842 and from 1849 until

1852, where he engineered the Compromise of 1850. Clay did not live long enough to see his vision of political economy implemented. He died on June 29, 1852. During the **Civil War**, however, everything that Clay had advocated was realized when Congress passed protective tariffs, created a national banking system, and financed the construction of a **transcontinental railroad**.

Clayton Antitrust Act of 1914

The **antitrust** movement had its beginnings in 1890 when Congress passed the **Sherman Antitrust Act**. **Progressive** reformers as well as small businessmen worried that the new industrial **monopolies** had established such control over markets that they had essentially suspended the laws of competition and supply and demand. In order to preserve competition and maintain low prices, the federal government needed to break up the monopolies into smaller, more competitive units. The antitrust movement gained momentum, and businessmen developed tactics to avert antitrust action. One method was to create **interlocking directorates**, in which competing enterprises shared boards of directors that set company policy and established a monopoly in all but name.

During the presidential administration of **Woodrow Wilson**, Congress worked at closing the loophole of interlocking directorates. The Clayton Antitrust Act of 1914 strengthened provisions of the Sherman Antitrust Act by outlawing monopolistic price discrimination, contracts requiring purchasers not to handle the products of competitors, and interlocking directorates in companies valued at more than $1 million. The law also included criminal and civil penalties for corporate officials convicted of violating the law. To satisfy organized labor, the Clayton Act prohibited antistrike injunctions unless the strike posed a major threat to property. The law also legalized strikes, boycotts, and peaceful picketing and demonstrations. Historians consider the Clayton Antitrust Act a linchpin of reform during the Progressive Era.

Coal

Coal was the fuel of the Industrial Revolution. Formed over eons of time as the result of the breakdown of petrified vegetable matter, coal is overwhelmingly composed of carbon. As the vegetable matter decomposed, the matter lost oxygen and hydrogen molecules, leaving behind carbon. Also, as the vegetable matter was gradually covered over by silt, pressure and heat from the earth's crust compressed the hardened carbon into several types of coal. The least efficient form of coal, in energy-producing terms at least, is peat, which possesses relatively low amounts of carbon and high amounts of moisture. Next in efficiency is lignite, which has a higher carbon content. Bituminous coal is higher still in carbon content and therefore has more potential for generating heat. The hardest coal with the highest carbon content is anthracite.

In the United States, the major coal deposits exist in several major regions. The so-called Appalachian bituminous field covers parts of Pennsylvania, West Virginia, Kentucky, Tennessee, Ohio, and Alabama. The Midwest bituminous field covers much of Illinois and parts of Indiana and Kentucky. Iowa, Missouri, Kansas, and Oklahoma constitute the third bituminous field. Together, these three fields supply the United States with most of its coal. North Dakota, South Dakota, and Montana have substantial bituminous deposits, as do Wyoming, Utah, Colorado, Arizona, and New Mexico. Finally, small reserves of bituminous coal can be found on the Pacific coast and in Alaska. The center of anthracite coal is in the vicinity of Scranton and Wilkes-Barre, Pennsylvania. The first coal mine in America opened in Virginia in 1756, and anthracite mines opened in Pennsylvania in the 1780s. During the 1820s, coal mines appeared throughout the mid-Atlantic states.

During the Industrial Revolution, coal had four primary uses in the United States. First, it was used to heat homes and businesses. Second, coal fired the furnaces that produced the steam for engines in steamboats, **railroads**, and industrial machinery. Third, coal provided the coke that, when mixed with iron, produced the makings of modern **steel**. Fourth, at the end stage of the Industrial Revolution, coal-fired generators supplied **electricity** to tens of millions of Americans. By 1918, coal production in the United States had reached an annual volume of 605,546,343 tons, by far the largest in the world.

Commerce Clause

One reason for calling the Constitutional Convention in 1787 was to deal with the chaotic problems caused by thirteen different states exercising independent trade policies, charging import and export tariffs on goods crossing state lines. The most difficult problem was the fact that each individual state began charging high tariffs to protect its own producers from outside competition. As a result, costs rose and economic growth slowed down because the efficient movement of goods became increasingly difficult. To address this problem, the Founding Fathers empowered Congress, in Article I, Section 8, Clause 3, to "regulate Commerce with foreign nations, and among the several States, and with the Indian Tribes." That clause giving Congress power to regulate interstate commerce evolved into the federal government's most important constitutional power.

In 1824, the Supreme Court under Chief Justice **John Marshall** made a landmark decision in ***Gibbons v. Ogden.*** Marshall overturned a New York law awarding a monopoly on steam navigation between New York and New Jersey. Only the federal government, Marshall claimed, possessed such regulatory authority. Throughout the nineteenth century, the U.S. Supreme Court had to deal again and again with jurisdictional disputes over the commerce clause—where state and local authority stopped and federal authority began. In the end, Congress steadily extended its authority over interstate commerce.

The commerce clause of the U.S. Constitution proved to be an enormous boost to the Industrial Revolution. Throughout the world, in the early nineteenth century, maps were divided and subdivided into countries and principalities, each with its own trade policies, including tariffs designed to limit competition from imports. Economists have identified the principle of comparative advantage to describe the process by which a free market makes economies more productive, more efficient, and more competitive. Because of the commerce clause of the Constitution, individual states in the United States could not retard the flow of commerce. As new territories came into the union, the size of the American market increased. While Europe, Africa, Asia, Latin America, and the Pacific were divided into literally thousands of nations and colonies, the United States became the world's largest free market, full of tens of millions of consumers to purchase the wealth of goods flowing out of new industrial factories. More than anything else, the commerce clause of the Constitution helped fashion a legal environment ideal for rapid economic growth.

Contracts Clause

An intimate relationship exists between an economy and the political and legal climate in which it operates. Businessmen and investors need political and legal stability before they will put investment capital at risk, and the Founding Fathers understood that principle. Before the Industrial Revolution could ever have occurred in the United States, a functional legal atmosphere had to be established. Central to that atmosphere is what constitutional historians today identify as the "contracts clause" of the U.S. Constitution.

In Article I, Section 10, Clause 1, of the U.S. Constitution, the "contracts clause" is spelled out clearly, directing that "No State shall . . . pass any . . . Law impairing the Obligation of Contracts." The clause was introduced at the Constitutional Convention in Philadelphia in 1787 by Rufus King of Massachusetts, where Shays's Rebellion in 1786 had led to widespread nullification of business and financial contracts. Daniel Shays had led an armed rebellion against foreclosures on the property of small farmers who had failed to pay their debts or their taxes. The rebellion had sent shivers of fear through the propertied classes of the thirteen states and had helped prompt the convening of the Constitutional Convention to alter or to repeal the Articles of Confederation, which, many concluded, had become too weak to maintain public order and social stability. Only a stronger federal government, they argued, could guarantee that contracts would be upheld and economic growth protected.

The importance of upholding contracts was obvious. Most economic growth comes from the agreements between businessmen and other businessmen and between employers and workers. When businessmen sign contracts, they expect the terms of those agreements to be fulfilled, and when one participant fails to do so, the law assists in the enforcement or the punishment. At the time of the Constitutional Convention, the Founding Fathers were particularly concerned about contracts between creditors and debtors, but their commitment to contracts extended well beyond that one relationship.

During the early decades of the nineteenth century, the Supreme Court, under the leadership of Chief Justice **John Marshall**, dealt repeatedly with the contracts clause and tended to interpret it quite liberally, generally protecting contractual relationships from the interference of state legislatures and state courts. In the case of *Fletcher v. Peck* (1810), for example, Marshall overturned the decision of the Georgia legislature to repeal an earlier piece of legislation that had provided for the sale of large amounts of the public domain at fire-sale prices. When it became clear that wholesale fraud had been involved in the legislation and the sale, the legislature tried to repeal the sale, but Marshall argued that in doing so, the state would violate the contracts clause of the U.S. Constitution, since many individuals who had purchased land under the original provision had done so in good faith. In *Dartmouth College v. Woodward* (1819), Marshall nullified a New Hampshire legislation that had changed the nature of the Dartmouth College charter in order to bring the institution under state control. The legislation, Marshall claimed, undermined the contracts clause.

As a result of the contracts clause of the Constitution and the Supreme Court's early vigilance in upholding it, the ability of state governments to interfere in private economic matters was severely limited. Marshall did agree that state intervention might be necessary during times of economic or military emergency, but those instances, he insisted, would occur only rarely. The contracts clause of the Constitution helped fashion a legal environment in which investors felt safe, politically and legally at least, in putting their capital to use. With that investment capital, the Industrial Revolution received the financial fuel necessary to move and accelerate.

Cooper, Peter

Peter Cooper was perhaps the Industrial Revolution's most unique character, an innovative businessman and inventor who also found his way into radical politics and philanthropy. He was born in New York City on February 12, 1791. When he left school, he apprenticed out to a coach maker, where he learned to fully exploit his mechanical genius. In 1828, Cooper went into partnership with several associates and established the Canton Iron Works in Baltimore, Maryland. In 1829, Cooper made his first major contribution to the Industrial Revolution when he designed and built *Tom Thumb,* the first steam locomotive, which the **Baltimore & Ohio Railroad** purchased. The steam locomotive made the **railroad** age possible and transformed the American transportation system. In 1845, Cooper used his experience in the iron business to construct a rolling mill in Trenton, New Jersey, where he specialized in manufacturing, for the first time, a strong structural iron for use in fireproof building construction. When that iron product came out of his mill, it revolutionized building construction in the United States. In 1856, Cooper refit his mills to make full use of the recently developed **Bessemer process** for manufacturing **steel**.

But his fertile imagination was not content with the iron, steel, and locomotive businesses. He was taken with **Cyrus Field**'s idea of laying a **telegraph** cable under the Atlantic Ocean, and he supplied Field with needed venture capital for the project. Cooper later became president of the New York, Newfoundland & London Telegraph Company. In 1859, he used a substantial portion of his personal wealth to establish Cooper Union in New York City, an institution of higher learning dedicated to science and engineering.

Later in his life, Cooper became interested in politics, and the ideas of **Specie Circular (soft-money)** advocates appealed to him. He became convinced that the country's economic problems could be solved through inflation of the currency by printing more paper money. In

1876, Cooper ran for president of the United States on the **Greenback-Labor Party** ticket, and the next year, he outlined his economic views in the book *Political and Financial Opinions of Peter Cooper with an Autobiography of His Early Life*. In 1883, he wrote *Ideas for a Science of Good Government*. Cooper died on April 3, 1883, just after the book was published.

Copyright. *See* Intellectual Property Rights

Corporation

The corporation was the business organizational vehicle that drove the Industrial Revolution in the United States. The corporation is a form of business organization with assets subdivided into shares, which may be owned by one or many individuals, known as stockholders. Also, the corporation exists independently of its stockholders, who may die or sell their shares without legally affecting the corporation. Also inherent in the concept of the corporation is the fact that individuals can form a corporation only with the legal permission of government.

In the United States, the law came to view the corporation the same as it would an individual. The corporation enjoyed the same rights as an individual and therefore could purchase and sell property, lend and borrow money, enter into contracts, and sue and be sued. Also, debts owned by the corporation are not considered to be the liability of its individual owners.

For businessmen, the corporation provided a number of advantages. First, it was a convenient way to raise long-term capital for businessmen interested in expanding production or marketing networks. The problems associated with securing capital from a bank included the need to post collateral and to repay the loan in full with interest in a limited amount of time. By incorporating and selling shares, on the other hand, a businessman received capital without having to pay interest or having to amortize the loan in a certain amount of time. His obligation, instead, was to pay stockholders their fair share of annual profits. Also, corporations limited a businessman's liability. Upon incorporating an enterprise, a businessman essentially legally segregated his personal assets from the assets and liabilities of the company. The corporation became legally responsible for its own debts, and even in cases of corporate bankruptcy, a businessman's personal assets could not be threatened. Such a limitation of liability encouraged businessmen to take risks that might not otherwise be undertaken if personal assets could be seized in case of failure.

Over the years, the federal courts helped establish a legal environment in which corporations could function successfully; for example, the case of *Santa Clara County v. Southern Pacific Railroad* in 1886 added to corporate legal rights. In the decision, Chief Justice Morrison Waite concluded that under the U.S. Constitution, a corporation should be viewed as a "person" and as entitled to the equal-protection clause of the Fourteenth Amendment to the Constitution. The decision provided corporations a strong hand in their economic dealings with consumers, other businessmen, unions, and employees.

Cotton Gin

After graduating from Yale in 1792, Eli Whitney headed south to Savannah, Georgia, to work as a tutor but soon became intrigued with the great problem faced by cotton planters. The short-staple cotton they produced was loaded with green seeds embedded into the balls of fiber. Before the cotton could be processed, the seeds had to be removed, a labor-intensive process that had to be done by hand, since the seeds clung tightly to the fiber. By 1793, Whitney had a working model of what he called the "cotton gin"—a mechanical device composed of a rotating metal cylinder with teeth—which could be operated by hand or by horsepower. As the cylinder rotated, the cotton was pulled through the teeth, which selected out the seeds. The gin permitted cotton planters to reallocate much of their slave-labor force from removing seeds to planting and harvesting, which made them infinitely more productive. As a result of the cotton gin, cotton production in the United States boomed. Whitney's gin revolutionized cotton production and played a key role in giving birth to the cotton **textile industry** in the United States.

Whitney moved back to New Haven, Connecticut, filed a patent on his new invention in 1794, and went into business manufacturing cotton gins. The business proved to be a financial disaster, primarily because patent law, although already on the books after passage of the first patent legislation in 1790, was unenforceable. Manufacturers throughout the North and South jumped into the gin-making business, and Whitney profited only slightly. One successful lawsuit, which took thirteen years to make its way through the legal system, eventually yielded him a modest settlement.

Coxey's Army

The **depression of 1893** threw millions of people out of work, and unemployment became a recognizable economic and political problem. Poverty and suffering seemed endemic, and some Americans called on the federal government to intervene. Jacob Coxey was one of them.

A local businessman in Massillon, Ohio, Coxey had become deeply concerned about the plight of poor families with unemployed fathers. He thought that the federal government should intervene with a program of public-works construction for unemployed workers. More specifically, he asked Congress to appropriate $500 million for road-construction projects that would hire the unemployed and a federal bonding program that would allow state and local governments to launch construction projects for unemployed workers. Coxey felt that $1.50 a day would be a fair wage for the workers. It was a radical idea for the time, and few people in power would listen to him. In fact, large numbers of businessmen and their allies in Congress denounced the ideas as radical and socialist.

Coxey decided to dramatize his demands with a march of unemployed workers in 1894 from Massillon to Washington, D.C. Although frightened conservatives predicted that Coxey would mass 100,000 radicals in Washington, D.C., and foment revolution, Coxey never managed to have more than 500 workers on the road at any given time, and fewer than 400 of them actually made it all the way to Washington, D.C. A few of them were arrested for disorderly conduct, while the rest simply disbanded and returned home. Police dispersed them. Coxey was arrested for stepping "upon certain plants, shrubs, and turf then and there growing." He posted bond and returned to Ohio. Coxey lived until 1951, having witnessed later and more successful efforts to help the unemployed. His so-called army never came even close to being one, but he had for the first time shown the potential political power of unemployed workers, and that power would finally be realized during the Great Depression of the 1930s.

Crocker, Charles

Perhaps the most significant development in the history of American transportation was the construction of the transcontinental railroad, which created a truly national market in the United States and provided eastern manufacturers with huge new opportunities for volume sales. A leading figure in the construction of the transcontinental railroad was Charles Crocker. He was born in Troy, New York, on September 16, 1822, and was raised in Marshall County, Indiana. He worked for a number of years as a farmer in Marshall County, but his life changed dramatically when he discovered a local iron-ore deposit and formed Charles Crocker Company to mine the deposits.

When gold was discovered in California in 1848, Crocker sold out his Marshall County properties and moved to Sacramento, where he opened a mercantile store serving miners. The business was a gold mine in its own right, making Crocker a wealthy man in a matter of just a few years. Active in state politics, Crocker became part of the fledgling Republican Party during the late 1850s, and his business interests branched out into **railroads** and banking, which brought him into close association with such prominent California businessmen as **Leland Stanford**, Collis P. Huntington, and **Mark Hopkins**. Lobbying diligently in Congress during the **Civil War** years, they secured the exclusive contract to form the **Central Pacific Railroad** and build it east from San Francisco to link up with the **Union Pacific Railroad**, which was under construction from Missouri to the West. The legislation offered both railroads lucrative construction subsidies as well as miles of land on each side of the track, which the railroads could sell to prospective settlers and land developers. Crocker supervised engineering and construction for the Central Pacific, and the transcontinental railroad was completed in 1869.

The Big Four—Crocker, Huntington, Stanford, and Hopkins—went on to become the dominant force in California politics and the California economy. They purchased railroads, steamship companies, port facilities, and the Southern Pacific Railroad, which gave them a stake in another transcontinental line. When Crocker died on August 14, 1888, he was one of the richest men in the United States.

Croly, Herbert David

Herbert David Croly, whom many economic historians regard as the intellectual father of the **Progressive movement**, was born in New York City on January 23, 1869. His father, a native of Ireland, became a New York editor and reformer committed to eliminating corporate and governmental corruption. Croly's mother was a successful journalist in her own right. During his late teen years and throughout his twenties and thirties, Croly attended Harvard sporadically due to poor health, finally graduating in 1910. He served as the editor of the *Architectural Record* between 1900 and 1906 and spent most of his spare time working on the book that became his magnum opus, *The Promise of American Life*, which was published in 1914 and established Croly as the leading intellectual light of progressivism. That same year, Croly became the founding editor of *The New Republic*, a liberal journal of social and political criticism.

Croly spared nobody in his critique of American public policy. Thomas Jefferson, he wrote, had been guilty of "intellectual superficiality and insincerity" and had confused democracy with extreme individualism. In doing so, Jefferson had erroneously concluded that the good society would emerge naturally out of the unhampered activities of individuals. On the other hand, Croly had only praise for Alexander Hamilton, who had pursued a public policy of "energetic and intelligent assertion of the national good." For Croly, contemporary progressives who hearkened to Jeffersonian values were misguided. Big business was a fact of life, a condition of a modern economy, and the government needed to enlarge its role in the economy. For Croly, "Reform is both meaningless and powerless unless the Jeffersonian principle of non-interference is abandoned. The experience of the last generation plainly shows that the American economic and social system cannot be allowed to take care of itself, and that the automatic harmony of the individual and the public interest, which is the essence of the Jeffersonian creed, has proved to be an illusion." Croly rejected all notions of **laissez-faire**, arguing instead that the economy, like all other human creations, was intimately connected to human culture and behavior. To argue otherwise, he insisted, was foolish. Just as human beings could create such economic problems as poverty, worker exploitation, and abnormally high prices, human beings could work out these problems.

But Croly had specific ideas about how government should be used. He rejected **antitrust** ideas aimed at breaking up all large **corporations** in order to maintain a competitive economy, which would then lead, according to classical economics, to lower prices. Croly insisted that big corporations had an advantage over smaller ones—economies of scale that would allow manufacturers to maximize savings and pass them on to consumers. Instead, the federal government should assume the responsibility of regulating the economy, eliminating whatever abuses large corporations produced without breaking them up and losing the advantages of economies of scale. The federal government should also tax the excess profits of the large corporations. Croly also insisted that it was the federal government's responsibility to provide a social-welfare economic safety net for its poor and most vulnerable citizens. Croly's ideas became the foundation of **Theodore Roosevelt**'s "**New Nationalism**" initiative during the presidential **election of 1912**. Although Croly did not live long enough to see his vision of public policy realized—he died on May 17, 1930—the New Deal during the Great Depression embodied most of his ideas. The activist federal government and welfare state that today characterize public policy in the United States are largely the creation of Croly's fertile mind.

 # Cumberland Road

The development of a national market was a prerequisite to the Industrial Revolution; otherwise, the production and marketing of goods would have been confined to local regions, and opportunities for **mass production** would have been curtailed. The first stage of the development of a transportation **infrastructure** was the construction of **turnpikes**, or paved toll roads, and one of the most notable turnpikes was the Cumberland Road or Pike, which also became known as the National Road. The federal government financed the construction of the Cumberland Road, and construction began in 1811, with Cumberland, Maryland, as the road's eastern terminus. Construction continued until 1838, when the road reached Vandalia, Illinois. During these years, a furious debate raged over whether or not the federal government should undertake such projects. States' rights advocates, especially those in the South, argued that the U.S. Constitution did not authorize such an activity by the federal government and that states should retain that responsibility. The Cumberland Road was a landmark in the development of the American transportation system, a pioneer of highways, **canals**, and **railroads** that would eventually link the Atlantic seaboard with the Midwest and help to create a single national market in the United States.

D

Debs, Eugene Victor

Eugene Debs, America's most influential socialist and critic of the Industrial Revolution, was born in Terre Haute, Indiana, on November 5, 1855. In his young teens, he left school to work in Terre Haute as a locomotive fireman. In the **railroad** yards of Terre Haute, where workers were badly exploited by railroad management, Debs began to develop a political consciousness and a commitment to labor organization. Active in the Brotherhood of Locomotive Firemen, Debs quit the railroad yard in 1875 for full-time work as a Brotherhood organizer. In 1880, he was appointed secretary-treasurer of the national brotherhood, and he also became editor of *Locomotive Firemen's Magazine*, the journal of the national union. His editorship gave him increasing influence in the movement to organize railroad workers and to secure recognition from management. At the same time, Debs became active in local Democratic Party politics, where he hoped to secure political support for the labor movement. He was elected city clerk of Terre Haute in 1880 and served until 1884, when he was elected to the state legislature of Indiana.

In 1887, Debs left the state legislature, which he had found too conservative and too unwilling to take the radical steps necessary to redress the power gap between labor and management and poor and rich. He returned to the Brotherhood of Locomotive Firemen, which had become increasingly radical in the intervening years.

Debs had also encountered too much conservatism, he believed, in the railroad craft unions, which were loath to organize less skilled workers. Debs had become convinced that the only way the working classes would ever exert real power in their struggle with management was through mass organization. In 1893, defying both management and the craft unions, Debs established the **American Railway Union** and opened membership to all railroad workers, skilled and unskilled. Workers joined in throngs, and Debs soon found himself the head of one of the largest unions in the United States.

Disaster soon struck the union. In 1893, the United States slipped into a serious depression, and unemployment rates skyrocketed. Economic historians and labor leaders today understand that taking workers out on strike during a depression is a calculated risk. Production is down and unemployment is high, and it is much easier for management to break the strike. Debs and the American Railway Union launched a strike against the Pullman Company, a Chicago manufacturer of luxury railroad cars that shamelessly exploited its workers. Pullman was a convenient target. To give himself complete control over his workers, **George Pullman** required them to live in a company town in which they rented their homes from him, shopped in stores he owned, and even received their pay in company scrip.

But the Pullman Company was also committed to breaking the strike. Across the country, American Railway Union workers refused to handle trains with Pullman cars, which created unprecedented traffic jams and interruptions in shipments. Pullman appealed to President Grover Cleveland for assistance, arguing that the strike had become a federal matter because the railroads shipped in interstate commerce and carried the federal mail. Attorney General of the United States Richard Olney sympathized with management and issued a court injunction ordering Debs to call off the strike. When Debs refused, Olney ordered federal troops to break the strike. Along the railroad lines of the Northeast, a virtual civil war erupted between workers and federal troops. The workers lost, the strike was broken, and Debs was convicted of criminal conspiracy and sentenced to jail.

When Debs was released after six months of incarceration in 1895, he proclaimed himself a socialist committed to government ownership of the means of production and distribution. Only when the federal government seized ownership of railroads and other major industries, he argued, and managed them with the interests of working people in mind could labor ever secure equity in the United States. He was also convinced that the Democratic and Republican parties would never take the country down the road to **socialism**, and he became a founding father of the Socialist Party of America and its standard-bearer in the presidential elections of 1900, 1904, 1908, and 1912. In the **election of 1912**, Debs managed to garner 901,255 votes, about 6 percent of the total vote cast, but that was where he peaked. Never again would the Socialist Party come even close to that electoral percentage.

When World War I erupted in Europe in 1914, Debs denounced it as a conspiracy by capitalists and their imperialist countries to expand their influence throughout the world. He opposed American entry into the war, and after Congress declared war in April 1917, he continued to speak out against American involvement. In doing so, he violated the Espionage Act and was sentenced to prison. During the presidential election of 1920, Debs ran as the Socialist candidate from his prison cell in Atlanta. He won 919,801 votes, or 3.5 percent of the total. In 1921, President Warren G. Harding paroled Debs.

Debs spent the rest of his life speaking at Socialist gatherings and writing as editor of *American Appeal*, the organ of the Socialist Party. He also became interested in prison reform. Eugene Debs died on October 20, 1926. His socialist critique of the American economy never resonated very well with American workers, perhaps because the productivity of the Industrial Revolution, the rise of the consumer culture, and the success of the labor movement eventually made American workers the most prosperous in the world.

Deere, John

John Deere, along with **Cyrus McCormick**, revolutionized the farm implements industry in the mid-nineteenth century. Deere was born on February 7, 1804, in Rutland, Vermont. After a short stint at Middlebury College, he dropped out and went to work for a blacksmith. In 1825, Deere went into business for himself. He moved to Grand Detour, Illinois, in 1836 and opened another blacksmithing enterprise. In his spare time he tinkered with the use of **steel**. Wooden plows had long since given way to iron plows, but iron was brittle, heavy, and inefficient. At the time, there were two varieties of iron plows. The Eagle cast-iron plow had been in use for a long time in the East and South, but it was not suitable for the thick grasses of the western prairies. The soil was too heavy and thick and stuck to the blade, forcing farmers to stop frequently to clean the muck off the plow. The so-called Prairie Breaker cast-iron plow was designed for prairie grasses, but its heavy weight required as many as seven oxen to pull it, and even then it could only manage a two-to three-inch cut in the earth.

Deere wanted to build a stronger, lighter, more efficient steel plow suitable for prairie grasses. He made his first prototype in 1837, and by 1846, he was manufacturing more than 1,000 of them a year. The Deere plow was slow to catch on at first because it was far more expensive than cast-iron plows, primarily because Deere hammered out his steel from German ingot imports. In 1847, he relocated to Moline, Illinois, and founded a manufacturing firm that later came to be known as Deere & Company. He also began to smelt his own steel and cast his own steel moldboards, which made his steel plows more price competitive. By the 1870s, the Deere plow dominated the industry and made the grasslands of the Great Plains a breadbasket through the production of corn and wheat. John Deere died in 1886.

Depression of 1873. *See* Panic of 1873

Depression of 1893

Economic historians identify the depression of 1893 as the first downturn in the business cycle in the United States after the onset of the Industrial Revolution. On previous occasions when the economy had suffered a downturn, relatively few people had been affected because the vast majority of Americans lived in rural areas where they could survive off milk cows, chickens, and a garden. Historians often use the term *panic* rather than *depression* to describe preindustrial economic downturns because the people most affected tended to be merchants and bankers. But because the Industrial Revolution stimulated urbanization, the economic collapse of 1893 had a much broader impact.

The depression of 1893 had its origins in the **railroad** economy, which overexpanded in the 1880s and 1890s and became badly overbuilt. The railroad sector of the economy consumed huge amounts of capital, most of it borrowed from banks or secured from private investors, and the companies went deeply into debt to finance their expansion. These investors expected regular dividend payments and banks needed their loans paid back, but because of overcapacity in the industry, freight rates plummeted and many railroads could not make loan payments or dividends. Late in February 1893, the Philadelphia and Reading Railroad declared bankruptcy, and bankers and shareholders with an interest in the road panicked. That panic soon spread through the credit markets. Large numbers of banks, **corporations**, and well-to-do Americans owned railroad bonds, and the threat of other defaults on these bonds sent the economy into a tailspin. During 1893, more than 500 banks failed, 16,000 businesses declared bankruptcy, and 3 million workers lost their jobs.

The depression of 1893 further loosened the moorings of **laissez-faire**. "I've never seen so many blank, hopeless stares," lamented a Chicago pastor. "Too many children with bloated bellies and dull eyes. They haunt me at night." Apparently they did not haunt President Grover Cleveland, who insisted that government "functions do not include the support of the people."

Industrial society, claimed the **Populist Ignatius Donnelly**, had failed "the great mass[es]. . . . the poor are coming to hate the rich. . . . society divides itself into two hostile camps. . . . They wait only for the drum beat and the trumpet to summon them to armed conflict." In the heartland, farmers accelerated their political organization, which soon evolved into the Populist Party.

In 1894, Jacob Coxey, an obscure businessman from Massillon, Ohio, staged a huge protest. He called on unemployed workers to join him in a march on Washington. Thousands responded, and Coxey massed them together as the Commonwealth of Christ and marched east to force Congress to issue $500 million in greenback paper money and hire hundreds of thousands of workers to construct new roads. Washingtonians panicked. Rumors had Coxey's "troops" raiding the U.S. Treasury and storming the White House. But **Coxey's Army** sputtered to an ignominious end. In April 1894, only 400 reached Washington, D.C. The others ran out of money or just quit. Police dispersed them and arrested Coxey for stepping "upon certain plants, shrubs, and turf then and there growing." After posting bond, he returned to Ohio. Coxey lived until 1951, having witnessed later and more successful efforts to help the unemployed.

Two months later, **Eugene V. Debs**, head of the **American Railway Union**, struck the Pullman Company, a manufacturer of luxury railroad cars. For Debs, Pullman employees suffered a unique form of exploitation. Their pay envelopes were stuffed with Pullman company scrip, not U.S. currency, which could only be used to buy food in Pullman Company stores or pay rent for Pullman-owned housing. Pullman charged exorbitant rents and elevated food prices in the company-owned stores. Union workers refused to handle Pullman cars, and by the end of June, railroad traffic had been disrupted throughout the country. Attorney General Richard Olney, a former railroad lawyer, with the blessing of President Grover Cleveland, crushed the strike with a court injunction outlawing activities that interfered with mail delivery. Federal marshals jailed Debs.

The depression did not begin to ease until late in 1895, and by that time it had become an issue in that year's presidential election. Democratic and Populist nominee William Jennings Bryan called for free coinage of silver, which he believed would help increase the prices of farm commodities and benefit poor farmers. Bryan also called for lower tariffs, which he thought would allow farmers to buy manufactured goods at lower prices. Republican candidate William McKinley opposed tariff reductions and free coinage of silver, and he made his case to industrial workers, especially those who had only recently been rehired as the depression eased. McKinley claimed that higher commodity prices for farmers would only mean higher food prices for workers, and lower tariffs would cost industrial workers their jobs. The workers listened and most of them eventually sided with McKinley and gave him the White House.

Donnelly, Ignatius

During the course of the Industrial Revolution, the rise of big business created great gaps in wealth between the rich and the poor and drew criticism from a variety of reformers. None was more vocal than Ignatius Donnelly. Born in Philadelphia, Pennsylvania, on November 3, 1831, Donnelly came to his radicalism late in life. Early in the 1850s, he toured the Old Northwest and concluded that the town of Nininger, Minnesota, was destined to become one of America's great cities. He was wrong and lost his savings in the **panic of 1857**. Heavily in debt, Donnelly remained in Minnesota and tried to farm the land.

During the **Civil War**, Donnelly became an ardent Republican and a supporter of high tariffs and conservative fiscal principles. He ran for Congress and served three terms, lobbying successfully to secure land grants, government subsidies, and **railroad** lines in his district. But he also grew disillusioned at how consistently businessmen tried to use the powers of government to enhance their own economic positions and how frequently they were willing to exploit other people in order to get them. The Republican Party, he concluded, was nothing more than an agent for business interests, pursuing high tariffs and **hard-money** policies at every turn. In 1870, Donnelly abandoned the Republican Party.

During the next twenty years, Donnelly tried to find a political home in the Liberal Republican Party, the **Greenback-Labor Party**, and the **Granger** movement, and his ideas about **soft money**—free coinage of silver—developed during these years. He served in the state legislature during these years and edited *The Anti-Monopolist*, a political journal dedicated to the **antitrust** movement. When Congress passed the **Sherman Antitrust Act of 1890**, Donnelly considered it a personal victory. He also wrote the book *Caesar's Column* (1890), which predicted the future of cooperative **socialism** for the United States.

As the plight of farmers worsened in the 1890s—declining incomes because of overproduction and rising rates from railroads, grain elevators, and banks—Donnelly joined the Farmers Alliance movement, which soon evolved into the **Populist** Party. In 1892, he wrote the preamble to the Ocala platform of the Populist Party. In 1896, Donnelly endorsed the presidential candidacy of William Jennings Bryan, who was running on the Democratic Party ticket but who had also been endorsed by the

Populists. For Donnelly, the free coinage of silver was the answer to all of the country's economic problems. If the money supply were expanded and commodity prices were inflated, farmers would escape the economic squeeze in which they found themselves, and since most Americans were farmers, the economy would improve. Most voters did not buy the idea, and the Republican candidate William McKinley won the election. Donnelly ran as a Populist for vice president in 1900 and lost, and he died on January 1, 1901.

Du Pont, Pierre

Pierre Samuel du Pont was the most influential individual in one of America's most influential families. His great-grandfather, Éleuthère Irénée du Pont, emigrated from France in 1800 and settled in New York City. The family eventually settled near Wilmington, Delaware, where he began to manufacture gunpowder. The business grew steadily until the War of 1812, when it boomed because of large government contracts. During the next half-century, the business prospered with technological improvements in gunpowder manufacture and international sales. The **Civil War** provided another boost in company profits and led to further expansion as well as some diversification with investments in **textile industry**, **railroads**, hotels, and **steel**. By 1900, the du Ponts controlled 90 percent of the explosives industry in the United States.

It was at this point that Pierre du Pont began to make his mark on the business. He was born in New Castle, Delaware, on January 15, 1870. He graduated from the Massachusetts Institute of Technology in 1890 and then joined the family business. Du Pont left the company in 1899 to become president of the Johnson Steel Company, and three years later, with two of his cousins, he engineered the purchase of all of the du Pont family's interests. He served as president of the company from 1915 to 1919, when the company vastly expanded its arms and chemical-manufacturing interests. Because of the production of pyroxylic lacquer, plastics, cellophane, and rayon, du Pont became the world's largest chemical manufacturer. In 1918, Pierre du Pont purchased $25 million of **General Motors** stock, and he served as president of GM from 1920 to 1923 and chairman of the board from 1920 to 1929. At GM, du Pont revolutionized the company's organizational structure and launched it on a period of enormous growth. In fact, because of his implementation of accounting and statistical control procedures, strategic planning, and relative independence of different operating divisions, he is considered a founder of the modern **corporation**. Du Pont spent the rest of his life overseeing his family's financial interests and working to promote a conservative agenda in the Republican Party. He died on April 15, 1954.

Duke, James Buchanan

Historians consider James Buchanan Duke to be the father of the modern cigarette industry in the United States. He was born outside Durham, North Carolina, on December 23, 1856. As a child, he worked with his father and older brother rolling cigarettes, packaging them, and then selling them along roadsides in North Carolina. Demand always outpaced supply because of the labor-intensive nature of crushing tobacco and wrapping cigarettes by hand. In 1881, his father established W. Duke & Sons Company to manufacture cigarettes, a process that was still done by hand. By 1883, however, they had adopted James Bonsack's machine for automatically wrapping cigarettes, and they were soon able to introduce the principle of **mass production** to their manufacturing process. In 1884, the Dukes opened a branch factory in New York City and began advertising nationally. By the end of the decade, they manufactured half of the cigarettes annually consumed in the United States—billions of cigarettes a year.

Competition, however, was fierce in the tobacco industry, and rival companies decided to limit competition by establishing a **monopoly**. The American Tobacco Company, a merger of the five major cigarette manufacturers, was formed in 1890, with James Duke as president. He soon introduced the Lucky Strike and Pall Mall cigarette product lines, which quickly became very popular with consumers, and Durham Smoking Tobacco, which farmers labeled *Bull Durham*. Plug tobacco manufacturers then decided on the same consolidation process, and in 1898, they established the Continental Tobacco Company and also named Duke as president. Profits soared, and Duke decided to consolidate the entire tobacco industry. In 1900, he formed the American Snuff Company and followed that up one year later by organizing the American Cigar Company, the Consolidated Tobacco Company, and the United Cigar Stores Company. Duke's enterprises, which soon totaled more than 150 factories and $502 million in assets, had become one of America's most powerful industrial conglomerates.

Critics, however, found Duke's business operations too powerful and monopolistic, resulting in an increase in the price of cigarettes. Under the authority of the **Sherman Antitrust Act of 1890**, the Justice Department during the presidency of **William Howard Taft** filed a lawsuit against the so-called Tobacco Trust that Duke had engineered. The case of *United States v. American Tobacco Company* reached the U.S. Supreme Court in

1911, and the Court's decision, which held that the company had deliberately engaged in restraint of trade, forced the reorganization of the American Tobacco Company. Duke remained in the tobacco business for the rest of his life, and during World War I, he distributed cigarettes free to millions of American soldiers. They returned home with lifelong cigarette habits and further enriched James Duke, making him one of America's wealthiest individuals. He died on October 10, 1925.

Durant, William Crapo

Until the rise of Microsoft in the 1990s, **General Motors Corporation** was the largest **corporation** in the world, a product of the Industrial Revolution, and William Crapo Durant was its founder. Durant was born in Boston, Massachusetts, on December 8, 1861, to a prosperous family. A fine mechanic, he supplemented his income from a job working in his grandfather's lumberyard with repair jobs on farm machinery. In 1881, at the age of twenty, he was named manager of the Flint Water Works in Flint, Michigan. The move to Michigan proved to be a fateful one for Durant because it placed him in the geographic region where the **automobile** industry was about to be born.

After working in the carriage business, in 1887, he founded the Durant-Dort Carriage Company. His division of the company into separate divisions specializing in spokes, timber, and wheels and implemented assembly-line techniques to boost production demonstrated his business acumen. By 1891, Durant-Dort was the largest manufacturer of horse-drawn carriages in the United States. Durant did not sell out his interest in Durant-Dort until 1914.

By that time, he was deep into the horseless-carriage, or automobile, industry. In 1904, Durant had purchased the Buick Motor Car Company, and within a few years he had turned the company into one of the leading automobile manufacturers in the country. To Buick he soon added his new purchases—the Cadillac Motor Company, the Oakland Motor Company (which assembled Pontiacs), and the Oldsmobile Motor Company—all four of which he combined into General Motors in 1908. Durant then purchased the Weston-Mott Axle Company of Utica, New York, relocated it to Flint, Michigan, and financed the development of Albert Champion's new porcelain spark plug.

In 1910, after badly overproducing automobiles and undermining company profits, Durant lost control of General Motors and teamed up with Louis Chevrolet, a race car driver and mechanic interested in designing automobiles. The two of them established the Chevrolet Motor Car Company, and their designs were so successful that Durant was able to take his profits and begin purchasing General Motors (GM) stock. In 1916, with extra capital from GM mogul John Jacob Raskob and **Pierre S. du Pont**, Durant managed to regain control of GM.

But his success was to be short-lived. During the depression of 1920–1921, Durant again overextended GM, manufacturing far too many cars and undermining company profits. Du Pont then took over GM. Ever determined, Durant founded the Durant Motor Company, but the company did not survive the onset of the Great Depression, and Durant declared bankruptcy in 1935. He died on March 18, 1947.

 ## Duryea Brothers

Historians credit the Duryea brothers—Charles Edgar Duryea and J. Frank Duryea—with building the first commercially successful **automobiles** in the United States. The two brothers were born in Canton, Illinois, Charles in 1861 and J. Frank in 1870, and they worked together as bicycle mechanics. In 1893, they developed their one-cylinder, two-cycle car, which they demonstrated in Springfield, Massachusetts, on September 21 of that year. One year later, they produced a second car, this one with a four-cycle, two-cylinder engine. The *Chicago Times-Herald* sponsored an automobile race that year, which the Duryea model won, bringing the Duryea brothers to the attention of the automobile-buying public. They then came out with a car that exhibited items important to modern automobiles—a four-speed gear shift; a water-cooled, four-cylinder engine; an electric ignition; a bevel-gear differential; and a front axle with steering knuckles. In 1895, they established the Duryea Motor Wagon Company to manufacture their automobiles. They dissolved the company in 1898 and went their separate ways. Charles founded and managed the Duryea Power Company and retired in 1914. For years Frank headed the Stevens-Duryea Company, a manufacturer of automobiles.

E

Eastman, George

George Eastman, one of the Industrial Revolution's most influential investors, was born in Waterville, New York, on July 12, 1854. As an adolescent, he developed a fascination with photography, and in 1880, he received a patent on his dry-plate invention for processing film and making photographic reproductions. With the patent in hand, Eastman went into business in Rochester, New York, manufacturing dry plates. He soon pooled his financial resources with Henry A. Strong, and together they invented a flexible film that had paper backing. In 1884, they went into the production of the invention, which they called the roll film. Eastman then built and patented a small, box-shaped camera and loaded it with his new film. He named the camera Kodak. It was a hit among consumers. Eastman then went to work developing motion-picture film and secured a patent he jointly held with Henry M. Reichenbach. In 1892, Eastman formed the Eastman Kodak Company.

Through aggressive use of borrowed capital, Eastman rapidly expanded production and market share, and by 1901, Eastman Kodak was the world's largest industrial manufacturer of photography supplies and equipment. Eastman pioneered the idea of industrial research and development, investing substantial sums in hiring and developing a cohort of scientists and technicians who worked full-time on product improvement and product development, and Eastman Kodak soon had a reputation for producing high-quality products. Eastman also pioneered the use of benefits and profit sharing with employees. As a result, he had the lowest turnover of workers of any major business in the United States. Finally, Eastman was a devoted philanthropist. He had never married or had children. His entire fortune went into the company or into such institutions of higher learning as the University of Rochester, the Massachusetts Institute of Technology, Tuskegee Institute, Hampton Institute, Oxford University, and the Eastman School of Music, which he founded in Rochester. A loner with few friends and no family, Eastman committed suicide on March 14, 1932.

Edison, Thomas Alva

Thomas Alva Edison was America's greatest inventor and a leading light in the technological advances that characterized the Industrial Revolution. He was also the first person in the history of the world to make "inventing" itself a business, and because of Edison's example, **corporations** made research and development a key component of strategic planning. He was born in Milan, Ohio, on February 11, 1847. As soon as he started elementary school, teachers decided that he was a slow learner. Historians have since concluded that the brilliant Edison was just so bored with school that he could not pay attention. In any event, his parents withdrew him from school and saw to his education at home. In his early teens, Edison went to work on the **railroads**, selling newspapers, candy, and toiletries from car to car. He also became acquainted with **telegraph** operators at the train stations and grew fascinated with **electricity** and the technology of communication.

In 1863, Edison stopped selling on the trains and became a telegraph operator himself. He also became largely self-educated, with occasional help from night-school teachers, in chemistry. Edison's fertile mind let him always inclined to figure out more efficient ways of completing ordinary tasks. He moved to Boston in 1868 to work for the Western Union Telegraph Company. In Boston, he tinkered with how to more efficiently record votes, and in 1869, he received a patent on his first invention, the electrographic vote recorder. Late in 1869, he relocated to New York as a partner with Pope, Edison & Company, an electrical engineering firm. Within a matter of months, a competing business purchased the firm, and in the transaction Edison received $40,000 as his share.

The money allowed Edison to pursue his dream of starting a business wholly dedicated to inventing new products. He hired creative, technologically adept assistants to work under his direction, and for the next five years they developed a series of improvements in the telegraph. Needing a research facility more conducive to contemplation and discussion, Edison decided in 1876 to build an office and laboratory in Menlo Park, New Jersey. Within a decade, his business operations outgrew the Menlo Park facility, and he transferred his research laboratories to West Orange, New Jersey. Between 1877 and 1879, after years of work and experimentation, Edison's research labs produced two inventions that dramatically changed domestic life. In 1877, his phonograph gave rise to an industry and a technology that allowed music and other forms of voice communication to be conveniently used at home, and in 1879, his first practical incandescent **light bulb** ended forever the need to light up homes and offices with fuel-burning lamps and candles. Edison then constructed a factory to

Relatively uneducated by today's standards, Thomas Edison proved to be one of the most prolific and revolutionary inventors in American history. (Library of Congress)

manufacture light bulbs. In 1896, Edison took Thomas Armat's invention of a movie projector and vastly improved it, producing his Edison Vitascope, which gave birth to the modern era of films and movies. Eventually, Edison received more than 1,000 patents, including those on the storage battery, the dictaphone, the mimeograph machine, the electric locomotive, composition brick, and electric safety lanterns.

In terms of the Industrial Revolution, Edison's greatest invention, however, was his improvements in the electric dynamo, which made possible the production and distribution of large volumes of electricity. In 1875, William A. Anthony had built the first working dynamo to generate outdoor lighting, and in 1881, Edison and his associates at Edison Machine Works constructed the first practical, operating dynamo, a twenty-seven-ton contraption. When the dynamos were combined with **steam turbines**, which were introduced to the United States in 1890, it became practical to generate electricity almost anywhere. These technological developments provided a great boost to **mass-production** techniques. In 1899, only 1.9 percent of electric-motor horsepower in American factories came from purchased electrical current. By 1914, that number had jumped to 17.3 percent.

Thomas Edison was also a successful businessman always interested in using his inventions to make money. He eventually consolidated his manufacturing and research enterprises into the Edison General Electric Company, the forerunner of today's **General Electric Corporation**. In the process of developing new technologies and building a successful business, Edison also became a near folk hero in American popular culture, an icon to America's fascination with the rags-to-riches, self-made-man ideology. Despite being a man with little formal education, Edison had managed to develop technologies that changed the world. He also had a homespun quality that endeared him to millions of Americans. Edison's death on October 18, 1931, made newspaper headlines throughout Europe and the United States.

Election of 1860

Although the Industrial Revolution was an economic phenomenon that transcended politics, economic historians nevertheless identify two presidential elections that had a defining impact on economic development. One of them was the election of 1860. After the election of 1856, the Whig Party disintegrated and the Republican Party filled the vacancy, while the Democratic Party split over the slavery issue. By the time the presidential election of 1860 rolled around, the Democrats had fractured three ways. The Republicans nominated Abraham Lincoln for president, and although he managed to secure only 37 percent of the popular vote, he won because of an electoral-college majority. He had prevailed in every Northern state.

Lincoln's election triggered panic throughout much of the South and precipitated the secession movement. Between December 1860 and June 1861, as Southern state after Southern state seceded from the Union, Democrats lost their majorities in Congress, and Republicans took the upper hand. With Republicans in charge, the **American System** that **Henry Clay** had promoted earlier in the century—high tariffs, a national bank, and federally financed **internal improvements**—enjoyed new currency, and Congress moved ahead on all fronts. To protect Northern industry from foreign competition, Congress passed the Morrill Tariff, which substantially raised rates. To stabilize the monetary system, Congress passed the **National Banking Act of 1864**, which provided for a new system of national banks and a new currency. To improve the nation's transportation system and create a truly national market, Congress passed the Pacific

Railway Act, which financed construction of a **transcontinental railroad**. Together, this **Civil War** legislation provided a boost and stimulus to business at the very time when the Industrial Revolution was accelerating.

Election of 1896

Like the presidential **election of 1860**, the election of 1896 had a defining impact on economic development. At the time, the economy was just beginning to emerge from the **depression of 1893**. Industrial workers, suffering unemployment and declining wages, focused on bread-and-butter issues, but farmers, after decades of declining commodity prices, focused on the free coinage of silver as the panacea for the economy. By inflating the prices of farm products, free coinage of silver would improve farmer income. The Democratic Party and then the **Populist** Party endorsed free coinage of silver, and their joint presidential nominee, William Jennings Bryan, traversed the country preaching the virtues of monetary reform and inflation.

Advocates of a single gold standard rallied to the Republican Party and its nominee William McKinley, who enjoyed considerable support within the business and banking communities. Republicans were convinced that free coinage of silver would be disastrous for both the industrial and the agricultural economies. Republicans told industrial workers that free coinage of silver would inflate the economy and raise the prices of food and clothing, a prospect that terrified most workers and their families. Republicans also warned workers that free silver would have a chilling effect on business investment and would lead to more unemployment. Republicans told bankers that free silver would build long-term inflation into the monetary system and undermine bank profits by devaluing the money bankers would receive as repayment for loans.

In the end, the Republican strategy worked. To win the election, William Jennings Bryan would have needed to win over the loyalties of industrial workers who, if they were allied with most farmers, would have delivered an electoral majority. But what farmers wanted—higher food prices—was exactly what workers feared. When the votes were counted, McKinley had garnered 7.036 million to Bryan's 6.468 million.

Election of 1912

Few presidential elections in U.S. history have revolved more around issues of public policy than the election of 1912. The side effects of the Industrial Revolution had created a new economy and a new society, and many Americans worried about the future of the country. Public policy especially concerned them. The **Progressive movement** was at its peak and produced a debate about the role of the federal government in regulating the new economy.

Democratic presidential candidate **Woodrow Wilson** employed the logic of Louis Brandeis and recommended a vigorous **antitrust** movement. Large companies that had the potential to evolve into **monopolies** should be broken up into smaller units. In doing so, the federal government would restore competition to the economy and guarantee consumers the lowest possible prices. Not surprisingly, Wilson called for a strengthening of the **Sherman Antitrust Act of 1890**. To make the economy even more competitive, Wilson also called for tariff reductions. Through direct election of U.S. senators, he argued, much corruption could be eliminated from the political process. Finally, Wilson advocated a constitutional amendment to authorize a federal income tax. These proposals collectively became known as the "**New Freedom.**"

President **William Howard Taft** and the Republican Party offered a much less ambitious agenda. Taft proposed to continue his antitrust activities, which had been considerable, but he had no credibility on the tariff issue because he had promised lower tariffs and then had delivered the Payne-Aldrich Tariff, which had raised rates substantially. Besides that, Taft paid lip service to the conservative wing of the Republican Party, which wanted to limit government interference in the economy.

Former president had grown more progressive since he had left the White House in **Theodore Roosevelt** 1909, and he had contested the Republican nomination with President Taft and lost. Roosevelt then bolted the Republicans and established the Progressive, or "Bull Moose," Party. Roosevelt proposed to voters the implementation of graduated income and inheritance taxes, federal legislation outlawing **child labor**, the right of women to vote, and government regulation of large **corporations**. Basing many of his proposals on the thinking of **Herbert Croly**, Roosevelt rejected the rigid antitrust approach of Wilson's New Freedom, which wanted all large companies broken up. Roosevelt believed that large companies brought economies of scale to the production process and therefore could benefit consumers if they behaved properly. The federal government had the responsibility to regulate large enterprises to make sure that they did not restrain trade, artificially manipulate prices, or abuse workers and consumers. Roosevelt called his set of proposals the "**New Nationalism.**"

Finally, Socialist candidate **Eugene V. Debs** delivered up the most radical proposals. He argued that **capitalism** was essentially a bankrupt system and that workers could only get justice when the federal government assumed ownership of major industries like **railroads**, the **telegraph** and

telephones, steel, and mining. Once the government had taken over, workers could manage the companies to their own advantage.

When the votes were counted, Wilson had a ticket to the White House. Although Debs and the Socialists did not win, they secured more than 900,000 votes, their best showing ever. Taft did not have a chance because Roosevelt drew away so many votes. Wilson ended up with 6.297 million popular votes to 4.119 million for Roosevelt and 3,487,000 for Taft. Never again would an American presidential election revolve around such clearly defined issues.

Electricity

No technology changed America more than the advent of electric power. In Europe during the 1870s, the first practical, cost-efficient electric generators, known as dynamos, were developed, primarily for factory use in electroplating. But their ability to generate electricity provided vast opportunities for the invention of new, electrically driven technologies. In the United States, the first inventor to really take advantage of the possibilities of electric power was Charles Brush, who specialized in arc lighting for building exteriors and streets. In 1875, sixteen-candle gas lamps were commonly used to light American streets, and more than 400 gaslight companies existed to maintain these systems. Brush believed that arc lighting would be an effective, cost-efficient replacement for gaslights.

Brush invested his energies into the development of a lighting system in which power was generated centrally and transmitted widely. He overcame a number of technical challenges. Brush invented several high-voltage dynamos to generate the power; automatic regulators that would keep current constant; automatic feeding systems to maintain gap distance; and automatic short circuits to preserve systems when lights burned out. In addition, Brush made major improvements in his arc carbons—rounding them, tapering their tips to generate longer life, and copper-plating their bases to reduce resistance. In 1879, Brush built the country's first arc-lighting system in San Francisco. By 1880, he had built similar systems in New York City, Philadelphia, and Boston. Competitors soon built more powerful and more efficient dynamos, and by 1890, the Thomson-Houston Company dominated the market in the United States.

Development of incandescent lamps was largely the work of **Thomas Edison**, who envisioned new systems of indoor lighting, which arc lights could not provide because of their brightness. He wanted to create a direct current (DC) that would supply incandescent lighting. Between 1878 and 1880, he succeeded, and in 1882, he opened the Pearl Street Station in New York City, which relied on jumbo generators to generate electricity. He also founded the Edison Electric Light Company in 1878 to market the electricity. Edison Electric spun off subsidiaries with each new city it penetrated. By 1888, it had subsidiaries in Chicago, Brooklyn, Detroit, Boston, New Orleans, St. Paul, and Philadelphia. Edison dominated the DC market, whereas **George Westinghouse** and his Westinghouse Lighting Company emerged as the leader in the alternating-current (AC) market. By 1892, Westinghouse had made more than 1,000 AC systems providing incandescent lighting.

New-generation systems also appeared. In 1896, Westinghouse Lighting Company completed its Niagara Falls project, which provided mega generation of electric power. Between 1895 and 1910, turbine power increased from 40,000 volts to 150,000 volts. Such large-scale generation capacity created immense new opportunities for the use of electric power.

The availability of centrally generated electricity created opportunities for the development of almost infinite uses for electric motors. Urban transportation provided the first opportunity. In 1880, throughout the United States, 100,000 horses tugged away at 19,000 streetcars. The horses' shoed hooves tore up streets, horse droppings polluted cities, and epizootic diseases accompanied the animals. Also, urban steam locomotives had drawbacks of their own, particularly soot pollution and sparks. Gradually during the 1880s and 1890s, electric traction systems propelled streetcars and replaced the horse-drawn cars and steam locomotives. Between 1888 and 1892, the number of electric streetcars jumped from 130 to 8,000, and by 1903, 98 percent of all streetcars were electrified.

The market for electric motors expanded in 1892 when Thomas Edison merged with Thomson-Houston to form **General Electric Corporation** and to begin developing AC products. At the same time, Westinghouse hired **Nikola Tesla** to build electric motors using AC power. Electrical power was soon applied to telegraphy, **telephones**, wireless communications, lighting, motion pictures, and motors for electric irons, washing machines, vacuum cleaners, and refrigerators. Between 1921 and 1939 alone, the electrical industry's gross annual production increased from $809 million to $2.3 billion.

Ely, Richard T.

Richard T. Ely offered one of the first and most accurate criticisms of America's new industrial society, and most of his critiques were eventually adopted in order to ameliorate some of the more devastating impacts of the Industrial Revolution. Ely was born in Ripley, New York, on April 13, 1854. He grew up in Fredonia, New York. After finishing high school, he matriculated at Dartmouth College and later transferred to Columbia in 1872, where New York City was infinitely more to his liking. After graduating from Columbia in 1876, Ely headed abroad for graduate studies. He earned a PhD in agricultural economics in Germany and came back to the United States in 1880 as a member of the faculty of the Johns Hopkins University in Baltimore, Maryland.

Ely was soon a leading figure in the "new economics movement," which rejected out of hand traditional classical notions that the economy operated according to immutable economic laws. Classical economics, he argued, was rigid and deductive, the product of a preindustrial world where businesses were small and markets local. In the new economic world of giant business enterprises and global markets, the theories of classical economics no longer explained reality. Ely found the idea of **laissez-faire** to be particularly loathsome, little more than a bankrupt theory employed cynically by businessmen who wanted to augment their own wealth by keeping government regulators out of their affairs. In 1885, Ely was a founding member of the American Economics Association, a group of young economists dedicated to promoting the "new economics."

In Ely's vision, human society was an organic whole of interrelated, interdependent parts. Human behavior, as individuals and in groups, determined the direction of the economy, and government had a responsibility to serve as a balancing mechanism, especially to restrain individual or minority behavior that was inconsistent with the welfare of the larger group. The federal government, he insisted, needed to deal with large **corporations** that operated in national markets and abused their privileges.

Ely was also convinced that government had a new role to play in addressing the needs of the workers and the poor. The Industrial Revolution had created, he argued, a new class of industrial workers who lived in cities and were completely severed from the rural, home economy. During downturns in the business cycle, when large numbers of people were out of work, they had a difficult time supporting themselves. The government, Ely said, needed to create a "safety net" of unemployment insurance, welfare benefits, and public-works jobs. He favored **immigration** restriction in order to prevent foreign workers from undermining wage and employment levels in the United States. He also believed that industrial workers needed to be able to organize into unions and engage in collective bargaining with their corporate employers. Otherwise they would have little leverage in improving wages, working conditions, and hours. Ely was passionate that government should not become an ally of the business community in making labor organization and collective bargaining more difficult. Eventually, Ely became an advocate of "limited **socialism**," which he defined as government ownership of public utilities and **railroads**.

But Ely was far more than an academician writing articles and giving presentations that only other academicians read or heard. In 1892, he accepted a job at the University of Wisconsin, and his presence at the state capital in Madison gave him access to state political leaders, none of whom was more important than Robert La Follette, who came under the influence of the reformers. Ely was a leading figure in the so-called Wisconsin school of social and economic reformers, a group of economists, historians, and sociologists who had great influence on public policy in the state. When La Follette was elected governor of Wisconsin in 1900, Ely became one of his most influential advisors, enthusiastically regulating railroads, utility companies, and grain elevators; launching the beginnings of a welfare state with unemployment insurance, workers' compensation, and aid to dependent children; and using experts to develop solutions to economic and social problems, and Wisconsin became one of the most progressive states in the country. It was not until the outbreak of World War I that the Ely–La Follette relationship disintegrated. Ely was a confirmed isolationist who believed that the United States should stay out of the war. La Follette was more of an internationalist. In 1925, Ely left the University of Wisconsin to teach at Northwestern University, where he also edited the *Journal of Land and Public Utility Economics*. He died on October 4, 1943.

Erie Canal

The Erie Canal was the most important artificial waterway in the United States in the first half of the nineteenth century. During the seventeenth, eighteenth, and early nineteenth centuries, Americans for the most part relied on their river systems and coastal shipping to transport goods, but it gradually dawned on many businessmen that the resources of the country could never be fully utilized as long as transportation arteries were confined to rivers and coastal traffic. Nor could the Industrial Revolution have really gotten under way because exploitation of the raw materials **factories** needed to produce finished goods would not have been available, or would have been available only at costs that would have made competition prohibitive.

Enterprising Americans began pondering methods of improving the transportation system by extending it beyond rivers; such thinking led to what historians now term the ***canal*** *boom*—a burst of canal construction linking different river systems and allowing for expansions in markets. By far the most important of these projects was the Erie Canal. New York City businessmen began suggesting the canal as early as 1792, but it took years before anybody was seriously willing to begin construction. The project,

A view of the Erie Canal at Salina Street in Syracuse, New York, in 1900. (Library of Congress)

too ambitious and expensive for individual businessmen or entrepreneurs to undertake, required government sponsorship, and in 1817, the New York state legislature authorized an appropriation of $7 million to construct a canal from Albany to Buffalo, New York. The Erie Canal, named after Lake Erie, was completed in 1825.

The Erie Canal was 363 miles in length and connected Albany with Buffalo. Water was diverted from the Hudson River in the east and from Lake Erie in the west to fill the canal, and teams of mules pulled large, multiple barges along the canal. When the canal was completed, it became possible to ship goods from New York City up the Hudson River to Albany; from Albany to Buffalo on the Erie Canal; and from Buffalo to Cleveland, Ohio, on Lake Erie. The canal opened up a huge hinterland to farmers and consumers in upstate New York, northern Ohio, northern Indiana, and western Pennsylvania, who could now ship farm products in bulk at cheap rates to eastern cities. The total volume of goods shipped into and out of New York City increased exponentially during the next two decades, making it the center of the American economy.

The economic success of the Erie Canal inspired a host of copycat projects all over the country, or at least wherever existing rivers supplied the necessary water. What undermined the Erie Canal was the development of railroads in the 1840s and 1850s. Railroads could ship goods in greater volume, at faster speeds, and therefore at cheaper rates than canal barges, and while canal traffic was limited geographically, railroads could be constructed anywhere, even over or through mountains. By the early 1850s, the Erie Canal was in a state of rapid decline, but during its heyday, it was a key component in a transportation system that gave rise to a national market and allowed businesses to increase vastly in size to supply that market. The Industrial Revolution in the United States owed at least some of its origins to the influence of the Erie Canal.

F

Factory

The term *factory* refers to a new method of organizing workers in manufacturing enterprises. Until the Industrial Revolution, most manufactured goods were produced at home or in small shops employing only a handful of workers. Because the development of a transportation **infrastructure** created a national market in the United States in the nineteenth century, with opportunities for innovative entrepreneurs to sell vastly greater volumes of products, new methods of production had to be developed. A transition to factory production was the so-called putting-out system, in which merchants distributed raw materials, production specifications, and tools to individual craftsmen who then fashioned the manufactured goods in their own home workshops. The merchants then traveled from home to home collecting finished products and marketing them.

Eventually, however, these merchants were tired of the putting-out system, since it required so much travel on their part. In looking for more efficient ways to organize their workers, they decided to bring all of the craftsmen under one roof. By bringing all workers under a single roof, the factory system allowed the former merchant/businessman to save time distributing raw materials and collecting finished goods and to take advantage of mechanized production, technology, and new energy sources, all of which greatly increased production and reduced the unit cost of goods. Bringing all workers under one roof in a factory setting also permitted the implementation of assembly-line production systems, in which raw materials and component parts were brought to stationary workers, who performed specialized tasks and assembled finished products.

Farming. *See* Agricultural Revolution

Federal Reserve Act of 1913

One of the consequences of the Industrial Revolution was the rise of a more activist federal government, primarily because most voters felt that banks and business **corporations** had grown powerful enough to subvert market economic forces and inflict damage on small businesses, poor workers, and farmers. The **Panic of 1907** was one event that prompted a serious consideration of proposals to increase the power of the federal government. In March 1907, the New York Stock Exchange suffered a free fall in securities prices, which triggered a run by panic-stricken depositors on banks. In a desperate attempt to come up with liquid funds to meet depositor demand, banks all over the country tried to call in business loans, which sent thousands of businesses into bankruptcy. Hundreds of banks closed their doors as well. Astute observers realized that the panic could have been avoided had bankers been able to acquire liquid reserves without selling securities or calling in business loans.

In order to avoid such financial emergencies in the future, Congress began to investigate ways for the federal government to supply those liquid reserves. An initial solution was the Aldrich-Vreeland Act of 1908, which allowed national banks to issue notes backed by the bonds of state, county, and municipal governments. Such notes would be permitted to circulate for a maximum of six years and would be considered legal tender. The legislation would allow banks during times of financial emergency to liquefy assets without imposing even more pressure on securities markets and private businesses. The Aldrich-Vreeland Act also established the National Monetary Commission to explore more comprehensive federal initiatives.

In 1912, Congress also had the House Committee on Banking and Currency launch a formal investigation of the banking industry. Democratic congressman Arsene Pujo of Louisiana headed the investigation, and journalists were soon referring to the group as the ***Pujo Committee.***" During the hearings, Pujo subpoenaed most of the country's major bankers and made them testify, and the press followed the witnesses carefully, publishing anything that seemed particularly salacious. In the process, the banking industry experienced a public-relations nightmare. The final report of the Pujo Committee, published in 1913, concluded that because of mergers, leveraged buyouts, the use of **interlocking directorates**, and consortiums—all of which engaged in the purchases of stocks, bonds, insurance companies, **railroads**, and public utility companies—a dangerous concentration of power had occurred in the financial industry in the United States.

The conclusions of the National Monetary Commission and the Pujo Committee helped pave the way for the Federal Reserve Act, which

Congress passed in 1913. The law established twelve regional federal reserve banks and allowed them to discount, or make loans, on the eligible securities of private banks that had joined the system. Such authority gave the federal government at least some power to provide liquidity during financial panics. Each federal reserve bank enjoyed considerable autonomy, although a national federal reserve board in Washington, D.C., served in an advisory capacity. Eventually, the Federal Reserve System acquired leverage over interest rates in the economy and came to wield great influence in public policy.

Federal Trade Commission Act of 1914

During the **Progressive** Era of the first two decades of the twentieth century, Americans vigorously debated the merits of **antitrust** action to break up large **corporations** in order to preserve a competitive economic environment where the lowest possible prices would prevail. In the presidential **election of 1912**, Democratic Party candidate **Woodrow Wilson** advocated what he called his "**New Freedom**"—vigorous use of the federal government to stop all corporate practices that resulted in monopolistic conditions and restraint of trade. Wilson won the election, and as soon as he was inaugurated, he began pushing for antitrust legislation. Along with the **Clayton Antitrust Act of 1914**, the Federal Trade Commission Act of 1914 embodied his antitrust vision. The law established a Federal Trade Commission and authorized it to "investigate, publicize, and prohibit all unfair methods of competition." The legislation was an important event in the history of the Industrial Revolution because it helped permanently render moot all serious **laissez-faire** ideas and helped make the federal government a player in the modern industrial economy.

Field, Cyrus West

Cyrus West Field was a businessman and innovator whose fertile mind produced major changes in the economic **infrastructure** of the United States and made the conduct of international business infinitely more efficient. He was born in Stockbridge, Massachusetts, on November 30, 1819. The family moved to New York City in 1834, and Field went to work in a dry-goods store. He returned to Massachusetts in 1837 to work for his brother, who owned a paper-manufacturing business in the town of Lee. Field learned the paper business and in 1839 opened his own paper mill in Westfield. He returned to New York and founded Cyrus W. Field & Company, and when he had accumulated a portfolio of $250,000, he retired.

Field had other interests by that time. He was fascinated with the notion of a transatlantic **telegraph** cable that would make communications between continents essentially instantaneous. In 1854, he met Frederick N. Gisborne, an engineer, who thought that the idea was feasible. To raise money for the project, Field worked the financial offices of New York City and eventually amassed $1.5 million in venture capital, much of it coming from **Peter Cooper**, an inventor and a prominent iron and **steel** manufacturer. The work of laying the cable began, and on August 5, 1858, it was complete from Trinity Bay, Newfoundland, in Canada to Valentia, Ireland. On August 10, Great Britain's Queen Victoria made history by telegraphing a message to President James Buchanan in Washington, D.C. The world had suddenly become smaller.

Unfortunately, Field's fortune was about to head in the same direction. Within months of the Queen's message, the cable went down and would transmit no messages. Unable to determine where the break had occurred, Field could not make any repairs, and he sustained huge financial losses. He never lost faith in the concept, however, and after the **Civil War**, he relaid a new cable. At the same time, he put his money into a series of bad **railroad** investments and urban elevated-railroad stock that rendered him bankrupt. Cyrus Field died on July 2, 1892, leaving behind a spotty financial legacy but a record as a visionary who believed in, and helped realize, the day when global communications would be instantaneous.

Firestone, Harvey Samuel

During the early 1900s, at the midstage of the Industrial Revolution, development of the **internal-combustion engine** gave rise to an **automobile** industry that quickly evolved into the heart of the economy. The innovations of **Ford Motor Company** and **General Motors Corporation** made the automobile a nearly ubiquitous consumer item in the American economy, but this would not have been possible without the development of the vulcanized rubber tire by Harvey Firestone. He was born in Columbiana, Ohio, on December 20, 1868. After graduating from a public high school, he attended a business school in Cleveland and then went to work for his uncle, who owned a buggy company. The company went bankrupt in 1896, and Firestone decided to go into business for himself selling rubber tires. It was an auspicious move because Firestone found himself in the tire business just when the automobile age began. In 1899, with $40,000 in savings, he moved to Akron, Ohio, and established the Firestone Tire and Rubber Company, manufacturing rubber tires for horse-drawn buggies and bicycles.

In 1903, Firestone developed a pneumatic rubber tire, and when **Henry Ford** placed a large order for the tires in 1906, Firestone was on his way to becoming a multimillionaire. Firestone followed that up in 1907 with a disposable-rim tire, which allowed flats to be fixed on the road. His sales skyrocketed from $100,000 a year in 1901 to $15 million a year in 1913. He invented the balloon tire, which became standard on automobiles in the 1920s, and he invested heavily in the infant trucking industry. Firestone realized that trucks could haul freight in ways **railroads** could not—from the point of production to the point of consumption. Beginning in 1928, Firestone pioneered the concept of "one-stop retail shopping," in which he built Firestone stores where consumers could purchase gasoline, oil, tires, and automobile parts and where automobile repairs could be done. By the time of Firestone's death on February 7, 1938, he had more than 600 stores operating nationwide.

Flying Shuttle. *See* Spinning

Ford, Henry

Henry Ford is widely regarded today as America's most innovative and influential industrialist, the individual who all but defined the Industrial Revolution and single-handedly revolutionized modern social life. A poorly educated man, he was a brilliant tinkerer, a mechanic who enjoyed taking things apart and discovering better ways of putting them back together. Ford was born near Dearborn, Michigan, on July 30, 1863. He attended school in Greenfield, Michigan, but dropped out in 1879 to apprentice himself as a machinist. A mechanical genius, he made money on the side as a traveling farm-machinery repairman. Between 1884 and 1887, he managed a small sawmill operation and then returned to Detroit as chief engineer for the Edison Illuminating Company.

By that time, however, Ford had already decided that an **automobile** driven by an **internal-combustion engine** was the future of American transportation, and he began building one himself. His great love was the gasoline engine. In 1896, he had completed a prototype automobile. Ford left Edison Illuminating Company and worked for a while with the Detroit Automobile Company, during which time he built his first racing car, which he dubbed the 999. In 1903, Ford established the **Ford Motor Company** to manufacture automobiles.

Ford's great achievement was making an affordable automobile. At his River Rouge factory, Ford produced in 1909 the Model T or, as it was dubbed, the Tin Lizzie—a simply designed and easily maintained vehicle that sold for $950. As Ford's volume went up, his prices came down; the Model T sold for $700 in 1911, $500 in 1914, $335 in 1920, and $290 in 1924. By 1925, a Ford factory turned out a Model T every ten seconds, and Fords sold almost as fast.

In 1919, 10 percent of families owned a car; by 1927, 82.8 percent did. By 1929, the industry employed 7 percent of all manufacturing workers and paid 9 percent of manufacturing wages. Related industries boomed since automobile plants needed **steel**, oil, glass, rubber, paint, leather, and other products. Drivers needed gasoline and better roads. On the outskirts of almost any town, other businesses mushroomed around the automobile—gas stations, body and mechanic shops, motels, used-car dealers, and finance companies. Providing Americans with the option of relocating outside downtown areas, automobiles prompted a boom in suburban home construction.

What Ford began was nothing short of a revolution; equally revolutionary was his belief that wages should be increased and hours reduced so that workers could buy and enjoy new cars. He paid some of his laborers $5 a day, shortened the workday from nine to eight hours, and adopted the five-day week. The idea of the "weekend"—time for working families, in Ford's words, to "enjoy the blessings of pleasure in God's great open spaces"—was novel. Toward the end of his life, Ford summarized his philosophy: "One day someone brought to us a slogan which read: 'Buy a Ford and Save the Difference.' I crossed out the 'save' and inserted 'spend'—'Buy a Ford and spend the Difference.' It is the wiser thing to do." Certainly for Ford himself, it made good business sense: by 1925, he personally earned $264,000 a day. Eventually other businessmen adopted the concept that higher wages and leisure time stimulated economic growth.

Ford served as president of Ford Motor Company until 1919, when his son Edsel assumed leadership of the company. During the 1920s, Ford devoted his time to political and philanthropic concerns. He was active in the world peace movement, which would have established him as somewhat of a liberal, but at the same time he was a rabid anti-Semite convinced that Jews were in control of international banking and politics. During the years of the Great Depression, Ford bitterly fought the Congress of Industrial Organizations' efforts to unionize automobile workers, and he was the last of the automobile manufacturers to capitulate to the union. When Edsel Ford died in 1943, Henry Ford once again took over management of Ford Motor Company and remained in that post until 1945. He died on April 7, 1947.

Ford Motor Company

The Ford Motor Company was the corporate embodiment of **Henry Ford**'s genius. He established the company in 1903 to manufacture **automobiles**, and in 1909, he introduced the Model T, a simple automobile that Ford mass-produced and was able to steadily reduce in price, from more than $700 in 1910 to only $300 in 1923. That year, Ford Motor Company sold more than 2 million Model Ts. In 1920, the sales of new Model T accounted for 60 percent of all automobiles sold in the United States. Ford did everything he could to design simply and cut costs, but at the same time Ford Motor Company pioneered in corporate paternalism. Ford prided himself on paying his workers a decent wage and giving them a reasonable workday. He was largely responsible for making the automobile affordable to mass numbers of consumers, which virtually revolutionized American social life. By the end of the 1920s, the vast majority of American families owned an automobile.

During the 1920s, however, Ford Motor Company began to enter a long period of decline. **General Motors Corporation** introduced the new Chevrolet model, which competed in the Model T price range but was considered much more stylish. Chevrolet sales were so high that Ford had to abandon the Model T in 1926, opting instead to produce the new Model A, a four-cylinder car designed to compete with the Chevrolet. In 1932, Ford discontinued the Model A and replaced it with a new, more powerful six-cylinder motor car.

But the decline continued. Ford Motor Company introduced the new lines of Mercury and Lincoln, but Chevrolet sales surged, at least in terms of market share, and late in the 1930s, Ford's sales dropped behind those of Chrysler, a relative newcomer in the automobile industry. Ford's bad luck changed after World War II. By then, Ford Motor Company's place in the history of the Industrial Revolution was fixed. Because of the automobile, the **steel**, glass, rubber, leather, and **petroleum** industries boomed, and the Industrial Revolution came to revolve around cars and the companies that produced them and their parts. The automobile made suburbs possible because governments built roads radiating out of the cities and allowing Americans to live in bedroom communities. It changed dating and courting practices as well as vacation and leisure. Without much debate, American economic historians identify the Ford Motor Company as the most important corporate vehicle, until the advent of computers and Microsoft in the 1980s and 1990s, respectively, in changing the way virtually every American lived his or her life.

Frick, Henry Clay

Henry Clay Frick was a leading figure in the early history of the American **steel** industry whose career eventually reflected much of what was good and bad about the Industrial Revolution. He was born in West Overton, Pennsylvania, on December 19, 1849. After quitting school, Frick went to work as a bookkeeper for his father's whiskey distillery, but he noticed that the steel industry was budding all over western Pennsylvania and decided that that was where his fortune was to be made. Since the demand for coke to supply the steel furnaces was booming, Frick threw his savings and some of his father's money into building coke ovens. By 1870, he had ovens operating throughout the region, and with financial backing from the wealthy Mellon family, he founded the H. C. Frick Coke Company. By 1880, Frick owned and operated more than 1,000 coke ovens and was a multimillionaire.

At the same time, **Andrew Carnegie** was building the country's biggest steel operation. In 1882, Carnegie Steel Company bought out H. C. Frick Coke Company, and the two men formed a fertile partnership. Frick became chairman of the board of Carnegie Steel in 1887 and accelerated the drive to establish a **monopoly** in the industry by merging with competitors, buying them out, or just driving them out of business. Frick slashed costs with a vengeance to make Carnegie Steel more competitive, and he integrated the company vertically, bringing under its roof **coal** mines, iron-ore deposits, **railroads**, and barges. Economic historians remember Henry Frick as an innovative businessman who made steel a relatively cheap commodity and the building block of the Industrial Revolution.

The **Homestead Strike** of 1892, however, proved to be a public relations disaster for Andrew Carnegie and Carnegie Steel. Frick was ruthless in breaking the strike, hiring armed Pinkerton detectives and other goons to crush it and killing many strikers in the process. The violence employed against the strikers, for most Americans, exceeded what any rational observer considered necessary and left Carnegie and Frick with images as cruel, self-centered multimillionaires who cared little for the plight of poor people. Carnegie never forgave Frick for his handling of the strike. Frick resigned in 1899 and took away from Carnegie a huge fortune of $60 million. **J. P. Morgan** later worked closely with Frick in organizing the **United States Steel Corporation**, and he had Frick serve for years as a member of the board of directors. Henry Frick died on December 2, 1919.

Frontier Thesis

In his 1893 speech "The Significance of the Frontier in American History," delivered at the World's Columbian Exposition in Chicago, historian Frederick Jackson Turner cited the westward expansion of the frontier as an essential facet of the continual development of American culture, namely, the rugged individualism at the source of American democracy and economy. This articulation of American values was done largely through the continual repetition of the stages of development as pioneers created settlements, which began with "the Indian and the hunter" and continued with "the disintegration of savagery by the entrance of the trader . . . the pastoral stage in ranch life; the exploitation of the soil by the raising of unrotated crops of corn and wheat in sparsely settled farm communities; the intensive culture of the denser farm settlement; and finally the manufacturing organization with the city and the factory system." Turner's thesis was and continues to be a controversial one among historians who take issue with his uniform view of the progression of industrialism and westward expansion as the hallmarks of American nationhood because such a viewpoint did not adequately consider the range of more complex forces, such as immigration, inclusion of women in the industrial workforce, and larger economic trends, at play in the unfolding of American history at the turn of the twentieth century.

Fulton, Robert. *See Gibbons v. Ogden* (1824)

G

Gary, Elbert Henry. *See* United States Steel Corporation

General Electric Corporation

The General Electric Corporation, one of the world's most powerful and influential companies, was a corporate by-product of the Industrial Revolution in the United States. It had its origins in 1878 when **Thomas Edison**, the great American inventor, established the Edison Electric Light Company to produce and sell the incandescent **light bulbs** he had developed. Within a few years, the Edison Electric Light Company was manufacturing and marketing a variety of the newly invented electrical technologies coming from Edison's fertile mind and laboratories. All of Edison's assets, including the Edison Electric Light Company, were reorganized in 1892 in a new corporate entity, General Electric (GE). It rapidly became the dominant force in the new industry of electrical appliances, dynamos, and electrical engines, and its appliance lines—GE and Hotpoint—became the best known in the country. After World War II, GE diversified into the design and manufacture of jet engines, the construction and management of electric-utility power systems, aerospace equipment, and nuclear energy.

General Motors Corporation

Until Microsoft Corporation replaced it in the 1990s, General Motors had long reigned as the world's largest **corporation**. When Microsoft assumed that position, it signified in a very concrete way how the Industrial Revolution had been succeeded in the modern economy by the information revolution.

General Motors had its beginnings in the early twentieth century when the advent of the **internal-combustion engine** had given rise to the **automobile** industry. In the early 1900s, automobile manufacturers appeared throughout the country, especially in and around Detroit, Michigan. One of them was **William C. Durant**, the country's largest manufacturer of horse-drawn carriages. Durant put some of his wealth into the Buick Motor Company, an automobile-manufacturing concern in Flint, Michigan, and soon controlled the company. Durant also purchased the Cadillac Motor Company, the Oldsmobile Motor Company, the Oakland Motor Company (which built Pontiacs), the Cartercar Company, the Elmore Company, the Reliance Truck Company, and the Rapid Truck Company. He formed the General Motors Company in 1908 to manage these enterprises, and in 1916, he renamed the company the General Motors Corporation.

The automobile industry boomed during the first three decades of the twentieth century, and General Motors adopted the **mass-production** innovations introduced by **Henry Ford**. The company also expanded rapidly, purchasing the Chevrolet Company in 1918, the Delco Company (spark-plug manufacturers) in 1918, the Fisher Body Company in 1919, and the Frigidaire Company in 1919.

During the 1920s, General Motors led the way in corporate organization systems in order to deal with its huge size. Alfred Sloan became president of General Motors in 1923 and pioneered the concept of corporate decentralization. The company was simply too large to manage in a highly centralized, top-down management style because bureaucratic inertia would have guaranteed serious inefficiencies. Instead, Sloan awarded near autonomy to the individual divisions—Chevrolet, Buick, Cadillac, Pontiac, Oldsmobile, Fisher Body, and so on. In doing so, he pioneered a pattern of decentralization that would become common among the Industrial Revolution's corporate giants.

George, Henry

One of the most visible consequences of the Industrial Revolution was a vast gap between the rich and the poor, and one of the most popular individuals addressing that problem was Henry George. Before the Industrial Revolution, wealth in America tended to be in the hands of a family, with most assets tied up in land and owned in a relatively confined geographical area. Income from these assets tended, for the most part, to flow in from that geographical area. Also, the country did not have a super-rich class of people whose incomes and net worth had reached incredible proportions. At the same time, most poor people in America owned their own land and were self-employed, often in a near-subsistence economy with a marginal existence, but they were nevertheless their own bosses.

The Industrial Revolution changed all that. Wealth became national and then global, with income flowing in from all over the world. People like **Andrew Carnegie** and **John D. Rockefeller** became billionaires whose assets were scattered throughout the country and whose political influence reached every corner of the country. Poor people were displaced from the land and brought to the cities, where new **factories** existed, and they found themselves working for invisible employers. They enjoyed little control over their lives and functioned so far below the poverty line that hunger and death always loomed on the horizon.

Such disparities between the rich and the poor raised serious questions about fairness and equity in America. Henry George thought that he had a solution to the problem. Born in Philadelphia, Pennsylvania, in 1839, George was raised in a middle-class family. As a fifteen-year-old, he enlisted as a cabin boy on a

Henry George helped launch an entire generation of economic and social reform in the United States with his best-selling book, *Progress and Poverty* (1880). (National Archives)

sailing ship and visited India and Australia, and when he returned, he became a printer's apprentice. He soon signed on as a seaman again and ended up in San Francisco, California, in 1858, where he spent the next twenty years working as a grocer, journalist, and printer. On a trip to New York in 1869, George noticed the huge mansions of the rich and the hovels of the poor, and the discrepancy triggered a desire to come up with a social and economic policy that would address the problem.

George identified the source of poverty in government land policies, which encouraged land grabbing. In his 1871 book *Our Land and Land Policy*, George contrasted the country's rapidly growing population with the shrinking volume of land in the public domain. Such a reality created rapidly rising land prices, which enriched those who owned the assets. Such income, he argued, was unearned, simply a by-product of inflation. He believed that a solution to the problem was to restrict land grants only to those people who would actually settle the land and to tax landholdings that were idle. In 1879, George published his most famous and influential book *Progress and Poverty*. The great irony of industrial society, George argued, was the fact that "where the conditions to which material progress everywhere tends are most fully realized. . . . we find the deepest poverty, the sharpest struggle for existence, and the most enforced idleness." As population increased, George claimed, the landowners' portion of wealth increased while that of businessmen and workers declined.

George's solution was what he called the *single tax*—have the government tax away all value on land that came from inflation rather than from improvements. Although Henry George's economic thinking was full of flaws, he made a huge contribution to social policy in the United States by convincing millions that poverty was not necessarily an inevitable by-product of human nature but was the result of specific policies, and that if those policies were changed, poverty could be eliminated. "Taking men in the aggregate," he said, "their condition is as they make it." For Henry George, social justice could become a reality.

During the 1880s, George became very popular on the speaking circuit, traveling widely throughout the United States and Great Britain and promoting the single tax. Single Tax Clubs sprouted in small towns and major cities. George returned to New York City in 1886 and tried to form a political party to push the single tax, but he failed in his bid to become mayor. He died suddenly in 1897 in the midst of another campaign to become mayor of New York City.

Gibbons v. Ogden (1824)

A prerequisite to the Industrial Revolution and the creation of a national market was an efficient transportation **infrastructure**, and **Gibbons v. Ogden** (**1824**) helped create a legal climate in which that infrastructure could develop. The U.S. Supreme Court heard the case on February 4–9, 1824, and decided it unanimously on March 2, 1824. The issue at hand revolved around the authority of Congress to regulate interstate commerce. In 1807, **Robert Fulton**, an inventor of the steamboat, began doing business on the Hudson River, and the New York state legislature essentially awarded him a **monopoly** on the route. When Thomas Gibbons tried to run a competing shipping business between New Jersey and Manhattan, New York outlawed the run because it violated the existing monopoly, and Gibbons sued. The case took several years before it reached the U.S. Supreme Court in 1824.

Daniel Webster of Massachusetts argued Gibbons's case before the Court. Webster insisted that authority over interstate commerce rested exclusively with Congress and that the state legislature could not legally prohibit Gibbons from running a competing business across state lines. Although the Court ended up deciding the case narrowly, Chief Justice

John Marshall nevertheless upheld Gibbons's case, writing that the power of Congress to regulate foreign and interstate commerce "does not stop at the jurisdictional lines of the several states." The decision was a boost to economic nationalism because it liberated interstate commerce from the legislative regulation of different states.

Gold Standard Act of 1900

During the 1880s and 1890s in the United States, an epic debate raged over the nature of the monetary system and whether gold should continue to serve as the only medium of exchange. Farmers facing falling incomes because of overproduction found a panacea in **soft-money** ideas, from the issuance of greenback paper currency in large volumes to free coinage of silver, all of which were designed to produce an inflation that would raise commodity prices, so the logic went, and improve farm income. The fact that costs would also rise did not seem to dawn on many farmers. For workers who were in debt, the idea of inflation seemed appealing because the money they paid back over time would be less valuable than the money they had borrowed. These inflationary ideas found political expression in such groups as the **Greenback-Labor Party** and the **Populist** Party.

During the **election of 1896**, the debate became the nation's primary political focus. The Democratic Party nominated William Jennings Bryan for president and endorsed free coinage of silver at a ratio of sixteen ounces of silver to one ounce of gold as the central idea in the party platform, and the Populists followed suit, similarly endorsing Bryan and free coinage. Republican candidate William McKinley denounced free coinage of silver and the inflation it would produce. He warned farmers that inflation would also increase their costs and leave them no better-off, and he warned workers that free coinage of silver would increase food prices. Finally, he warned the entire country that free coinage of silver would destabilize the financial markets and lead to another economic depression—far worse than the **Depression of 1893**—and mass unemployment. When the votes were counted, McKinley won handily, and free coinage of silver had been thoroughly discredited.

The culmination of the monetary debate came on March 14, 1900, when Congress passed the Gold Standard Act. In the previous two years, gold discoveries around the world had allowed an expansion in the money supply, relieving some of the problems in financial markets and easing deflationary pressures. The Gold Standard Act guaranteed the dollar by declaring its standard unit value to be 25.8 grains of nine-tenths fine gold. A gold reserve of $150 million was established to redeem legal-tender notes. The legislation put to rest the demands for coinage of silver until the 1930s, when the Great Depression resurrected the notion as an economic panacea.

Gompers, Samuel

Samuel Gompers was the first successful national labor-union leader in the United States. Because of the Industrial Revolution, the nature of work in the United States had changed dramatically. For centuries, laborers in manufacturing businesses had worked at home or in small shops. When laborers worked for someone else, the employer-employee relationship was characterized by personal and paternalistic feelings. Problems could be worked out on a personal level. But the Industrial Revolution gave rise to huge business enterprises and at the same time depersonalized labor-management relations. Workers found it more difficult and often impossible to negotiate personally with owners. As a result, many workers began to see the need for collective action, to have a union representing all of them do the negotiating with management. Samuel Gompers found himself on the cutting edge of that change. Gompers was born in London, England, on January 27, 1850. He immigrated to the United States as a thirteen-year-old and went to work rolling cigars. Gompers sensed almost immediately the need for workers to organize, and he joined the Cigarmakers' International Union. He quickly demonstrated a gift for labor politics and rose in the union. The Cigar Makers' International Union became a core craft union in the fledgling **American Federation of Labor** (AFL), and Gompers became its president in 1886. Gompers headed the AFL until 1894, when socialists ousted him, but their control of the union was quite brief. He was reelected in 1895 and remained at the helm until his death on December 13, 1924.

Gompers remains today perhaps the most influential labor leader in U.S. history. Other national labor unions, such as the **National Labor Union** and the **Knights of Labor**, had foundered, but the AFL succeeded, largely because of Gompers's leadership. The original AFL consisted of thirteen craft unions composed exclusively of skilled workers. Gompers refused to organize unskilled workers because they had no leverage against management. Striking unskilled workers could too easily be replaced by strikebreakers. Gompers knew that only skilled workers could force management to decide whether or not to respond to union demands. He also decided to stay away from direct political action or running the AFL as a political party. Instead, he envisioned the AFL as a powerful lobbying organization because it represented millions of people, and he turned his vision into reality. To make sure that the individual craft unions inside the AFL did not feel threatened, he extended complete autonomy to the unions.

Gompers also focused on conservative economic objectives, the bread-and-butter issues of better wages, improved working conditions, and shorter workdays. Also, convinced that faith in **capitalism** and private property was woven into the fabric of American culture, he was an outspoken critic of **socialism** and communism. Finally, Gompers was a tactical genius, launching strikes only when victory was guaranteed. AFL membership grew steadily, reaching 297,000 in 1897 and 1.676 million in 1904. When Gompers finally stepped down as AFL president in 1924, the union claimed a membership of 2.865 million and was recognized by business management and politicians as one of the most influential economic interest groups in the United States.

Goodyear, Charles. *See* Vulcanization

Gould, Jay

The Industrial Revolution generated vast accumulations of wealth in the United States, and critics used the term *robber barons* to describe the new class of super-rich industrialists, as if they had intentionally imposed poverty on the rest of the country in order to enrich themselves. Some of them indeed were rascals—corrupt and exploitive—and none more so than Jay Gould. Born to a poor family as Jason Gould in Roxbury, New York, on May 27, 1836, Gould spent his early career as a clerk, a surveyor, a blacksmith, and then a leather merchant, but he took his profits and invested in **railroads**. In 1867, he owned enough stock to become a director of the Erie Railroad, one of the East Coast's major carriers.

Gould had little interest in running the railroad as a successful enterprise and preferred to spend his time manipulating railroad stock through what is today called insider trading. Along with Daniel Drew and James Fisk, the treasurer and a director of the Erie Railroad, respectively, Gould illegally released 100,000 new shares of Erie stock in an attempt to prevent **Cornelius Vanderbilt** and the **New York Central Railroad** from seizing the line. To avoid New York courts, Gould fled to New Jersey and opened another office. A few bribes to powerful New York legislators got him off the legal hook.

But he had not learned his lesson. He appointed Boss Tweed, the famous and corrupt head of the Tammany Hall political machine, to the Erie board of directors. They then issued more fraudulent shares, and in 1869, Gould tried and failed to corner the U.S. gold market, a ploy that triggered the Panic of 1869. A huge public outcry against Gould led to his dismissal as president of the Erie Railroad.

Gould then headed west and put his money into the **Union Pacific Railroad** and became a director. To boost the stock's value and the value of his own portfolio, Gould released fraudulent information on the line's profits, and in the process he made up to $10 million, selling his stock just in time. Gould then invested in the **Central Pacific Railroad**, the Kansas Pacific, the Denver Pacific, the Missouri Pacific, and the Wabash. By 1881, Jay Gould was a railroad czar, controlling more mileage than anybody else in the country. He also owned the Western Union Telegraph Company.

Gould's railroad empire, badly undercapitalized, came crashing down in the panic of 1884–1885, and he emerged with only the Missouri Pacific. He recovered quickly and built ownership of the Manhattan Elevated Railway. Gould spent the rest of his life doing what he had been doing for years, ruthlessly manipulating stock prices and taking advantage of the fact that the law had not yet developed prohibitions against the activities Gould specialized in. When Gould died on December 2, 1892, he had an estate worth more than $72 million and a reputation for greed and corruption that helped shape negative public perceptions of big businessmen during the Industrial Revolution.

Granger Laws

Severe economic problems in Midwestern and Southern agriculture prompted the beginnings of government regulation of the private sector in the United States. Gross overproduction had placed downward pressure on commodity prices, and farmers had seen, during the early post–Civil War years, severe declines in income. Millions of farmers felt squeezed between the prices they received for their crops and the prices they had to pay to railroads, banks, and grain storage facilities.

In 1867, Oliver Kelley, a clerk in the federal government's bureau of agriculture, organized the Patrons of Husbandry, nicknamed the Grange, to bring farm families together. Initially, Kelley was concerned about relieving the drudgery and loneliness of isolated farm life by providing group social outlets, but at Grange picnics and barn raisings, talk inevitably drifted to economics and politics. Complaining about banks and railroads inspired some farmers to lobby state legislatures for assistance, primarily through the regulation of bank, warehouse, and railroad rates. What emerged were the so-called Granger laws, a series of state laws imposing government regulation on private business. In 1873, for example, Illinois set maximum rates that grain storage companies could charge farmers.

Banks, railroads, and grain storage companies protested bitterly, claiming that the Granger laws deprived them of their Fifth Amendment property rights and that such legislation was more properly the domain of Congress, not state legislatures, since farm produce was largely part of interstate commerce. They claimed that the Fourteenth Amendment to the Constitution protected the property rights of corporations as well as citizens. They sued in the federal courts, and in 1873, the U.S. Supreme Court heard the case of *Munn v. Illinois*. The justices insisted that private property could come under the regulatory authority of state legislatures, upholding the Granger laws as long as the states were legitimately acting for the welfare of their citizens.

But in the 1880s, the U.S. Supreme Court began to backpedal from that conclusion. In the case of *Santa Clara County v. Southern Pacific Railroad* (1886), the justices ruled that corporations as well as individuals enjoyed the right to due process outlined in the Fifth and Fourteenth Amendments. In awarding civil rights to corporations, the decision asserted that some types of business regulation could constitute violations of due process. That same year, in *Wabash, St. Louis & Pacific Railroad v. Illinois*, the court overturned its own decision in *Munn v. Illinois* and declared unconstitutional an Illinois statute that created a state commission to regulate the railroads. Because the Wabash, St. Louis, and Pacific Railroad operated across state lines, the Illinois law had illegally preempted the authority of Congress. Other Granger laws were declared unconstitutional as well. In 1890, the Supreme Court rendered its verdict in the *Chicago, Milwaukee & St. Paul Railroad Company v. Minnesota* case, overturning a Minnesota law that had established a state commission to set railroad freight rates and grain storage company rates. The legal foundation of the Granger laws had effectively been destroyed.

Discontented farmers then turned to the federal government for help, insisting that what states could not legally do, Congress needed to do. Railroads came under scrutiny first, primarily because eastern merchants joined western and Southern farmers in complaining about high freight rates. Even some railroad chief executive officers and investment bankers asked for government help. In the process of constructing 80,000 miles of new track between 1880 and 1893, the railroads had gone deeply into debt, but they soon discovered that they had expanded too rapidly, and that the economy suffered from excess railroad capacity. Railroads found themselves engaging in cutthroat competition and suffering from falling income. Many railroads began defaulting on their debts, threatening many bankers with disaster. If the federal government would agree to set freight rates, some argued, the vicious competition would come to an end.

In 1887, Congress responded with the Interstate Commerce Act, which created a federal Interstate Commerce Commission (ICC) to regulate railroads. In particular, the ICC was committed to preserving competition in the industry and protecting the interests of consumers. The ICC outlawed rebates (kickbacks of a certain percentage of freight rates to the richest customers); banned the formation of pools, in which competing roads cooperated to set minimum rates; and outlawed the practice of charging less per ton mile for short haul freight than for long hauls on the same line. Railroads were compelled to impose only "reasonable and just" freight rates. The ICC was the first federal regulatory agency in U.S. history.

As an organization, the Grange had its heyday in the late nineteenth century. Early in the twentieth century, economic conditions on the farm improved, and the Grange lost some of its political sting. Also, the rapid increase in the pace of urbanization drew millions of Americans into the cities, reducing the farm population and Grange membership. The Grange still survives in some rural areas today, sponsoring dances, lectures, and picnics, but its influence is nowhere what it was in the nineteenth century.

Great Atlantic and Pacific Tea Company

The creation of a national market and the advent of **mass-production** techniques made possible a consumer culture in which social life in America revolved largely around the purchase of goods. Manufacturers were capable of producing vast amounts of goods, but these goods also had to be distributed efficiently. Perhaps the most effective form of retail distributorship was the chain store, a concept pioneered by a number of prominent Americans, including George H. Hartford. A native of Augusta, Maine, Hartford worked for several mercantile concerns in New England before moving to New York City in 1860, where he went to work for George F. Gilman's Great American Tea Company. An immediate success, the store soon expanded its retail line from tea to include spices, milk, baking powder, corn, wheat, and rice. Gilman and Hartford then opened several more retail outlets in New York City, each of which was just as successful as the original store. Part of the reason for their success was a "cookie cutter" approach to retailing. Each store had the same floor plan with the same products displayed in the same places and in the same way. Customers shopping at one store could enter another and instantly find what they were looking for, and the similarities built a feeling of comfort and predictability among the chain's clientele. A host of other retailers eventually mimicked Gilman and Hartford's style.

In 1869, with a total of ten stores, Gilman and Hartford renamed the enterprise the Great Atlantic and Pacific Tea Company, or the A&P. They continued to expand, both in the variety of products they marketed to consumers and in the number of stores they owned. The A&P's increase in the variety of products began an evolution toward the modern supermarket, while the increase in the number of outlets gave rise to what economists today call the "chain store." By 1878, the A&P possessed 67 stores, and by 1900, the number had increased to more than 200. As a chain store, the A&P enjoyed annual gross sales that put it at the top of the industry. The company was not surpassed in gross annual sales until 1964, when Sears, Roebuck and Company reached the top spot, but it remains one of the country's widely known chain stores.

The A&P had a dramatic impact on American retailing, pioneering the chain store that would eventually become a hallmark of shopping and economic life in the United States. Customers felt comfortable with the familiarity and routine of the stores, and chain-store retailing eventually helped create a consumer culture in the United States in which the process of purchasing and consuming the same products nationwide built a sense of community in a society noted for its ethnic and racial diversity.

Great Migration, The

Several decades after the United States had outlawed slavery, African Americans began to flee the South in huge numbers in a movement that became known as the Great Migration. Resettling in Northern cities, where they sought better lives, employment, some degree of social equality, and an escape from daily violence, the migrants (numbering approximately 500,000) found more opportunities and transplanted some of the most vibrant aspects of their culture. However, they also faced brutal violence reminiscent of what they had left behind in the former Confederate States of America.

The mass migration transformed both the South and the North. Most notably, black migrants settled in Chicago, Cleveland, Detroit, and the Harlem section of New York City. Those cities became the first U.S. urban centers with large African American populations. What attracted them to the North? The answer lies not only in the opportunities they believed existed there but also in the fact that the South was a brutal place for those former slaves and their descendants. In the years following emancipation, Southern whites, who were desperate to retain social and political dominance over African Americans, enacted black codes that very closely replicated slave codes—a series of laws that severely circumscribed the personal and social behavior of slaves.

The new black codes, known as Jim Crow laws, enforced a strict racial division in every aspect of Southern life. That system of segregation

Typesetters work at their keyboards at *The Chicago Defender,* an African American newspaper founded in Chicago in 1905. (Library of Congress)

extended to all areas of society, including education, transportation, and the legal arena. Although Jim Crow laws were a blatant violation of civil rights guaranteed to black Americans in the post–Civil War era, they received the sanction of the U.S. Supreme Court in its ignominious *Plessy v. Ferguson* (1896) decision that codified the separate-but-equal doctrine.

Economic suffering compounded the humiliation and depredations African Americans suffered under Jim Crow laws. Former slaves endured crushing poverty and continued subservience to whites under "sharecropping"—a form of pseudoslavery in which white landlords retained economic control over blacks. A boll weevil infestation that obliterated cotton crops across the South beginning in 1915 further exacerbated the state of economic dependence.

In addition to those economic and political challenges, African Americans faced entrenched and violent racism in the South. For example, the Ku Klux Klan and more mainstream white citizens regularly lynched blacks as a means of maintaining social control through terror. In short, the American South was an especially dangerous and unfriendly place for African Americans by the time World War I opened up new opportunities in the North. Labor agents traveled to the South to entice African Americans northward, while Southern employers and landholders often intimidated and brutalized those who tried to leave the South. The mass exodus of black laborers left the already economically troubled South in an even worse condition.

In addition to the lure of jobs, African Americans were persuaded to move northward by the encouraging letters of friends, family, and others who had themselves made the trip and found the North to be a more hospitable place. Black churches in the North extended assistance to potential migrants as well. Perhaps most importantly, *The Chicago Defender*, a newspaper edited by African American Robert Abbott, railed against Southern injustices and encouraged blacks living in the South to migrate to Chicago and other Northern cities, where conditions were far better for African Americans. The power of the *Defender* was such that many Southern localities banned its distribution, fearing that it would tempt former slaves to leave the South.

On arrival in the North, African Americans found that there were jobs to be had. Those newfound job opportunities were due to the recruitment of native-born white men into the military during World War I and recent immigration laws that severely restricted the influx of European immigrants who would normally fill the positions. In the absence of native-born whites and European immigrants, the jobs were filled by black migrants, although the newcomers received substantially lower pay than their white counterparts and were often excluded from promotions or higher-paying positions. Nevertheless, wartime industrial production increased exponentially, creating many new positions that African Americans eagerly filled.

Great Northern Railway

Before the Industrial Revolution could really take off and sustain itself over the long term, manufacturers needed access to a truly national marketplace, and nothing contributed more to the creation of that national market than the construction of the **transcontinental railroads**. Completion of the roads linked the West Coast with Midwestern and Eastern manufacturers and marked the beginnings of the so-called Pacific Rim, which opened Asian markets to American manufacturers. The Great Northern Railway was one of those transcontinental railroads.

The Great Northern Railway was the brainchild of **James J. Hill**. Hill acquired the Minnesota & Pacific Railroad, which had been chartered in 1857, and in 1879 renamed it the St. Paul, Minnesota & Manitoba Railroad. Anxious to extend his reach across North America, Hill in 1889 renamed the railroad again, this time the Great Northern Railway. He also oversaw the expansion of the line, building track from Minneapolis and Duluth, Minnesota, to Seattle and Vancouver. After Hill's death, the Great Northern Railway expanded into Oregon and northern California and eventually was absorbed into today's huge Burlington Northern Railroad system. As a result of the Great Northern Railway, the vast wheat fields and timber stands of the Pacific Northwest became available to East and West Coast producers and consumers.

Great Railroad Strike of 1877. *See* Railroad Strike of 1877

Greenback-Labor Party

During the 1870s, 1880s, and 1890s, the United States witnessed a ferocious debate over the nature of the monetary system and the merits or demerits of paper currency. Experience had taught that in earlier periods when the U.S. government issued greenback paper currency, such as during the American Revolution and the **Civil War**, price inflation was the result. After the Civil War, because of productivity gains made possible by Industrial Revolution technologies, crop production boomed, saturating American markets and leading to falls in commodity prices. Millions of farmers found themselves in difficult circumstances, caught between falling commodity prices and rising **railroad** freight rates and bank interest rates. Seeking a political solution for their economic plight, some focused on convincing the federal government to issue paper currency, which they believed would bring about price inflation and raise farmer income. The idea also had the support of many workers, especially those in debt who felt that inflation would cheapen the dollars they had to pay back on their loans. In 1874 in Indianapolis, Indiana, representatives of the National Grange, the **Knights of Labor**, and several other reform groups founded the Greenback Party or Greenback-Labor Party.

After the **panic of 1873**, banking interests wanted to remove more than $400 million in paper currency, also called "greenbacks," from circulation. The federal government had issued the currency during the Civil War, and bankers and financiers held the paper money responsible for the instability that had hit the money markets. Backers of the Greenback-Labor Party, however, opposed the idea for fear that it would induce deflation and require them to pay back their loans with more valuable money. In 1876, the Greenback-Labor Party nominated **Peter Cooper** for president and called for the issuance of more paper currency and suspension of gold bond sales to foreign investors. Cooper won only 81,737 votes, but in 1878, when the party ran a slate of congressional candidates, it elected fourteen representatives to Congress. Much of its success was due to fallout over the great **railroad strike of 1877**, which had produced much violence. James Weaver received the Greenback-Labor presidential nomination in 1880 and won 308,578 votes, more than in 1876 but far less than Republican James Garfield's winning total of 4.449 million votes. Under Weaver's leadership, the party expanded its platform from increased volumes of paper currency to also include an end to convict labor, free coinage of silver, and an eight-hour workday.

As it turned out, however, 1880 marked the peak in popularity for the Greenback-Labor Party. Businessmen and bankers lambasted its proposals and argued that if they were enacted, they would destabilize the money markets and lead to a depression and widespread unemployment. They also convinced workers that issuance of greenbacks might badly inflate food prices and make life more miserable for them. In 1884, with Benjamin Butler as the nominee, the party secured only 175,000 votes and soon disappeared.

H

Hamilton, Alexander. *See* Bank of the United States

Hammer v. Dagenhart (1918)

During the **Progressive** Era, reformers became increasingly concerned about the impact of **child labor** on individual children as well as on the society as a whole. In some **factories**, especially in the **textile** mills of the South and the **coal** mines of Pennsylvania, Ohio, and West Virginia, children essentially left school before they were ten years old and went to work full-time. They labored for long hours, often in unsafe and unhealthy circumstances, and fell victim to accidents and disease. Social workers and family advocates began calling for regulatory legislation at the federal level to outlaw child labor. Legislation at the state level, they claimed, did little good because it punished states that passed the laws. Businessmen would simply relocate their factories in states without regulatory laws. Only federal legislation, the reformers claimed, could ameliorate the problem. In 1916, during the **Woodrow Wilson** administration, Congress responded with the Keating-Owen Child Labor Act, which prohibited the shipment in interstate commerce of goods manufactured by children. Congress felt constitutionally justified in passing the legislation because of its authority over interstate commerce.

Manufacturers regularly employing children in their factories filed lawsuits, claiming that Congress had exceeded its constitutional authority. The case of *Hammer v. Dagenhart* was argued before the U.S. Supreme Court on April 15–16, 1918, and decided on June 3, 1918. By a narrow fi5–4 decision, the Court overturned the Keating-Owen Child Labor Act, arguing that Congress had exceeded its constitutional authority and had interfered in matters that, under a federalist system, should best be left to state governments. In reaching this decision, the justices had essentially denied the reality of a national economic market, or at least had chosen to ignore its existence. *Hammer v. Dagenhart* seriously limited the power of the federal government to regulate problems created by the new industrial economy. These limitations, however, proved short-term, since the Great Depression of the 1930s gave rise to the New Deal and a vastly empowered federal government.

 # Hard Money

The term *hard money* was widely used during the late nineteenth century in the debates over the merits and demerits of paper currency and silver and gold coin or silver- or gold-backed currency. "Hard money" was the equivalent of gold and silver bullion, while "**soft money**" equaled paper money.

 # Harriman, Edward Henry

Edward Henry Harriman was a leading figure in the **railroad** industry of the late nineteenth and early twentieth centuries. Harriman was born in Hempstead, Long Island, New York, on February 10, 1848. The family moved to Jersey City, New Jersey, when he was a small boy, and Harriman grew up there. He quit school in 1862 and got a job as an office boy on Wall Street. In 1870, with a $3,000 loan from his uncle, he opened his own brokerage firm, which enjoyed immediate success. In 1872, he founded Harriman and Company, an investment bank. He married Mary Averell in 1879; her father was president of the Ogdensburg and Lake Champlain Railroad. The industry fascinated him, especially its vast opportunities.

In 1881, Harriman engineered a takeover of the Lake Ontario Southern Railroad, and two years later he sold it at a substantial profit. With the capital he gained from the sale, Harriman invested in a number of other lines, including the Dubuque and Sioux City Railroad and the Illinois Central Railroad. In 1893, because of the depressed economy, with financial assistance from **J. P. Morgan**, Harriman took over and reorganized the Erie Railroad. That set the stage for a grand attempt to take over much of the American railway industry. In 1898, Harriman organized a syndicate that purchased the **Union Pacific Railroad**, and by 1901, he had added the Kansas Pacific, the Southern Pacific, the Denver Pacific, and the Oregon Short Line to his collections, making him one of the most powerful railroad magnates in the world.

Early in the 1900s, Harriman staged an attempt to seize control of the Northern Securities Company from **James J. Hill** and J. P. Morgan. Had he succeeded, Harriman would have enjoyed near-monopolistic control of the entire industry. He failed in his takeover bid, but in the final negotiations he managed to secure for himself a profit of $50 million. He died on September 9, 1909.

Haymarket Riot

By the 1880s, as unions increasingly challenged the freedom of action of corporate giants, labor-management relations were steadily deteriorating, primarily because company owners could not conceive any circumstances in which workers were justified in going on strike. The Industrial Revolution produced a labor-management confrontation of epic proportions. Some of these confrontations became particularly symbolic, and none was more ideologically loaded than the Haymarket Riot of 1886. Workers at the McCormick Reaper Works in Chicago had gone out on strike, and the company appealed for police to serve as strikebreakers. On May 3, 1886, Chicago police discharged their weapons when the strikers became unusually unruly, and several workers died in the melee. On May 4, 1886, a local anarchist group decided to exploit the killings in order to promote its own political agenda. It held a protest meeting at Haymarket Square, but late in the afternoon, just as the meeting began to break up, police arrived on the scene and proceeded to wade into the anarchists. An outraged anarchist lobbed a bomb toward the police. The explosion killed seven police and wounded twenty-seven.

The police charge rioters in old Haymarket Square in Chicago, Illinois, on May 4, 1886. The riot occurred when a bomb exploded among a group of policemen as they attempted to disperse a giant labor rally in the city's Haymarket Square. Eleven people died in the incident. (Library of Congress)

In the wake of the disaster, eight anarchists were arrested, tried, and convicted of murdering police. The state's case was a weak one, since nobody had ever been able to identify the individual who actually threw the bomb, but four of the anarchists were eventually executed. Another committed suicide in prison. Governor John Peter Altgeld of Illinois eventually pardoned the others.

Haywood, William Dudley. *See* Industrial Workers of the World

Hill, James Jerome

James J. Hill was one of America's best-known **railroad** magnates during the late nineteenth and early twentieth centuries and a key individual in the development of the country's transportation **infrastructure**. Before the Industrial Revolution could gain full momentum, the United States needed to be linked into a single national market, which, more than anything else, railroad construction made possible.

Hill was born in Rockwood, Ontario, Canada, on September 16, 1838. When he was just fourteen years old, after the death of his father, Hill got a job as a clerk. In 1856, he moved to St. Paul, Minnesota, setting himself up as an agent for several steamships and railroads. It was good work that made him some money and taught him much of what he needed to know about railroad construction, freight shipment, and passenger travel. He branched out into his own wholesale fuel business and built the Red River Transportation Company, a steamship business working the Mississippi River.

In 1878, after an economic decline in the United States had bankrupted a number of railroads, Hill joined several associates in purchasing the St. Paul and Pacific Railroad, which was in receivership. Hill had a keen eye for management, and he turned the St. Paul and Pacific Railroad around, constructing new tracks all the way to Puget Sound in Washington, Oregon, and Canada. Hill managed the railroad's day-to-day affairs like a conductor working an orchestra, leaving nothing to chance and insisting on cooperation and efficiency. He began buying up other railroads in the Midwest and Northwest, and in 1889, he consolidated all of his holdings into the **Great Northern Railway**.

Like other prominent business leaders, Hill wanted to reduce the cutthroat competition that had long characterized the railroad business and had led to volatile swings in railroad profits. His purchase of the **Northern Pacific Railway** achieved just that, as did his purchase of the Chicago, Burlington, and Quincy Railroad, which gave Hill access to the Chicago market. Hill also worked diligently and effectively as a major player in the construction of the Canadian Pacific Railroad.

Late in the 1890s, **E. H. Harriman** of the **Union Pacific Railroad** made a hostile bid to snatch the Northern Pacific Railway from Hill's holdings. The two engaged in a financial battle so tangled and bitter that it prompted the panic of 1901 on Wall Street. Eventually, the two settled the issue privately by giving Harriman a minority voice in management of the Northern Pacific. In 1901, Hill formed the Northern Securities Company, a holding company that controlled all of his railroad assets.

The Northern Securities Company soon became the object of **antitrust** action in the United States. By effectively controlling all railroad traffic in the Northwest, federal government lawyers argued, Hill had created a **monopoly** that violated the **Sherman Antitrust Act of 1890**. The case wound its way through the federal courts, and in 1904, the U.S. Supreme Court decision in *Northern Securities Company v. United States* ordered the breakup of the Northern Securities Company. Hill continued to manage his companies until his death on May 29, 1916.

Hoe, Richard March

Richard March Hoe was responsible, technologically speaking, for the rise of the modern newspaper and printing business. He was born in New York City on September 12, 1812. After graduating from high school, he went to work in his father's factory, which manufactured **printing presses**. The elder Hoe retired in 1830, and Richard took over the operation. The business had done well manufacturing a single small-cylinder press, but the technology was insufficient for the demand being generated, and Hoe began tinkering with improving the press so that its volume would increase. In 1837, Hoe developed an operational double small-cylinder press, and he soon went into production. His next improvement in printing technology came the next year when he developed a single large-cylinder press characterized by the large flat bed.

The advent of mass-circulation newspapers created the need for an even better, more efficient press, and in 1845 and 1846, Hoe worked on a rotating printing press with the capacity to print more than 8,000 newspapers in an hour. In 1847, he sold the first one to the *Philadelphia Public Ledger*. Within a few years, every major newspaper in the country was using one of the rotary printing presses Hoe had invented.

Still, demand outstripped supply, and Hoe set his mind to work on a new printing-press technology. In cooperation with Stephen Tucker and building on the work of inventor William Bullock, who constructed in 1865 a web printing press, Hoe designed, built, and patented the first web press, which printed two sides of a page simultaneously from a single roll of paper. The web press, which he introduced in 1871, had a maximum capacity of 18,000 newspapers per hour, and it too soon became the standard in the industry. Finally, in 1881, he came up with the triangular form folder, which automatically folded the papers coming off the web press. With that development, the modern newspaper printing press, and a new industry, was born. Richard Hoe died in Florence, Italy, on June 7, 1886.

Holding Company

During the Industrial Revolution, a national market appeared, and larger and larger **corporations** developed to exploit that market. Some of the companies became big enough to establish near-monopolistic control over certain segments of the economy. Economists use the term *horizontal integration* to describe the imposition of monopolistic power, and a holding company was one way of doing so. In order to secure greater control of a certain market, a holding company purchased controlling interests in several companies competing in that market. The holding company then dictated pricing rules or allocated markets to the subsidiaries in order to establish a monopolistic environment. With the passage of the **Clayton Antitrust Act of 1914**, the use of **interlocking directorates** of several companies was outlawed, which limited the ability of holding companies to control markets.

Homestead Strike

One of the most memorable of the Industrial Revolution's labor-management confrontations occurred in 1892 at the Carnegie Steel Works in Homestead, Pennsylvania, and it took on all the dimensions of civil war. The city had 12,000 residents, and 3,800 worked at **Andrew Carnegie**'s mill. Nearly 800 were members of the **Amalgamated Association of Iron, Steel, and Tin Workers of the United States**. In 1892, Carnegie decided to break the union. He possessed absolutely no sympathies with labor unions, which he felt interfered with corporate prerogatives and with private property. At the same time, however, Carnegie did not want a public relations disaster, so he handed the assignment of breaking the union over to **H. C. Frick**, his trusted assistant. Frick converted the steel plant into a fortress, stringing barbed wire, erecting searchlights, and hiring 300 armed Pinkerton detectives to man the barricades. Frick then cut wages 20 percent, repudiated the union, and hired strikebreakers. The workers howled in protest and immediately went on strike.

As barges hauled Pinkertons up the Monongahela River on July 6, 1892, armed workers attacked. By late afternoon, nine workers and three Pinkertons lay dead. A week later, the governor of Pennsylvania mobilized the state militia. Frick accused the workers of radicalism, an exaggeration that gained credibility on July 23 when Alexander Berkman, a Russian émigré anarchist, shot and stabbed Frick in Frick's office. Frick survived, but the strike did not. Berkman had single-handedly broken the back of the strike, convincing much of the public that the Amalgamated Association of Iron, Steel, and Tin Workers shared his penchant for revolutionary violence. After five months, the union caved in, formally ending the strike on November 20, 1892. The remaining workers faced twelve-hour days and debilitating wage cuts.

The Homestead strike proved to be a public-relations nightmare for Andrew Carnegie, who did not enjoy being portrayed as a crass, insensitive magnate. He never forgave Frick for bungling the entire matter. The strike also demonstrated clearly that businessmen in the 1890s could count on the power of the state to reinforce their political views and economic needs.

Hopkins, Mark

Mark Hopkins was an influential figure in the construction of the **transcontinental railroad**, which helped create a national market in the United States, thus accelerating the pace of the Industrial Revolution. Hopkins was born on September 1, 1813, in Henderson, New York, where his family owned a mercantile business. After leaving high school, he went to work in the store, continuing on to study law and bookkeeping, sell farm implements, and even work as a postmaster. When gold was discovered in California in 1848, Hopkins headed west to find his fortune. He settled in Sacramento and soon learned that real money was not to be found in digging for gold but in selling food and supplies to those who did. He went into business with Collis P. Huntington selling hardware and tools. Huntington had close business and personal relationships with **Leland Stanford** and **Charles Crocker**, and the four men soon turned their attention to **railroads**, particularly the feasibility of a transcontinental road linking San Francisco with the East Coast.

All four men possessed strong credentials in the California Republican Party, and they lobbied in Congress for a contract to build the west-to-east portion of the transcontinental railroad. In 1862, Congress passed the enabling legislation, and the four men founded the **Central Pacific Railroad**. Employing large numbers of immigrant and Chinese laborers, they built a railroad toward the east, finally linking up with the **Union Pacific Railroad** at Promontory Summit, Utah, in 1869. Hopkins then turned his attention to building trunk lines off the Central Pacific. The most important trunk line, which reached deep into Southern California, evolved into the Southern Pacific Railroad. At the time of his death on March 29, 1878, Hopkins's net worth exceeded $20 million.

Horizontal Integration

The term *horizontal integration* is employed by economists to describe the process by which a business enterprise establishes control over an economic market with the goal of securing enough power to restrain trade and commerce and fix prices, thus creating a **monopoly**. During the course of the Industrial Revolution in the United States, horizontal integration was achieved in a variety of ways. **Andrew Carnegie**'s application of cost-cutting technologies was so successful that he priced competitors out of the market. Prominent railroad magnates like **Cornelius Vanderbilt** often established **pools**, which amounted to private arrangements to eliminate competition by price-fixing conspiracies or by regionally allocating markets to create monopolistic conditions. **James B. Duke** horizontally integrated the tobacco business by engineering a series of corporate mergers. **John D. Rockefeller** helped achieve horizontal integration of the oil-refining business by creating the **trust**, a business arrangement in which competing enterprises sold trust certificates to a trust, authorizing that body to make corporate decisions and set prices. During the late nineteenth and early twentieth centuries, reformers became quite critical of horizontal integration because they felt that it destroyed competition and led to the exploitation of workers, consumers, and small businessmen. The **antitrust** movement was designed to block the process of horizontal integration.

Howe, Elias

Elias Howe, who invented the **sewing machine** and gave rise to the ready-to-wear clothing industry, was born in Spencer, Massachusetts, on July 9, 1819. At the age of sixteen, Howe apprenticed at a cotton **textile** mill in

Lowell, Massachusetts, where his mechanical gifts soon came to the forefront. Insatiably curious and a tinkerer, Howe began designing machines to make the mill work more efficient. After finishing his apprenticeship in 1837, Howe went to work for a toolmaker, and after hours he developed a prototype sewing machine. He built the machine during the winter months of 1844–1845, applied for a patent, and received it in 1846. Despite his best efforts to convince textile businessmen of the efficacy of the machine, he failed to secure any real interest. He then headed for Great Britain to market the device and there signed a deal with William Thomas, a London corset manufacturer, giving Thomas the English rights to the sewing machine. The two men soon had a falling-out, and in 1849, Howe returned to the United States.

There he learned that a number of textile manufacturers, among them Isaac M. Singer, had copied his invention and had put it to work without his permission. Howe filed patent-infringement lawsuits against them, but the legal battles lasted for years. In 1854, however, Howe won the suit, and the U.S. government ordered him to be paid a royalty for every machine illegally used. By the early 1860s, Howe's royalties exceeded $250,000 a year, and he had become a multimillionaire. When he died suddenly on October 3, 1867, Howe was widely considered the father of a new clothing industry that no longer relied on individual seamstresses sewing cloth together by hand. The advent of Elias Howe's sewing machine allowed the techniques of **mass production** to be applied to clothing manufacturing.

Hydroelectric Power

The basic principle of hydroelectric power is the generation of **electricity** by harnessing the energy of falling water. The best sites for the construction of hydroelectric power stations are those where large volumes of water fall steep distances. On September 30, 1882, the world's first hydroelectric power station went into operation on the Fox River in Appleton, Wisconsin. The power station there employed a waterwheel that was forty-two inches in diameter and two **Edison** direct-current generators. The station provided power for incandescent lamps and generated a total of twenty-five kilowatts of power. An alternating-current power station was built on the Willamette River near Oregon City, Oregon, in 1890, and 4,000-volt lines carried the power to Portland over a distance of thirteen miles. At that same site four years later, the country's first concrete dam was constructed to generate hydroelectric power. In 1895, the first large hydraulic turbines were used to generate electricity when a huge power station was built at Niagara Falls, New York. They generated 3,750 kilowatts of power, which supplied customers in Buffalo, New York. Soon, hydroelectric power stations were being constructed throughout the world. Although **coal**-, natural-gas-, and nuclear-generated electricity eventually came to be more important in terms of volume, hydroelectric power remains a critical source of power in the United States.

I

Immigration

The rapid economic expansion that the Industrial Revolution set in motion depended upon a steadily increasing supply of labor, and the United States found itself in a unique position. During the early to mid-1800s, the abundance of land in America acted as a magnet attracting large numbers of landless European immigrants, and the United States soon acquired in the Old World a reputation as a land of opportunity. Between 1800 and 1870, more than 6 million immigrants settled in the United States. Most of them came from the countries of Northern and Western Europe, and most ended up farming in America. After the **Civil War**, however, as the available land decreased, the immigrants found themselves increasingly involved in **factory** labor. The waves of immigration continued. Between 1870 and 1920, as many as 25 million immigrants settled in America, most in the cities and towns of the Northeast and Midwest. Most of these became known as the "new immigrants"—Poles, Czechs, Slovaks, Italians, Slovenians, Greeks, Russians, and Serbians—and they became industrial workers in mills, mines, and factories. The steady flow of new immigrants into the American workforce had the effect of keeping wages down, profits up, and business investment prodigious.

Until the late nineteenth century, opposition to immigration often had an overwhelming religious dimension to it, particularly from old-line Protestants who resented the arrival of Catholics, Jews, and Eastern Orthodox. But the opposition also took on an economic dimension, especially when labor unions began appearing in the 1870s and 1880s. Such groups as the **Knights of Labor** and the **American Federation of Labor** began calling for immigration restriction, arguing that the flood of immigrants from Eastern and Southern Europe was driving down prevailing wage levels and increasing unemployment among Native American workers. Such business-oriented groups as the **National Association of Manufacturers** and the Chamber of Commerce, naturally interested in keeping wage costs down, wanted immigration to remain unrestricted. The political lines were drawn in state legislatures and in the halls of Congress.

A group of immigrants at New York harbor's Ellis Island, around 1900, wait patiently to enter the examination hall, the first step in processing immigrants prior to their formal entry into the United States. (Library of Congress)

Chinese immigrants seemed to generate the most opposition, especially on the West Coast, where most of them were concentrated. Native Americans found them exotic and inscrutable, and the fact that they lived cheaply and sent much of their earnings to China aggravated resentments. Responding to intense pressure from California politicians, Congress in 1882 passed the Chinese Exclusion Act, prohibiting future immigration from China. The law was the first such measure in American history. Subsequently, Congress also passed legislation requiring immigrants to be literate, healthy, and without criminal records. In each instance, labor unions backed the laws and business groups opposed them. Finally, in 1924, Congress passed the National Origins Act, which imposed a nation-by-nation quota system and severely reduced immigration to the United States. The pattern of business interest groups backing liberal immigration laws and unions favoring restrictive practices became a standard in American economic history that still holds true today.

In re Debs (1895)

The case of *In re Debs* revolved around the **American Railway Union**'s 1894 strike of the Pullman Company. Pullman workers struck the company spontaneously, and **Eugene Debs**, president of the American Railway

Union, took up their cause. Debs's strategy was to have union workers refuse to handle any railroads equipped with Pullman cars. Attorney General of the United States Richard Olney sided with the railroad managers, filed a case of criminal conspiracy against Debs and the union, and secured an injunction in federal court shutting down the strike. When workers learned of Olney's actions, they rioted throughout the Midwest. In response, Olney ordered in federal troops, and Debs was sentenced to six months in jail for contempt of court. Debs and the American Railway Union appealed Olney's actions to the U.S. Supreme Court, demanding a writ of habeas corpus and his release from jail. The Supreme Court rendered a verdict on May 27, 1895, and denied the writ. In doing so, the Court sanctioned Olney's injunction and declared the union's actions a public nuisance worthy of government restraint. The Court also claimed that the strike had threatened the property rights of the railroads. The Court's decision in *In re Debs* established federal protections for **corporations** trying to deal with labor unrest.

Industrial Workers of the World

The only truly radical labor union to ever secure even a modest following in the United States during the course of the Industrial Revolution was the Industrial Workers of the World (IWW), nicknamed the "Wobblies" because so many of its immigrant members could not pronounce the acronym. The only national union to have long-lasting success in the nineteenth and early twentieth centuries was the **American Federation of Labor**, which limited membership to skilled workers in craft unions. **William "Big Bill" Haywood**, a leader in the Western Federation of Miners (WFM), was convinced that such craft-union elitism actually made life even more miserable for unskilled industrial workers. In 1905, along with Clarence Smith, Haywood convened a delegation of WFM leaders in Chicago and formed the IWW. They were convinced that corporate leaders in the United States were conservative, indeed reactionary, and controlled federal and state governments, and that only revolutionary violence could bring real change to America and improve the lot of working-class people. In 1907, Haywood was tried and acquitted of murdering the governor of Idaho, but the publicity surrounding the case convinced most Americans that the IWW was simply too radical. The union became involved in a series of violent strikes and work stoppages, free-speech movements, and organizing campaigns among migrant farm workers, miners, and timber workers. When the IWW formally opposed U.S. entry into World War I as a capitalist, imperialist measure, most Americans lost what little respect they had for the organization. The IWW then went into a rapid period of decline.

Infrastructure

Economic historians today realize that a major prerequisite to economic development, and therefore to the Industrial Revolution, is the development of a reliable infrastructure, which consists of dependable transportation, communication, and monetary systems. Without decent transportation and communication systems, the Industrial Revolution could never have occurred, since commerce would have been inevitably confined to local markets because the costs of transporting goods and information would have been so expensive as to render them uncompetitive, in terms of price, once they reached their destination. A talented, efficient shoemaker, for example, might have been able to make a high-quality product at a low price, but if roads, highways, and railroads did not exist, the shoemaker could not sell the product in distant markets. Freight costs would make the shoes too expensive for sale there. Without a reliable monetary system, the Industrial Revolution also would not have occurred. An unreliable medium of exchange discourages the efficient sale and purchase of goods, since determining product value is difficult. Once reliable transportation, communication, and monetary systems were in place, the most efficient producers could sell their products in distant markets, which then allowed them to increase volume and take advantage of economies of scale. Systems of **mass production**, which vastly reduced the unit cost of the commodity, then became possible, since goods could be widely distributed throughout larger and larger markets.

In the United States, vast improvements in the transportation system took place during the nineteenth century. In the 1790s, to link up frontier settlements with eastern towns and cities, entrepreneurs and local governments embarked on an ambitious program of turnpike construction. A turnpike was a paved toll road. Early in the 1790s, the Philadelphia-Lancaster Turnpike was completed in Pennsylvania, while the Knoxville Road and Old Wilderness Road opened the Ohio River Valley to settlement. In 1795 in Tennessee, the completion of the Old Walton Road linked up Knoxville and Nashville. Throughout the country in the early 1800s, with more than 300 turnpike companies in operation, new highways changed rural life, ending older subsistence patterns of production in favor of commercial agriculture, since produce could now be distributed in distant markets. The Cumberland Road, also referred to as the National Road or Old National Road, connecting Cumberland, Maryland, with Wheeling, Virginia, was finished in 1818. Subsequent extensions of the Cumberland Road took it all the way out to Vandalia, Illinois. By the 1830s, however, turnpike construction leveled off because roads now connected the major towns and cities of the Northeast.

Canals constituted the next phase in the development of the transportation infrastructure. The advantage of canals over turnpikes was obvious. While goods transported over turnpikes had to be hauled in wagons pulled by teams of oxen or mules, canal traffic was conducted on large, floating barges, which could carry much larger volumes of goods and greatly reduced freight costs. The Middlesex Canal, completed in 1793, connected the city of Boston with the Merrimack River, and in 1800, the Santee Canal joined the Cooper and Santee rivers in South Carolina. The greatest of the canals, the **Erie Canal**, was completed in 1825 and extended from Albany to Buffalo, New York. The Erie Canal opened up a vast hinterland to commerce, since it was now possible to move products by ship across Lake Erie, then east from Buffalo to Albany, and then south along the Hudson River from Albany to New York City. The success of the Erie Canal inspired a boom in canal building in the 1820s and 1830s, such as the Morris Canal across New Jersey (1832); the New Haven and Northampton Canal (1835); the Chesapeake and Ohio Canal (1850), which linked Georgetown with Cumberland, Maryland; and the Pennsylvania Portage and Canal System (1840), which tied Philadelphia, Pennsylvania, with Pittsburgh. The Illinois and Michigan Canal, completed in 1848, connected Lake Michigan with the Illinois River and gave the young city of Chicago an enormous economic boost. The longest canal—452 miles in length—was the Wabash and Erie Canal, which linked Toledo, Ohio, with Evansville, Indiana.

Although canals allowed the first bulk movement of goods, they had a distinct disadvantage. Geography dictated that canals follow river systems, and Americans did not want their economic and settlement activities constrained by the limits of geography. Technology gave them a way out and at the same time brought the canal boom to a complete halt. In 1825, the Stockton and Darlington Railroad began operations in England, and the technology spread quickly to the United States. Like canals, **railroads** provided opportunities to haul huge volumes of freight, but unlike canals, railroads had no geographic limitations. The Mohawk and Hudson Railroad was completed in New York in 1826, and construction on the **Baltimore & Ohio Railroad** began in 1828. During the 1830s and 1840s, railroad construction boomed throughout the United States, linking the country together and helping to create a national market for agricultural commodities and manufactured goods. After the **Civil War**, construction of the **transcontinental railroads**—the **Union Pacific** and the **Central Pacific**, the **Great Northern**, the **Northern Pacific**, the Atchison, Topeka, and Santa Fe, and the Southern Pacific—eventually created a national market that stretched from coast to coast. By 1866, the total track mileage in the United States reached 36,801, and the boom continued, reaching 198,964 miles in 1900. In 1920, it peaked at 263,821 miles. Freight increased from 39 billion ton miles in 1861 to 142 billion ton miles in 1900. Because of railroads, manufacturers could market their goods competitively anywhere in the United States, which made possible the expansion of **factories** and the rise of large, national **corporations**.

In addition to a revolution in transportation, the country's communication system underwent similar development. Throughout history, the movement of information has been no better than a country's transportation system. Turnpikes, canals, and railroads did make the shipment of letters and packages much more efficient, but it was the advent of electronic communication systems that revolutionized the sending and receiving of information. In 1832, **Samuel Morse** invented the first practical **telegraph** machine, and in 1844, the age of electronic communication was born when he transmitted a message from Baltimore to Washington, D.C. Soon telegraph lines were being constructed along railroad routes. In 1858, a telegraph cable linked Newfoundland, Canada, with Ireland, making instantaneous communication between Europe and the United States possible. Congress passed the Pacific Telegraph Act, authorizing the construction of a telegraph line from Washington, D.C., to San Francisco, and the first message was transmitted on October 24, 1861.

But the telegraph had its limitations, since the electronic messages had to be coded and then decoded to be understood, which made it impractical to connect all homes and businesses, since the vast majority of Americans did not understand Morse code. The invention of the **telephone** overcame that handicap by permitting the electronic transmission of voices. In 1876, **Alexander Graham Bell** invented the telephone, and by 1880, there were a total of 148 telephone companies operating in the United States. All of these systems ultimately came under the control of American Telephone and Telegraph Company. Long-distance lines were operating between Boston and New York in 1884, New York and Chicago in 1895, and New York and San Francisco in 1915. The total number of telephones in the United States went from 1,355,900 in 1900 to 17,424,406 in 1932. The transmission of information throughout the country had become instantaneous.

Finally, the United States had to develop a reliable monetary system before its infrastructure could permit the Industrial Revolution to proceed. Although the U.S. Constitution had confined the power to coin and print money to the federal government, the monetary situation was nevertheless chaotic until Congress passed the **National Banking Act of 1864**. Until that legislation, money consisted of gold and silver coins and paper ("greenback") currency issued by the federal government and paper banknotes issued by hundreds of banks throughout the country. The banknotes encouraged rank speculation and fraud, and it became difficult for merchants and consumers to understand the real value of money, which made the exchange of goods more difficult. The National Banking Act imposed a 10 percent tax on private banknotes, which quickly drove them out of circulation, and required national banks to have one-third of their capital invested in U.S. government securities, upon which they could issue national banknotes up to 90 percent of their holdings. The national banknotes provided the United States a reliable currency.

Because of these infrastructural developments in the nineteenth century, the American economy boomed. The creation of a national market in which goods and information could be efficiently shipped, and the existence of a reliable currency in which buyers and sellers understood the values of their transactions, encouraged entrepreneurial enterprise, economic expansion, and economies of scale, all of which became the building blocks of the Industrial Revolution.

Injunction

During the late nineteenth and early twentieth centuries, the injunction was used frequently by corporate leaders to crush strikes. The injunction was a court order enjoining certain union-sponsored, organized activities, most often strikes, boycotts, demonstrations, and work stoppages. Corporate lawyers, often acquainted from law-school days or from cooperative legal work with federal judges, would seek injunctions requiring labor unions to end strikes, boycotts, picketing, and in some cases political lobbying. When union leaders refused to obey the demands of the injunction, judges could order in federal troops to restore order, which essentially broke the activity. Labor leaders considered injunctions an unacceptable use of government resources and campaigned for their prohibition. They did not succeed until 1932, when Congress passed the Norris—La Guardia Anti-Injunction Act.

Intellectual Property Rights

Seventeenth-century English political philosopher John Locke held that the right to own and dispose of private property was the key to individual liberty, and the Founding Fathers of the United States agreed. The Fifth Amendment to the U.S. Constitution prohibited the federal government from taking from individuals their "life, liberty, or property without due process of law." The Fourteenth Amendment subsequently imposed a similar prohibition on state and local governments. The Founding Fathers also defined the term *property* widely, including not only bullion, currency, land, and physical assets but also ideas—"intellectual properties"—and the money that flowed from them, as well. To provide incentives for the production of new ideas and new technologies, their creators needed the protection of the law.

Intellectual property rights revolved around patent and copyright law. Article I, Section 8, of the Constitution proclaimed that Congress had the responsibility "to promote the progress of science and useful arts" by granting to authors and inventors, "for limited times," exclusive right to the use of their work. In 1790, Congress passed the federal government's first patent law, which provided for the issuance of patents to "whosoever invents or discovers any new and useful process, machine, manufacture or composition of matter." The individual who held the patent owned the exclusive right to profit from it. Others could not copy the invention and profit from it without the patent holder's permission. The law held that the invention needed to have "utility" and "novelty" in order to qualify for patent protection. Later, in the case of *Hotchkiss v. Greenwood* (1850), the Supreme Court added "inventiveness" to the criteria. At the heart of patent law was the desire of the Founding Fathers and later of Congress to create a legal environment that encouraged technological innovation by allowing innovators to profit from their creativity.

The Constitution established federal copyright law by specifically empowering Congress "to promote the Progress of science . . . by securing for limited Times to Authors . . . the exclusive Right to their . . . writings." In other words, an individual could not profit from the publication and sale of another individual's writings. If such activities could legally occur, individuals would have no incentive to write, publish, and sell their ideas to others. At first, the law applied copyright protection only to literary property, but in subsequent years it expanded to include music and artistic works. The key U.S. Supreme Court decision upholding copyright came in 1834 in *Wheaton v. Peters*. The Court argued that copyright protection provides incentive to individuals to create and therefore benefits society as a whole by unleashing the creative endeavors of large numbers of people.

The combined effect of patent and copyright law was to provide a firm foundation for intellectual property rights in the United States. With ideas and inventions protected from unauthorized use by those who did not create them, creativity and innovation were encouraged, which helped accelerate the development of new technologies and the Industrial Revolution.

Interlocking Directorate

As the Industrial Revolution produced larger and larger corporate entities in the late nineteenth and early twentieth centuries, concerns developed about the future of competition in a monopolistic economic environment. The movement to preserve competition through **antitrust** action by the federal government culminated in the **Sherman Antitrust Act of 1890**, which outlawed manufacturing **monopolies** in businesses that operated across state lines. One way around the Sherman Antitrust Act, some company leaders divined, was interlocking directorates, in which several firms selling the same product or delivering the same service appointed boards of directors that consisted of the same people. Although each company retained its individual identity, they collectively skirted the restrictions of the Sherman Antitrust Act. The single board of directors would then fix prices, allocate markets, and restrict production in order to restrain trade and artificially jack up prices, creating essentially monopolistic conditions. In 1914, Congress passed the **Clayton Antitrust Act** outlawing interlocking directorates.

Internal Improvements

During the first half of the nineteenth century in the United States, the term *internal improvements* was used to describe **infrastructure** improvements in the nation's transportation system. Most people who used the term *internal improvements* were referring to the construction of **turnpikes**, **canals**, and **railroads**. Such improvements were central to the progress of the Industrial Revolution, since they helped create a vast, national market in which new mass-produced factory goods could be distributed.

How to finance the construction of internal improvements became a hotly contested political issue in the 1820s and 1830s. Among such National Republican and Whig politicians as John Quincy Adams and Henry Clay, the federal government, not state governments, should assume responsibility because it would be able to engage in comprehensive national transportation planning and set national standards. Most people in the Northeast enthusiastically supported federally financed internal improvements in order to build transportation links with the western interior. But most Democrats, especially southerners, tended to oppose federally financed internal improvements. They did not think that the federal government should be in the business of building highways, canals, or railroads. Southerners objected particularly because they thought they would be taxed to finance projects that would be built in the North and West. The South's abundant river system already made it easy to ship products downriver to Gulf of Mexico ports. The debate continued, off and on, throughout the 1820s, 1830s, 1840s, and 1850s. Not until the Civil War did it end. When the Southern states seceded from the Union in 1860–1861, Congress lost large numbers of Democrats, and the Republicans took over.

Descended from the National Republican and Whig traditions, Republicans believed in federally backed internal improvements, and in 1863 Congress approved the biggest internal improvement of them all. The Pacific Railway Act authorized the construction of the transcontinental railroad. Today, the federal government continues to be a key partner in the construction and maintenance of the nation's transportation system.

Internal-Combustion Engine

The modern internal-combustion engine creates energy by burning fossil fuels. In 1859, Étienne Lenoir, a Belgian engineer, modified a **steam engine** and placed in it a volatile mix of air and **coal** gas. When he ignited the concoction with an electric spark, the exhaust gases drove a piston. This proved to be the world's first workable internal-combustion engine. Lenoir's engine delivered one horsepower and was used to drive water-pumping devices. Three years later, the French engineer Alphonse Beau de Rochas developed the four-stroke engine, which was more powerful and practical than Lenoir's invention. Nikolaus Otto, a German engineer, then improved on the four-stroke engine so much that his work remains known today as the "Otto cycle." Other German engineers worked on the internal-combustion engine, and in 1885, Carl Benz developed a horseless carriage run by a single-cylinder, gasoline-driven engine. One year later, Gottlieb Daimler and Wilhelm Maybach invented the carburetor for mixing fuel and air more efficiently.

At the same time, Rudolf Diesel, a German engineer, was approaching the internal-combustion engine from another direction. He knew that compressing air raises its temperature, and he used that physical principle to do away with the need for an ignition device to generate the spark that ignited the mix of air and petrol. In 1892, he developed a system for squirting fuel into a cylinder of pressurized air at 800°C, which then ignited spontaneously. The soon-to-be-called diesel engine was more efficient because combustion took place in a smaller-volume cylinder, which produced twice the compression. It was also a commercial success because it could use a cheaper, less flammable type of crude oil.

The internal-combustion engine led to the **automobile**, which was essentially a European invention. By the mid-1890s, horseless carriages had become very popular among the French, British, and German upper classes. Until the internal-combustion engine was perfected, the carriages were powered by electric and **steam engines**. The disadvantage of the steam engine, however, in driving an automobile was that it required huge volumes of water, which proved to be expensive and inconvenient.

The electric motors also had disadvantages, primarily because the huge batteries required had a very limited range before they needed to be recharged. Americans quickly became infatuated with the idea of the automobile, and hundreds of inventors and entrepreneurs began employing the internal-combustion engine to develop products.

Interstate Commerce Act of 1887. *See* Interstate Commerce Commission

Interstate Commerce Commission

Demands for federal regulation of the **railroads** intensified in the 1870s and 1880s, especially after the Supreme Court, in such decisions as *Wabash, St. Louis & Pacific Railroad Co. v. Illinois* (1886) and *Chicago, Milwaukee & St. Paul Railroad Co. v. Minnesota* (1890), overturned a variety of state regulatory laws. Western farmers and eastern merchants wanted the federal government to force reductions in what they considered to be exorbitant railroad freight rates. Even some railroad executives hoped for federal intervention. Because of too much railroad construction in the 1880s, the industry suffered from excess capacity. As railroads engaged in cutthroat competition for customers, freight rates fell, and they hoped that the federal government would set minimum rates and guarantee profits.

In 1887, Congress passed the Interstate Commerce Act. The law prohibited **rebates**, in which railroads kicked back portions of freight payments to wealthy customers; prevented roads from charging more money per ton mile for short hauls than for long hauls on the same line; and banned the formation of railroad **pools** in which several roads conspired to set minimum rates. Congress insisted that the railroads levy "reasonable and just" charges. A five-member Interstate Commerce Commission (ICC) would enforce the law by investigating complaints.

In subsequent years, Congress strengthened the ICC. In the Elkins Act of 1903, Congress outlawed all forms of rebates to favored shippers or other discriminatory rate cuts, forced railroads to charge according to their published rates, empowered the ICC to police their actions, and authorized the ICC to seek federal court **injunctions** against railroads defying the law. ICC authority grew substantially greater in 1906 when Congress passed the Hepburn Act. The new legislation allowed the ICC to set railroad freight rates, renewed the prohibition against rebates, severely limited the use of free passes, and, most importantly, prohibited appeals of ICC decisions in the federal courts. Finally, the Mann-Elkins Act of 1910 expanded ICC authority to cover the wireless, **telephone**, **telegraph**, and cable companies doing business across state lines. The ICC could suspend all rate increases and subject them to court review, and the ICC could force railroads to prove that their rates were "reasonable." These legislative amendments to the original Interstate Commerce Act provided the first chapter in the development of the regulatory state in which government agencies and their administrative decisions enjoyed the force of law. Eventually, however, critics argued that the ICC and other regulatory agencies had become captured by the very industries they were supposed to oversee, rendering the regulatory function all but moot.

J

Jones, Mary Harris ("Mother Jones")

The Industrial Revolution gave rise to serious labor-management problems as workers began organizing collectively to promote their own needs. No labor leader was more committed than Mary Harris Jones, affectionately nicknamed "Mother Jones" by the workers who followed her. She was born in Cork County, Ireland, on May 1, 1830, and immigrated to Canada when

Mother Jones (second from left) with Theodore Roosevelt Jr. and president and Mrs. Coolidge in 1924. (Library of Congress)

she was five years old. She was raised in Toronto. Jones later moved to Memphis, Tennessee, where she married and had four children. There she worked as a schoolteacher and dressmaker. During the infamous yellow-fever epidemic that swept through Memphis in 1867, she lost her husband and all of her children. She moved to Chicago and tried to restart her life, but the Chicago fire of 1871 left her homeless. A local office of the **Knights of Labor** gave her a temporary place to stay, and she was converted to the labor-union cause. During the great **railroad strike of 1877**, Jones held picket signs and was assaulted by private detectives and federal troops, but the abuse only made her more indefatigable.

Early in the 1890s, Jones became an organizer for the **United Mine Workers** of America (UMW). Her experiences with **coal** operators radicalized her even more, and in 1905, she joined with **William Haywood** in founding the **Industrial Workers of the World** (IWW), becoming a charter member of the "Wobblies." Mother Jones eventually became one of the best-known and most recognizable figures in the labor movement. She participated in the Arizona copper-mine strikes of 1910; the West Virginia, Pennsylvania, and Ohio coal strikes of 1912–1913; the lead-mine strike in Colorado in 1914, which resulted in the Ludlow Massacre; the New York City garment workers' strikes in 1915–1916; and the great **steel** strikes in Ohio, Indiana, Illinois, and Pennsylvania in 1919. While planning strikes and demonstrations by unemployed workers, Mother Jones died at the age of 100 on November 30, 1930.

The Jungle. *See* Sinclair, Upton Beall

K

Knights of Labor

Even though it did not survive the nineteenth century, the Knights of Labor was the Industrial Revolution's first national labor union to enjoy any longevity. The Industrial Revolution had given rise to a national market and large and powerful **corporations**, and workers increasingly found themselves isolated from management, which became more and more impersonal. Labor unions confined to local areas had neither the resources nor the influence to deal with large, national corporations. That problem gave rise to national labor unions, and the Knights of Labor was the first of them to wield any real power.

Once known as the Noble Order of the Knights of Labor, the Knights of Labor evolved from the Garment Workers Association of Philadelphia, which had been founded in 1862. In 1869, the Garment Workers Association disintegrated, and several of its members formed the Knights of Labor. Because of the prevailing hostile atmosphere about unions and the workers' conviction that the Garment Workers Association had failed because management knew too much about the union members, the Knights of Labor was formed as a secret fraternal lodge. Leaders of the union agreed to organize all workers, whether or not they were skilled.

The Knights of Labor was confined to Philadelphia until the panic of 1873, which laid waste to labor unions throughout the country. Organizers from the Knights of Labor actively recruited these former union members, and the organization grew rapidly, from a total membership of 9,000 in 1872 to more than 19,000 in 1881. When the Knights elected Uriah Stephens grand master in 1878, he abandoned the secret order and actively recruited. In 1885, the Knights of Labor claimed 111,000 members. That year, it organized a successful strike against the Wabash Railroad, and in the wake of the strike, membership soared, exceeding 700,000 by early 1887.

But 1887 was the peak year in the history of the Knights of Labor. **Terence Powderly** succeeded Uriah Stephens as president and led the Knights down the ill-fated road of workers' cooperatives. He tried to establish these cooperatives to actually compete with large corporations in producing goods, with workers sharing the profits. The scheme did not work, losing money and subjecting the workers to frustration and ridicule.

But the real disaster for the Knights of Labor came in 1886, when Powderly launched a strike against **Jay Gould** and the Southwestern Railroad. The strike was a miserable failure, and the union lost credibility. Powderly's refusal to endorse the eight-hour workday hurt even more, giving the fledgling **American Federation of Labor** the upper hand in recruiting drives. By early 1888, membership in the Knights of Labor had fallen to 250,000 workers, and the decline continued, to 100,000 in 1890 and 75,000 in 1893. When the economy fell into the **depression of 1893**, socialists managed to take over the union, and its membership all but collapsed completely.

The failure of the Knights of Labor changed the course of labor-management relations in the United States. Not for two generations would any prominent labor leader try to organize skilled and unskilled workers into the same union, and never again would labor unions attempt to compete with industrial corporations in the actual production of goods.

L

Laissez-Faire

The French term *laissez-faire*, which in English essentially means "hands off," became in the nineteenth century a political ideology aimed at limiting government interference with private business. Laissez-faire had its intellectual beginnings in Adam Smith's ground-breaking book *The Wealth of Nations*, published in 1776. Historians believe that publication of *The Wealth of Nations* marked the beginning of modern economics. A Scottish philosopher, Smith argued that economic behavior was no less a science than the behavior of heavenly bodies, whose movement was controlled by the law of gravity. Just as the law of gravity was impervious to human interference, so was the economy best left alone. Human interference through the agency of government would only introduce inefficiencies, interruptions, and productivity declines.

Smith postulated three laws of economics. According to him, the first law of economics revolved around human nature, which was programmed by God into the individual personality. Individuals, Smith wrote, were uncontrollably committed to their own self-interest. Everything else in the world, regardless of the camouflage of rhetoric, philanthropy, and charity, was secondary to individual self-interest. Self-interest, Smith claimed, was good, a positive virtue that produced long-term benefits for society as a whole.

As a result of the operation of self-interest, the law of competition was introduced into the economy. As thousands of producers compete to sell their products, competition drives down prices, and the quality of goods and services improves. Smith claimed that there was no moral dimension to prices. They were neither too high nor too low because the law of competition determined them. At any given moment, the prices of goods and services are in balance. To complain about prices, for Smith, was as foolish as complaining about the law of gravity.

While thousands of producers compete to sell, millions of consumers compete to purchase goods and services, and the interaction between producers competing to sell and consumers competing to buy generated Adam Smith's third law—the law of supply and demand. According to Smith, the price and availability of goods and services were always in intricate balance. The price of a product was directly related to consumer demand for it and inversely related to the supply of it. If large numbers of buyers were clamoring for a product, its price would rise. If few people wanted the product, its price tended to fall. On the other hand, if a product was abundantly available, its price fell; if it was in short supply, its price went up. As producers saw prices rising, they would work to produce more goods.

The operation of the laws of self-interest, competition, and supply and demand created what Smith described as the "invisible hand" regulating the economy. The "invisible hand" guaranteed that at any given moment, the economy was in perfect balance, as stable as the planets in the solar system that orbited the sun. The functioning of a free market, without government interference, would allow competing producers to supply ever-increasing volumes of goods. Supply and demand would provide fair prices to producers, low prices to consumers, and a living wage to workers.

Beginning in the 1790s, disagreements over laissez-faire became central to public policy debates in the United States. Secretary of the Treasury Alexander Hamilton who became a leading figure in the Federalist Party, believed passionately in using the power of the federal government to help develop the industrial economy. Hamilton and the Federalists argued that the government should pass high tariffs on imported manufactured goods to protect nascent American **factories** and establish a national, government-backed bank to provide a stable currency and loan money to industry. Within decades, the successors to the Federalist Party—first the Whigs and then the Republicans—advocated use of government to promote the construction of such **internal improvements** as **turnpikes**, **canals**, and **railroads** to build **infrastructure** and make the transportation of goods more efficient.

Opponents of Hamilton's ideas, particularly Thomas Jefferson and James Madison of the Democratic-Republican Party, employed the ideology of laissez-faire to justify their opposition to tariffs, a national bank, and federally financed internal improvements. Hamilton's program, they argued, gave unfair advantage to bankers and industrialists and discriminated against workers and farmers. They called for operation of the "invisible hand" of the free market—to let the laws of self-interest, competition, and supply and demand determine production, prices, and profits. Only laissez-faire, they claimed, would guarantee a level economic playing field where all could compete. Such arguments dominated public debates in the United States until the post–**Civil War** era.

After the Civil War, however, economic change turned that debate upside down. The rise of large **corporations** that dominated economic markets altered the ideological game. As fewer and fewer corporations gained more and more market share, fears of **monopoly** developed. Adam Smith's laissez-faire philosophy had never contemplated an economy in which a few producers, or even just one producer, controlled an entire industry and charged whatever the market would bear. The existence of a monopoly upset the laws of competition and supply and demand and undermined faith in an economy that regulated itself.

The erosion of that faith changed American politics. Groups representing workers and farmers, like the Democratic Party and the **Populist** Party, which had long employed laissez-faire arguments to prevent government from subsidizing business schemes, now rejected laissez-faire and began demanding government action to ameliorate and prevent the worst abuses of monopoly. In such legislation as the Interstate Commerce Act of 1887 and the **Sherman Antitrust Act of 1890** and a host of laws in subsequent decades, the federal government began regulating large corporations. In response, many business leaders reversed themselves too, adopting laissez-faire arguments, claiming that the federal government had no business interfering with the economy. Government intervention, they argued, increased business costs and rendered businesses less efficient, which only increased costs to consumers. On the other hand, whenever business leaders wanted government assistance—in the forms of protective tariffs, currency measures, and subsidies—they abandoned laissez-faire. In the end, laissez-faire arguments were usually employed only when they suited particular purposes. Few Americans were ever ideologically wedded to laissez-faire.

By the mid-twentieth century, few Americans believed in or advocated laissez-faire in any real way. Except for extreme conservatives in such groups as the Libertarian Party, most Americans acknowledged that in a modern political economy, the federal government has an important role to play. The debate between Republicans and Democrats today revolves around the nature of government intervention, not the morality of it.

Light Bulb

Development of the incandescent light bulb was one of the Industrial Revolution's most enduring technologies. The key to the light bulb was producing long-lasting filaments and so completely evacuating air from cylinders as to make combustion impossible. Before **Thomas Edison** put his fertile imagination to the task of inventing the incandescent bulb, several European inventors had tinkered with the idea. They employed electric batteries as their power source but failed to evacuate cylinders successfully. It was not until the late 1870s that Joseph Swan, a British pharmacist, succeeded in the evacuation process using a pump developed in Germany.

In 1878, Edison launched his own effort to develop practical incandescent lighting with a public-relations blitz designed to assist him in raising investment capital. He also established the Edison Electric Light Company to manage the business he expected to come from the invention. During 1878, he experimented with a variety of materials to develop the most durable filaments, and in 1879 he invented the light bulb. Always with an eye on the economic market, Edison also developed low-cost copper wiring and cost-effective, low-internal-resistance dynamos to generate electricity. In 1880 and 1881, he added special fire-resistant fuses, lighting fixtures, bulbs, and sockets. Late in 1881, he constructed his first commercial central power station at 257 Pearl Street in New York City. In 1882, the Pearl Street Station was selling electricity, and the market for residential and business incandescent lighting was huge.

The incandescent light bulb transformed social life around the world, liberating human schedules, for the first time, from the natural cycles of the sun. People began to stay up later, reading, playing games, and engaging in other forms of entertainment. Employers added new shifts to work schedules, and most people began sleeping less. Life became even more scheduled as electric clocks dictated day-to-day activities, and families were drawn increasingly to activities outside the home.

Lochner v. New York (1905)

As the Industrial Revolution matured in the nineteenth century, and major **corporations** grew in size and influence, critics began turning to state and national governments to prevent abuses of workers and consumers. The New York state legislature in May 1894 passed the Bakeshop Act, which limited hours in bakeries to no more than sixty per week or ten per day. The legislature justified its decision on the grounds that limiting hours would improve the family life of the workers, protect worker health and safety, and therefore strengthen society. At the time, a typical workweek for bakers exceeded 100 hours. Joseph Lochner, owner of a small bakery in Utica, New York, sued in state court, employing **laissez-faire** logic to condemn government interference in the marketplace. He also claimed that the Bakeshop Act violated his Fourteenth Amendment rights to due process of law by depriving him of liberty and property. Lochner lost his case in state court and eventually took it all the way to the U.S. Supreme Court. The Supreme Court heard arguments on February 23–24, 1905, and rendered its fi5–4 decision on April 4. The justices held in favor of Lochner, declaring the Bakeshop Act unconstitutional on the grounds that it interfered with the right of an employer to enter into a contract with an employee. The decision was a setback to progressive reformers interested in ameliorating the exploitation of labor in the United States and expanding corporate rights.

M

Marshall, John

John Marshall, chief justice of the U.S. Supreme Court from 1801 to 1835, helped create a legal environment in which the Industrial Revolution could flourish. Rapid economic growth depends upon the sanctity of contracts; the safety of private property; and fluid, reliable transportation, communication, and monetary systems, all of which garnered Marshall's wholehearted support.

Marshall was born on the northwestern Virginia frontier in Germantown, Fauquier County, Virginia, on September 24, 1755. Although the frontier gave him a sense of democratic values, he nevertheless came from a family rich in landed holdings, and this gave him a profound respect for private property and the sanctity of contracts. He proved to be a very remarkable young man, one with an appreciation for the virtues of democracy embedded in a conservative, nationalistic, philosophic framework. During the American Revolution, Marshall enlisted in the revolutionary cause, fought alongside his father, and developed a deep respect for George Washington.

Although he had only two years of formal education, Marshall studied law privately and attended law lectures at William and Mary College. He then opened his own practice in Fauquier County, where his keenly analytical, retentive mind made him an outstanding attorney. He later moved his practice to Richmond, Virginia, which placed him in the vortex of state politics. A confirmed supporter of the U.S. Constitution and a patriotic nationalist, Marshall became active in the Federalist Party. He served several terms in the state legislature, one term in Congress (1799–1800), and a brief stint as secretary of state under President John Adams before Adams appointed him to the Supreme Court. On March 5, 1801, Marshall assumed his duties as chief justice. In *Marbury v. Madison* (1803), one of the Marshall court's first major decisions, the principle of judicial review was established, giving the U.S. Supreme Court authority to declare congressional statutes unconstitutional.

Marshall's greatest impact on the economy and in providing legal impetus to the Industrial Revolution came in a series of critical decisions. Unlike most other attorneys of the time, Marshall understood the intricate connections between law and economics, and he was conscious of the need to create a legal environment in the United States in which the economy would flourish. A confirmed nationalist, Marshall believed that the federal government, not the state governments, was sovereign, and that for a truly national marketplace to evolve unfettered by unnecessary state and local regulations, federal supremacy had to be inviolate. In the case of *M'Culloch v. Maryland* (1819), Marshall made that a reality. The state of Maryland had passed legislation taxing the Second Bank of the United States, an institution of the federal government. The Second Bank of the United States refused to pay the tax, and the case made its way through the federal court system. Under Marshall's direction, the Supreme Court unanimously held that state governments did not possess the sovereign authority to tax the federal government or any of its agencies.

Chief Justice Marshall also believed that **capitalism** in general and economic growth in particular depended upon the protection of property rights through the **contracts clause** of the U.S. Constitution. In order for investors to put capital at risk, they had to be reasonably certain that their rights to property would be protected. In *Fletcher v. Peck* (1810) and *Dartmouth College v. Woodward* (1819), Marshall firmly established that principle in the law. With legislative authorization in 1794 from the legislature, Georgia sold 35 million acres of public land, at 1.5 cents an acre, to four land companies. A number of state politicians held stock in the land companies and profited handsomely when the companies resold the acreage. When charges of graft and corruption surfaced, the state legislature in 1796 rescinded the 1794 bill. But Georgians who had innocently bought land under the original legislation opposed the rescind law. Robert Fletcher sued John Peck, owner of one of the land companies, claiming that he had purchased his land in good faith and that taking it from him now constituted a violation of contract. Chief Justice John Marshall, in *Fletcher v. Peck*, concurred and overturned the legislation on the grounds that it violated a legal contract. The decision contributed to the creation of a legal environment in which funds could be safely invested and business transacted in security.

The case of *Dartmouth College v. Woodward* (1818) also contributed to that legal environment. In 1816, Republican Governor William Plumer of New Hampshire fired the trustees of Dartmouth College. Most of the trustees were members of the Federalist Party. At the same time, the Republican-controlled state legislature altered the college's charter and brought the school under state control. The fired trustees sued, claiming that the legislature had violated the contract clause of the U.S. Constitution. In the case of *Dartmouth College v. Woodward*, Chief Justice John Marshall found in favor of the trustees, claiming that the original college charter, which had come from King George III of England, constituted a contract that guaranteed the college's status as a private, not public institution. By dissolving that charter—a legal contract—the state had illegally interfered with Dartmouth College's property rights. In essence, the decision awarded Fifth Amendment property rights to a **corporation**, treating it as an individual under the law. The case helped insulate business investors from capricious interference from state government and in the process helped create a pro-business environment in the United States.

Marshall also sought to establish a legal setting in the United States where the shipment of goods from region to region was efficient and unencumbered by legal and political restrictions. Marshall embedded that principle into constitutional law in 1824 with the ***Gibbons v. Ogden*** case. Since 1807, Robert Fulton had a ***monopoly*** from the New York state legislature to operate a steamboat on the Hudson River. The state also passed legislation prohibiting others from running a steamboat across the Hudson from New York soil to New Jersey. Thomas Gibbons, who wanted to run a competing steamboat on the Hudson River, sued in federal court. The case of *Gibbons v. Ogden* reached the Supreme Court in 1824. Marshall and the other justices overturned the New York monopoly on the grounds that only Congress had the authority to interfere with interstate commerce. Historians consider the decision a victory for economic nationalism. Because of *Gibbons v. Ogden*, the United States was able to develop a truly national market, which was a prerequisite to the Industrial Revolution.

Finally, Marshall understood the importance of a reliable monetary system, since the efficient exchange of goods was essential to economic growth. The U.S. Constitution had confined the power to produce a currency to the federal government and had prohibited state governments from doing so. In *Craig v. Missouri* (1830), Marshall invalidated a Missouri law in which the state issued loan certificates and treated them as legal tender. Only Congress possessed the constitutional authority to issue money.

John Marshall presided over the Supreme Court as chief justice longer than any other individual in U.S. history. During his term, he helped fashion a legal environment in which businessmen and investors could confidently operate, goods could move freely between various political jurisdictions, and private property was protected by the contracts clause of the U.S. Constitution. Marshall died on July 6, 1835.

Mass Production

As the United States erected **turnpikes**, **canals**, and **railroads** in the nineteenth century, the shipment of goods became steadily more efficient. The

United States gradually became integrated into a single national market, which provided entrepreneurs with enormous opportunities to sell goods anywhere. When the country's **infrastructure** was still in its infancy, it was impossible to ponder national marketing because shipping goods efficiently was difficult. Once this became possible, businessmen felt the need to produce manufactured goods in ever-increasing volumes. Mass-production techniques developed out of that need to exploit a new opportunity.

The first step in mass production was to bring workers under one roof— a **factory**. Until the rise of factories, goods were produced under a "putting-out" system in which entrepreneurs traveled to and from the homes of their workers, delivering raw materials and picking up finished goods. Businessmen soon found themselves wasting too much time on the road. Efficiency demanded the gathering of workers under one roof, and **textile** mills in New England pioneered the technique beginning in the 1790s.

Once workers had been collected into a factory for their daily work, businessmen developed new techniques for improving productivity. One of the most important steps was specialization of labor. Instead of having employees sitting at workbenches assembling complete goods from scratch, businessmen assigned them specific, repetitive tasks, which saved time and helped eliminate wasted motion. Workers specialized in one phase of the production process, which increased their speed.

In addition to factories and specialization of labor, mass production also depended upon the development of interchangeable parts. Until then, individual goods were made from scratch by craftsmen, and therefore each product was unique in terms of its engineering specifications and tolerances. Among others, **Eli Whitney** pioneered the idea of interchangeable parts, with detailed, precise specifications that made for greater precision and less time assembling finished products or repairing them. By 1800, Whitney had developed interchangeable parts in his gun-manufacturing enterprise. Other industries soon adopted the idea. Scientific management also increased productivity and made mass production possible. Largely the brainchild of **Frederick Taylor**, scientific management at first concentrated on eliminating unnecessary movements by workers, but its greatest contribution to mass production was the idea of the assembly line, in which workers, instead of moving about to pick up raw materials and deliver finished goods, stayed put. Raw materials were delivered to them and finished products taken from them, at first by unskilled workers and later by power-driven conveyor systems, which brought materials automatically to the workers.

Mass production exerted a dramatic impact on American economic and social life. Economically, mass production brought about great reductions in the per unit cost of industrial goods, which rendered them affordable to larger numbers of people and then, in a reinforcing cycle, stimulated even more mass production. The result was the world's first consumer culture, in which masses of people came to define the meaning of life through the purchase of certain finished goods.

McCormick, Cyrus Hall

Cyrus McCormick, an inventor, played a key role in promoting the revolution in agricultural production in the United States that accompanied the revolution in industrial manufacturing. He was born in Rockbridge County, Virginia, on February 15, 1809. His father, Robert McCormick—a farmer, a blacksmith, and a "tinkerer," in McCormick's word—searched for more efficient ways of performing mechanical tasks. While the younger McCormick was growing up, his father worked diligently to develop a better way of harvesting grain. At the time, farmers reaped grain by hand, cutting the stalks down with a sickle. The work was labor intensive and limited the number of acres a farmer could work.

Robert McCormick worked unsuccessfully for years to come up with a mechanical reaper, and his son watched prototype after prototype fail. When his father gave up, Cyrus took up the crusade. Other inventors, such as Obed Hussey, were engaged in the same quest. In 1831, McCormick had a workable prototype. His reaper, a contraption on wheels that was pulled by horses, included a rotating reel that pushed the grain against a reciprocating cutting blade and a metal platform that caught and trapped the fallen grain. In 1834, McCormick filed for a patent on his reaper.

Cyrus McCormick invented the first practical grain reaper and went into large-scale production of the farm machines in the 1840s. His invention (shown here in 1878) enabled a huge increase in grain production. (Parsons, J. Russell, et al. *Memorial of Robert McCormick,* 1885)

McCormick worked at the family's iron-foundry business until its bankruptcy in the **panic of 1837**, when he began working on improving the reaper. By 1840, he was manufacturing reapers and selling them locally, even though most farmers found them hard to use. The heavy metal in the reaper easily tired the horses working to pull it through fields, and the contraption often clogged up, requiring farmers to stop and clean tangled plants from the metal teeth. Most farmers found it cheaper to reap by hand. Still, in 1842, McCormick was able to license others to manufacture and sell his invention.

In 1844, hoping to improve sales, McCormick traveled to Indiana, Illinois, and Missouri, where he found the topography much more amenable to the reaper. The land was flat, not hilly like back east, and the reaper clogged up less frequently. Also, because labor was less available and more expensive out west, the reaper had a better market. He moved his manufacturing operation to Chicago in 1847.

McCormick also made dramatic improvements in the reaper. He replaced all of the cast-iron parts with wrought iron, which made the reaper lighter and easier for horses to haul. He sharpened and strengthened the cutting blade and made it so that operators could adjust the cutting height. He also added a seat for the raker, who no longer had to walk along with the reaper.

In addition to being a successful inventor, McCormick proved to be a highly successful businessman. He developed a modern **factory** that revolutionized industrial production. The factory employed standardized, machine-tooled parts, which increased productivity and permitted farmers to make some repairs in the field. McCormick's factory in Chicago during the 1850s and 1860s was considered the most modern in the world. He also employed modern marketing methods, advertising the reaper in farmer publications. By the time of the **Civil War**, McCormick was a millionaire. He lived until May 13, 1884. By that time, his son had taken over the business, which eventually evolved into the corporate giant International Harvester.

Meat Inspection Act of 1906

The Meat Inspection Act of 1906 was the first major example of government consumer regulation in U.S. history. The Industrial Revolution had brought about a revolution of its own in food processing, and the size and power of the major food-processing companies created demands for government regulation. In 1890, Congress passed the Meat Inspection Act, allowing the Department of Agriculture to inspect live animals as well as beef, pork, and chicken headed into export markets. In 1891, Congress amended the law and empowered the Department of Agriculture to perform the same inspections on meat destined for domestic markets.

But early in the 1900s, new pressures mounted for more government regulation. These demands came from two sources. **Progressive** reformers advocated more government regulation in order to make processed meat products safer, and the publication of **Upton Sinclair**'s best-selling novel *The Jungle* in 1906, which exposed the scandalous sanitary standards in many meat-processing plants, provided reformers with increased public political support. The large packing houses supported more regulation, primarily because they had the capital needed to upgrade their facilities to meet government standards, while smaller competitors did not. In 1906, at the request of President **Theodore Roosevelt**, Congress passed the Meat Inspection Act, amending the 1890 legislation and permitting the Department of Agriculture to establish meat inspections throughout the country to grade beef quality and to enforce processing standards.

Meat-Packing Industry

Mass-production techniques revolutionized **factory** output of industrial goods, but they similarly revolutionized food production in the nineteenth century. The beef and pork industries were examples. Until the mid-nineteenth century, beef and pork production was a business affair in which community butchers purchased livestock from neighboring farmers, slaughtered the animals, and then retailed the meat locally. The work was usually confined to winter months so that the meat would not spoil. Fresh beef was a luxury that few Americans could afford, and even those who could afford it could not get it year-round, while pork production was typically done during the winter months so the pork would not spoil.

But after the **Civil War**, change swept through the industry when midwestern beef and pork merchants greatly expanded production. Because of its climate and location, Chicago became the center of the beef meat-packing industry, and Cincinnati the hub of pork production. In both locales, cool weather permitted spoilage-free processing most months of the year.

Chicago became the receiving area for cattle raised in Texas, Oklahoma, Missouri, Kansas, Nebraska, Montana, and Wyoming. Without **refrigeration**, it was impossible to slaughter cattle in the hinterland and then get the products to market. Ranchers drove large herds overland to major railroads in Kansas, where the cattle were loaded onto boxcars and shipped to Chicago. During the overland drives, the cattle had lost weight, so they had to be bulked up in Chicago feedlots before slaughter.

Huge slaughterhouses, owned by such entrepreneurs as **Gustavus Swift** and **Philip Armour**, were built in Chicago, and the cattle were slaughtered utilizing assembly-line techniques. After being stunned or killed by a sledgehammer blow to the head, the animals were attached to pulleys, were hung by their feet, and had their throats cut to bleed them. While the bleeding was occurring, the carcasses were towed along the pulley systems to butchers assigned different tasks. Butchers armed with sharp, narrow knives removed the hides, which were immediately collected and sold to tanners. Another crew removed the heads. Other butchers then gutted the animals, and the entrails were collected and saved for processing. A fourth group of butchers wielding large handsaws and knives split the carcasses in two along the spinal column and then quartered them. The beef quarters were then packed in ice in zinc- or tin-lined wooden boxes and were placed in insulated railroad cars for shipment to cities and towns in the Midwest and Northwest—markets that could be accessed in less than thirty-six hours. The invention of the refrigerated boxcar later in the century permitted the shipment of fresh beef throughout the country.

Cincinnati similarly became the center of the pork industry. Huge local salt deposits made curing and pickling the meat economical. Also, abundant hardwood forests provided wood for smoking the meat. Finally, the city's location along the Ohio River and its railroad nexus made it an entrepôt for shipping finished products—fancy hams, common hams, bacon, shoulders, and bulk pork, which was divided into such grades as clear, mess, prime, and cargo. The hog slaughterhouses became assembly-line factories. After being stunned into unconsciousness by a hammer blow to the head, the animals were dragged indoors, where their throats were cut and the carcasses were hung to bleed out. Once the bleeding stopped, the carcasses were dumped in vats of boiling water and then laid out on tables for removal of the ears and scraping of the skin. The carcasses were then rehung for gutters to remove the entrails. After spending the night in basement cooling rooms, the carcasses were butchered into marketable products and cured.

The beef industry became the source of two huge political controversies in the early twentieth century. In 1906, **Upton Sinclair** published his novel *The Jungle*, in which he described the fictional trials of a Lithuanian immigrant family living in Chicago. A committed socialist, Sinclair hoped that the novel would awaken Americans to the exploitation of workers, but it was his description of the filthy conditions in Chicago meat-packing plants that captured the public imagination and helped bring to pass such federal legislation as the **Meat Inspection Act of 1906** and the **Pure Food and Drug Act of 1906.**

The meat-packing industry also became the subject of **antitrust** action when a series of business consolidations produced what critics called the "Beef Trust." Entrepreneurs like Gustavus Swift and Philip Armour had established huge corporate entities controlling much of the beef market, and progressive critics accused them of having formed a **monopoly**. The Justice Department filed an antitrust lawsuit, *Swift & Co. v. United States*, to break up the so-called Beef Trust, a virtual monopoly enjoyed by Swift & Company and closely related firms over the beef-processing industry. The case reached the Supreme Court and was decided unanimously on January 30, 1905. The Court concluded that although Swift's meat-processing plants were indeed intrastate, the company had nevertheless intended to wipe out all competition and establish a monopoly.

Mesabi Range

If the **steel** industry was the driving force behind the Industrial Revolution, iron was the fuel of the steel industry. The major source of iron ore in the United States was the Mesabi Range of northern Minnesota. In 1842, the Webster-Ashburton Treaty between the United States and Great Britain awarded the United States sovereignty over territory south of a line that stretched from Lake Superior to Lake of the Woods, which gave America the Mesabi Range. Iron ore was not discovered there until 1866, but the find was huge, the largest known deposit of iron in the world, and it was easily transportable by Great Lakes barges to steel mills in Indiana, Ohio, and Pennsylvania. Because of the ready accessibility of the Mesabi Range iron, American steel became the most competitive in the world.

Molly Maguires

The term *Molly Maguires* was used in the 1870s to describe America's most radical labor movement. The panic of 1873–1878 sent most American labor unions into a rapid decline because the prevailing unemployment rate made jobs precious. Prospective workers feared that union membership would keep them from getting hired. The political atmosphere in Washington, D.C., and in most corporate boardrooms was decidedly antilabor. But one group of workers remained unintimidated and exceedingly radical. Known as the "Molly Maguires," they were a secret group of **coal** miners, mostly of Irish descent, who had once been members of the Ancient Order of Hibernians. They organized into a union in 1862, but poor treatment at the hands of coal operators over the years gradually radicalized them.

When the United States sank into an economic depression in 1873, the Molly Maguires decided that only revolutionary violence could ameliorate their situations, and they murdered a number of mine owners and management personnel. Mine owners hired detectives from the Pinkerton company to locate the murderers, and the Pinkertons resorted to violence themselves, harassing union members in general, whether or not they had participated in the violence. Late in 1875, dozens of Irish union organizers, many of them Molly Maguires, were arrested and charged with murder. Twenty-four were convicted, and in 1876, ten were executed. The convictions crushed the Molly Maguires as a labor organization. Nevertheless, the Molly Maguires provided an initial stage of union organization in the mine fields that the **United Mine Workers** later assumed.

Monopoly

The term *monopoly* is employed by economists to describe a situation in which a single individual, or more likely a single business enterprise, has secured complete or nearly complete control of a market. The monopolistic entity has so eliminated its competition that it can set prices at will, charging whatever the market will bear. During the late nineteenth and early twentieth centuries in the United States, monopolies assumed several forms. A company could simply buy out its competitors or drive them

An early-twentieth-century political cartoon depicts the Standard Oil monopoly as an octopus with many tentacles wrapped around the steel, copper, and shipping industries, as well as a state house, the U.S. Capitol, and one tentacle reaching for the White House. (Library of Congress)

out of business, becoming the last player on that particular economic playing field. Monopolies could also be created through collusion when several competing companies conspired to set prices or allocated markets geographically, essentially creating monopolies in certain regions. Critics accused the **railroads** of engaging in such conspiracies during the late nineteenth century in the United States. Several companies could also form a **trust** in order to restrain trade. In a trust arrangement, companies would surrender voting rights to an independent corporate body that would set corporate pricing and marketing policies for all of the participating entities, which received trust certificates entitling them to a share in the profits. A **holding company** was another monopolistic arrangement, in which a company would be set up that would purchase a controlling interest in several competing companies. The holding company would then establish pricing and marketing policies, essentially creating monopolistic conditions. The **antitrust** movement—embodied in such laws as the **Sherman Antitrust Act of 1890** and the **Clayton Antitrust Act of 1914**—worked against the formation of monopolies in order to preserve competitive markets. *See* **ANTITRUST**.

Morgan, John Pierpont

John Pierpont Morgan is remembered by economic historians as the greatest financier during the age of the Industrial Revolution and the man who became the living embodiment of Wall Street and its culture. He was born in Hartford, Connecticut, on April 17, 1837. Morgan's father, Junius Spencer Morgan, a successful merchant in Hartford, moved to London, England, where he became a partner in George Peabody's private banking company. Peabody had made a fortune in the dry-goods business and recognized in Morgan a real business acumen. The elder Morgan passed those talents to his son, J. Pierpont Morgan.

J. Pierpont Morgan attended secondary school in Switzerland and then studied mathematics at the University of Göttingen in Germany. In 1857, the senior Morgan had his son hired as an accountant in New York with Duncan, Sherman & Company, a subsidiary of Peabody's London banking house. J. P. Morgan opened his own firm in 1861, and when Peabody retired in 1864, he and his father, in cooperation with Anthony Drexel of Philadelphia, jointly built a banking house that came to be known as Drexel, Morgan & Company. Beginning in 1895, after the retirement of Drexel and the senior Morgan, J. P. Morgan took over and renamed the firm J. P. Morgan & Company.

J. P. Morgan appeared on the American financial scene just when the Industrial Revolution had created a huge demand for investment capital. The rise of a national market had provided unprecedented opportunities for manufacturers to build more **factories** and for **railroads** to build more tracks, but U.S. capital markets were notoriously short of cash. American businessmen needed long-term capital and wanted to issue corporate securities, but they needed investors. Because of his contacts in Great Britain, Morgan was able to match European investors with American companies. He pulled off his first big deal in 1879 when he sold $25 million worth of stocks in the **New York Central Railroad** to English investors. For each sale of corporate securities, he collected a percentage fee. In order to generate more income for himself, Morgan entered the business of engineering mergers, new public offerings, and corporate reorganizations, all of which provided opportunities to float new corporate securities. Because his English investors often gave him control of their proxy votes, Morgan often found himself on corporate boards of directors, where he could protect his investors' interests. When he could not personally sit on a board, Morgan appointed his own subordinates to the positions.

During the **depression of 1893**, Morgan acquired huge influence. In advance of the economic collapse, most American railroads had overexpanded, taking on huge debt structures that they could not maintain. Most railroads turned to what was now known as "the House of Morgan" to help restructure their debts and raise more capital. In 1901, Morgan engineered the reorganization plan that transformed **Andrew Carnegie**'s holdings into the **United States Steel Corporation**. Many people accused or credited Morgan with controlling the flow of capital in the United States.

The extent of Morgan's power was revealed first in 1895 and again in 1907. In 1895, with the country in a depression and financial institutions facing a run by depositors, the U.S. Treasury experienced a serious depletion of its gold reserves. President Grover Cleveland, worried that the United States might be forced to abandon the gold standard, turned to Morgan for assistance, and in a matter of days, the financier floated $65 million in government securities. In 1907, when the banking system experienced a meltdown and panic, Morgan intervened and stabilized the capital markets. That power alarmed some. In 1912, the **Pujo Committee** of the House of Representatives charged that the American financial system had fallen completely under his control, a charge that was certainly an exaggeration but nevertheless said a great deal about Morgan's influence. By the time of his death on March 31, 1913, J. P. Morgan had helped create a financial system in which investment bankers, of whom he was the patriarch, effectively controlled access to the sources of capital and its flow throughout the economy.

Morse, Samuel Finley Breese

Samuel F. B. Morse was the father of the **telegraph** industry and, as such, one of the Industrial Revolution's most influential figures. Because of the telegraph, personal and business communications ceased to be dependent upon surface transportation—wagons, barges, **railroads**, and ships—and instead became electronic and instantaneous, allowing businessmen to more efficiently conduct business and to do so at great distances from their bases of operations. Until Samuel Morse came along, a businessman in the East would have to wait at least six weeks to get a turnaround letter from Europe or the West Coast, and any letter sent to South America, Africa, or Asia would take months.

Samuel Morse was born in Charlestown, Massachusetts, on April 27, 1791. His father was Jedediah Morse, a Congregational minister and intellectual who devoted his personal scholarship to the study of geography. The younger Morse graduated from Yale in 1810 and then spent several years studying painting in London. In London and then back in the United States, Morse made a living as a portrait artist, teaching painting and sculpture at the City University of New York and founding the National Academy of Design. Morse's best-known portraits were those of the Marquis de Lafayette, which he completed in 1825.

During his stay in Europe, Morse had begun contemplating the idea of wireless communication, since he found the long delays in communicating with his family in the United States frustrating. Off and on over the years, he experimented with the idea, trying to design a workable technology, and he had a working model of the telegraph built as early as 1832. In 1837, he gave up his artistic career to pursue what he called the "telegraph" full-time. He designed the electromagnetic recording telegraph and then developed a code of dashes and dots to send messages. The code later became known as "Morse code" to generations of telegraphers. Morse also developed electromagnetic relays to permit the transmission of coded messages over long distances.

Over the years, Morse received financial assistance from Alfred Vail, who became his business partner. They filed a patent on the telegraph in 1837 and received the patent in 1843. Morse lobbied Congress for money to build an experimental line, and in 1843, Congress came up with $30,000 for the project. A line was run between Baltimore and Washington, D.C., and on May 24, 1844, Morse transmitted the message "What hath God wrought," giving birth to a new industry. Samuel Morse died on April 2, 1872.

Muckrakers

The Industrial Revolution introduced vast changes in society and the economy, changes that most Americans were unprepared for and had difficulty confronting. The old rural, agricultural economy—in which most people lived on farms or in villages and small towns and made their living off the land or from small businesses—gave way to an economy of **factories** and **mass production** and a society in which most people lived in larger towns and cities. The Industrial Revolution also produced a large, visible working class of people who suffered from low wages, dangerous, long workdays, and dangerous working conditions. In sharp contrast, the Industrial Revolution also produced a new upper class of fabulously wealthy individuals, most of whom, like **John D. Rockefeller** and **Andrew Carnegie**, owned the new factories and businesses. During the nineteenth century, these men came to control larger and larger shares of the economic market, and their **corporations** became national in scope. They also used their economic resources to influence the political process to secure from government the subsidies and market protections they needed to augment their wealth.

By the end of the nineteenth century, critics appeared who worried that the new industrial economy and the super-rich businessmen who controlled it threatened individual democracy. The rise of the critics came at the same time that new publishing technologies made books, magazines, and newspapers cheaper and available to mass audiences. Books and articles, mostly nonfiction, appeared in the 1890s and early 1900s that took the new industrialists to task for introducing corruption and exploitation into the American economy. President **Theodore Roosevelt** coined the term *muckrakers* to describe the sensational articles because he believed that many of the writers were "wallowing in the mud" and exaggerating their stories.

In 1894, Henry Demarest Lloyd wrote the book *Wealth against Commonwealth*, a vicious attack on John D. Rockefeller and **Standard Oil Company**, which he had created. Lloyd claimed that Rockefeller had monopolized the oil-refining industry by using unfair competitive practices to drive smaller refiners out of business, that he exploited workers, and that he gouged consumers because of his monopolistic powers. A similar indictment of John D. Rockefeller's business practices came in *McClure's Magazine*. In serialized form, Ida M. Tarbell's *The History of the Standard Oil Company* confirmed Lloyd's claims. Tarbell had a bias: her father had been driven out of business by Rockefeller. She praised the efficiencies Standard Oil Company had brought to the industry, but she accused Rockefeller of industrial espionage and ruthlessness in driving competitors out of business.

McClure's Magazine also published *The Shame of the Cities* in 1904, a series of serialized essays by Lincoln Steffens on urban corruption in the United States. Steffens claimed that in too many American cities, mayors and city councilors accepted bribes and kickbacks from businessmen interested in selling goods and services to city government. Steffens called for reforms that would reduce influence peddling by public servants.

Other muckraking publications included Thomas Lawson's *Frenzied Finance*, which revealed unfair and illegal machinations in the stock markets; David Graham Phillips's *The Treason of the Senate*, which showed how big business controlled public policy in the United States by exercising undue and corrupt influence on the U.S. Senate (at the time, before the Seventeenth Amendment, U.S. senators were elected by state legislatures, and big business had a relatively easy time corrupting such a relatively small number of electors); and Charles Edward Russell's *The Greatest Trust in the World*, an attack on monopolistic practices in the meat-packing industry.

Perhaps the greatest piece of muckraking was **Upton Sinclair**'s *The Jungle* (1906), a novel about the trials of immigrant life in Chicago and working conditions in the meat-packing industry. The novel became a best seller because of its descriptions of the filthy, unsanitary systems employed in processing meat. Readers ended up caring much more about what was in their sausage than in what was happening among poor immigrants. Readers did not buy, however, Sinclair's answer to the problems of poverty and corporate abuse. He advocated **socialism**, which the vast majority of Americans rejected.

The muckrakers, though often guilty of exaggeration and hyperbole to sell copy, nevertheless had a huge impact on American public policy. At the time, the **Progressive movement** was just gaining momentum, and the drive to use federal and state governments to regulate big business and eliminate its most abusive economic practices received a boost from muckraking journalists, who helped shape the opinions of large numbers of Americans and helped generate a new moral authority for those Americans committed to reform. Since then, investigative journalism has become a key ingredient in the political process in the United States.

Muller v. Oregon (1908)

Muller v. Oregon is among the most significant Supreme Court cases in the history of American jurisprudence. In 1903, the Oregon state legislature passed a law limiting the working hours of women, declaring that women in **factories** and laundries could not work more than ten hours a day. The law came during the **Progressive** Era when reformers at the state and national levels were trying to ameliorate some of the harsh and dangerous working conditions that had emerged during the Industrial Revolution. On September 4, 1905, Curt Muller's Grand Laundry in Portland, Oregon, required several of its women employees to labor more than ten hours. A local court found Muller guilty of a misdemeanor violation of the law and fined him $10. Aware of the U.S. Supreme Court's recent decision in *Lochner v. New York*, which had struck down a New York law limiting the hours worked by bakers, Muller sued. The case was argued before the U.S. Supreme Court on January 15, 1908, and was decided by a unanimous vote on February 24, 1908.

Louis Brandeis argued Oregon's case before the Court and employed a highly innovative legal strategy. Instead of relying on precedent and legal tradition, he assembled overwhelming evidence from social workers, nurses, and physicians that excessive working hours for women damaged women and their families. Brandeis cited the Court's recognition in *Lochner* that states possessed jurisdiction in concerns related directly to health, safety, and welfare, and the Oregon statute, he argued, was justified because of the state's interest in women's health. Brandeis convinced the justices, who upheld the statute. Since *Muller*, the courts have taken into consideration social and economic data, as well as legal precedent, in making regulatory decisions, and in the history of the Industrial Revolution, *Muller* is a landmark case in giving government regulatory powers over corporate decisions.

Munn v. Illinois (1877)

The Industrial Revolution, by giving rise to large, powerful private **corporations**, also gave rise to the demands for government regulation of these corporations. The case of *Munn v. Illinois*, also known as one of the so-called **Granger** cases, revolved around the legitimacy of state governments employing their police powers and regulating private corporate entities and whether or not such regulation violated company property rights. At the time, Midwestern and Southern farmers, extremely frustrated with rising freight costs and declining incomes, began forming what became known as the "Granger movement." The Grange, more formally known as the Patrons of Husbandry, had started out as a social organization to bring some relief from the loneliness of farm life in the United States, but when farmers got together for picnics, dances, and lectures, talk inevitably turned to politics. Grangers began being elected to state legislatures in the 1870s.

In 1875, the Illinois legislature passed a law allowing the state to set the rates grain elevators could charge farmers to store crops, as long as the grain-elevator operators did business in an Illinois city with a population in excess of 100,000 people. The only Illinois city with such a population was Chicago, where farmers were convinced that grain operators were fraudulently fixing rates. The grain operators filed suit, arguing that the legislation violated the Fifth and Fourteenth Amendment to the Constitution by depriving them of their property and, therefore, violating the due-process clause.

The case of *Munn v. Illinois* was argued before the U.S. Supreme Court on January 14–18, 1877, and was decided by a 7–2 vote on March 1, 1877. The justices upheld the Illinois law and declared that such legislation was clearly within the jurisdiction of the state's police powers. The majority opinion argued that when property is devoted to a "use in which the public has an interest . . . [it] in effect grants to the public an interest in that use, and must submit to be controlled by the public for the common good, to the extent of the interest [it] has created." *Munn v. Illinois* was a landmark decision in the legal history of the Industrial Revolution because it established a foundation for the creation of the regulatory state.

N

National Association of Manufacturers

The Industrial Revolution led to larger and larger business enterprises and also produced a political economy in which different interest groups—workers, middle-class professionals, farmers, and small businessmen—tried to use government to promote their own interests. Big business needed to organize as well, and one of the consequences was the National Association of Manufacturers (NAM). Founded in Cincinnati, Ohio, in 1895, the NAM had as its mission the promotion of business values and the meeting of business needs. Within a decade, however, the NAM had become the primary business trade group of major industrial enterprises, and it spent much of its time and resources fighting any increases in government authority, especially that of the federal government. The NAM targeted labor unions as its main enemy and fought against strikes, boycotts, demonstrations, and prolabor legislation. As far as the NAM was concerned, labor unions violated private property rights. But the NAM was not interested simply in **laissez-faire**, since it campaigned for tariff protection of American industry and various subsidies and tax breaks for big business. By 1922, the NAM had a total of 5,350 dues-paying members, making it one of the most powerful trade associations in the country. The NAM was also wired into politics, lobbying effectively at the federal and state levels to promote business needs and to protect business from other interest groups.

National Banking Act of 1864

One key to the development of a modern industrial economy was a stable currency and a reliable banking system, and these were provided for in the National Banking Act of 1864. In 1791 Secretary of the Treasury Alexander Hamilton proposed and Congress created the **Bank of the United States**. The bank was essentially an agency of the federal government with a mission to provide capital to industrial enterprises and to give the country a stable currency. Creation of the bank fractured the country politically.

Such Americans as Thomas Jefferson and James Madison, who would soon become known as Democratic-Republicans, argued that since the U.S. Constitution had never provided for a national bank, the institution was unconstitutional. Southerners objected to the bank because their own economy was so overwhelmingly agricultural; while never benefitting from any of its loans, they would nevertheless be taxed to support the bank. At the same time, most Americans who were in debt opposed the bank because it would stem the tide of inflation. They would no longer be able to repay their debts in dollars worth less than those they had originally borrowed. On the other hand, such Americans as George Washington, John Adams, and Alexander Hamilton, who would soon become known as Federalists, backed the national bank because it would strengthen other banks and businesses.

For the next twenty years, debate over the merits of the national bank became central to political discourse in the United States. In 1811, when the bank's original twenty-year charter expired, President James Madison chose not to renew it, and the Bank of the United States ceased to exist. Less than a year later, Madison realized that he had made a mistake. The outbreak of the War of 1812 created financial demands that only a central bank could meet, and in 1816, at Madison's request, Congress founded the Second Bank of the United States.

Controversy over the bank, however, erupted again in 1819. An epidemic of land speculation in the western states inspired state banks to issue vast amounts of paper notes, none of them backed by hard currency. Inflation became endemic. To suppress the speculation, the Second Bank of the United States ordered that tax and land payments be made in specie, not paper money. The order led to the **panic of 1819**, which brought about widespread bankruptcy among banks, businesses, and small farms in the West. Poor farmers blamed the bank for their misery. Anxious to win votes among them, President Andrew Jackson in 1832 vetoed an attempt by Congress to recharter the Second Bank of the United States. He subsequently withdrew all federal money from the bank. The Second Bank of the United States closed its doors in 1836, when its twenty-year charter expired.

Once again a war, this time the **Civil War**, exposed the problems of a modern government without a central bank. In 1864, the Republican-dominated Congress passed the National Banking Act of 1864, which required all national banks to have at least one-third of their capital assets invested in U.S. government securities. They could then issue national bank notes (paper currency) up to 90 percent of the values of those securities. The bill also imposed a 10 percent tax on private bank notes, which essentially drove them out of circulation. Finally, after decades, the United States enjoyed a stable paper currency that made for a stable economic environment conducive to capital investment.

National Labor Union

As the development of **turnpikes**, **canals**, and **railroads** in the first half of the nineteenth century began creating a national economic market, many business enterprises began manufacturing and distributing goods all over the country. The size of the new industrial **corporations** also changed labor-management relations from the paternalistic models of the past to new competitive relationships based on economic class. Many workers became convinced that only labor unions—and the threat of strikes, work stoppages, demonstrations, and boycotts—could give employees the leverage they needed to negotiate with management, and because of the advent of a national market characterized by larger and larger organizations, only a national union could truly compete. Such national unions as the National Typographical Union (1852) and the Iron Molders International Union (1860) appeared, as did several dozen others in the 1860s.

In 1866, **William Sylvis**, the founder of the Iron Molders' International Union, established the National Labor Union (NLU), an umbrella group of dozens of other national labor unions. Sylvis's purpose in founding the NLU was to promote the idea of the eight-hour day. He also tinkered with the formation of workers' cooperatives, employees' associations designed to produce goods and compete with the large corporations. The workers' cooperatives were doomed, however, because they could never generate sufficient capital to install cost-cutting technologies. Eventually, the NLU evolved into a political party, the National Labor Reform Party, and in the election of 1872, it nominated Judge David Davis of Illinois for president. At the last minute, Davis withdrew from the race, and the National Labor Reform Party collapsed. The NLU declined as well, and its demise was made certain when the economy entered the depression caused by the **panic of 1873**. Nevertheless, the NLU was the first episode in the development of viable national labor unions in the United States.

National Road. *See* Cumberland Road

New Freedom

During the early decades of the twentieth century, **Progressive** reformers debated the relative merits and demerits of **antitrust** action and federal regulation of big business. One group, led intellectually by **Herbert Croly** and **Theodore Roosevelt**, felt committed to regulating large enterprises rather than breaking them up, even if they did threaten **monopoly**, since economies of scale could keep prices down for consumers. Instead of dissolving such large enterprises, the federal government should develop techniques for regulating the companies and eliminating abuses, even if it meant setting prices accordingly. Another approach was simply breaking up any business enterprise that threatened to exercise control over an industry and to undermine market forces. The leading figures in such an approach were Louis Brandeis and **Woodrow Wilson**. Brandeis used the term *New Freedom* to describe his belief that monopolistic companies should be broken up by the federal government. Only then could society enjoy the advantages of a free market and real competition. The federal government's role in the political economy, according to New Freedom advocates, was to arbitrate conflicting interests, not to assume a partisan role and promote the needs of one interest group over another. During the first administration of President Woodrow Wilson (1913–1917), the New Freedom found institutional expression in the **Federal Trade Commission Act of 1914** and the **Clayton Antitrust Act of 1914**.

New Nationalism

The term *New Nationalism* emerged in the United States during the late **Progressive** Era as part of a larger debate over the proper role of the federal government in the private economy. At the time, large numbers of Americans were afraid that the rise of such large **corporations** as **Standard Oil Company** of New Jersey or **United States Steel Corporation** had created a monopolistic or oligopolistic economy in which the free market had been subverted. The laws of competition and supply and demand that market economics had long postulated were being undermined by corporations large enough to control entire industries. The federal government, some reformers argued, had a responsibility to address the economic problems created by such large business enterprises.

Progressives debated, however, just what form that intervention should take. Those who believed in the so-called **New Freedom** wanted the government to unilaterally break up all companies that threatened **monopoly**. The "New Nationalism" of such people as **Herbert Croly** and former President **Theodore Roosevelt** held that large corporations were not inherently evil by virtue of their size but only by their behavior. Those guilty of abuse, exploitation, and artificial manipulation of prices needed to be regulated by the federal government so that the worst abuses could be eliminated. But breaking up all large corporations, Croly and Roosevelt argued, would deprive the country of the economies of scale that only large enterprises could bring to the research, production, and distribution process. Roosevelt called his ideas to regulate large corporations rather than dissolve them the "New Nationalism" and promoted his point of view in the presidential **election of 1912**, when he ran as a third-party candidate. He lost the election, but many of his ideas about the role of the federal government in public policy have endured. Such agencies as the **Interstate Commerce Commission**, the Federal Trade Commission, the Federal Aviation Agency, the Federal Reserve System, and the Federal Communications Commission all testify to the enduring vision of the New Nationalism, that the federal government has a responsibility to see that business enterprises do not abuse their power.

New South

The term *New South* was coined in 1870 by Edwin de Leon, a South Carolina businessman who wanted to bring the Industrial Revolution to the South. He wanted the "Old South" of plantation agriculture, forced labor, and racial confrontation to give way to a "New South" of technological development, industrialization, and **railroad** construction. A leading advocate of the New South was Henry W. Grady, editor of the *Atlanta Constitution*, who knew that modernization of the Southern economy would require huge amounts of Northern capital, and that attracting Northern investors would require promotion of three key ideas: industrialization, agricultural diversification, and racial accommodation. Grady did so by celebrating the romanticized virtues of the Old South and by enlisting the support of black leader Booker T. Washington, whose message of education and segregation reassured both northerners and southerners.

During the late 1800s, the vision of the New South enjoyed some initial success, although full realization of the dream would have to wait until the late twentieth century. After the **Civil War**, a boom in railroad construction occurred in the South, and **textile** mills were built there to take advantage of cheap labor costs, especially the availability of **child labor**. **James Duke** brought the cigarette industry to North Carolina, taking advantage of the state's abundant tobacco crop. Finally, a burgeoning **steel** industry developed in and around Birmingham, Alabama.

New York Central Railroad

More than any other technology, the development of **railroads** created an economic environment in which the Industrial Revolution could flourish. During the 1830s and 1840s, dozens of railroads were constructed in the northeastern United States, and in 1853, twelve of them were consolidated into the New York Central Railroad. During the **Civil War**, the New York Central came under the financial control of **Cornelius Vanderbilt**, who renamed it the New York Central & Hudson River Railroad. Ambitious and anxious to control a good portion of American railroad traffic, Vanderbilt added the Erie & North East Railroad and the Buffalo & Erie Railroad to the New York Central system. Vanderbilt continued his acquisitions and expansions, and by the early 1900s, the New York Central operated in New York, Massachusetts, Pennsylvania, Ohio, Michigan, Indiana, and Illinois. It was widely considered to be the most powerful and politically influential railroad in the country.

 # Northern Pacific Railway

More than any other transportation development in U.S. history, construction of the **transcontinental railroads** helped create a truly national market in the United States and opened up the Pacific Coast and Intermountain West to economic development. The Northern Pacific Railway was one of these transcontinental lines. In 1864, Congress chartered the Northern Pacific Railroad, a transcontinental railroad from Lake Superior, Michigan, to Puget Sound, Washington. Construction did not begin until 1870, and the project was completed in 1883. The **depression of 1893** sent the Northern Pacific into bankruptcy, and in 1896, financier **J. P. Morgan** intervened and reorganized the line as the Northern Pacific Railway. In 1901, railroad

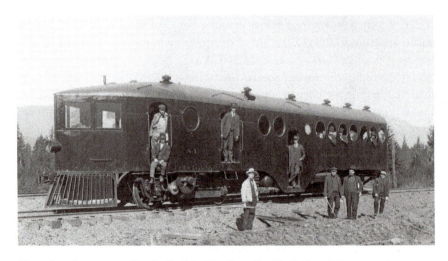

The railroad motor car "Roslyn" of the Northern Pacific Railroad Company in Alberta, Canada. (Library of Congress)

magnate **James J. Hill** took control of the Northern Pacific Railway and made it part of the Northern Securities Company, a **monopoly** on railroad traffic in the Pacific Northwest. In 1904, when the Supreme Court acted positively on an **antitrust** suit against the Northern Securities Company, the Northern Pacific Railway was separated out again and run independently. Until the Great Depression, it was one of the most profitable railroads in the United States.

O

Ocala Platform

During the 1880s, as overproduction led to falling commodity prices for farmers in the South and the West, a political movement emerged to address these problems through government intervention. The problem was that American farmers produced too much, but that problem would not be seriously addressed until the years of the Great Depression in the 1930s. The Southern Farmers' Alliance, an interest group dedicated to dealing with the plight of American farmers, met in Ocala, Florida, in 1890 to discuss the possibility of forming a political party to contest Democrats and Republicans in the elections of 1892. As part of these discussions, they produced the so-called Ocala Platform, which called for government ownership of the **railroads**, a graduated federal income tax with the heaviest burdens falling on the rich, federal loans to farmers at a 2 percent interest rate, lower tariffs on imported manufactured goods, and expansion of the money supply to $50 in circulation for each American. Most of the delegates at the Ocala convention believed in free coinage of silver as the best way to expand the money supply. Their logic in expanding the money supply was their conviction that it would produce an inflation that would raise commodity prices as well as their incomes. For unknown reasons, it never dawned on them that inflation would also raise their costs and wipe out whatever gains they secured from rising commodity prices. When the **Populist** Party was formed soon after, it adopted the Ocala Platform as its main focus.

Ohio and Erie Canal

During the boom in **canal** construction during the 1820s and 1830s, state and local governments and private investors cooperated to construct canals as a means of improving the nation's transportation system. One of the most important projects was the Ohio and Erie Canal. Construction began on the canal in 1825 and was not completed until 1833. The Ohio and Erie Canal stretched 308 miles from Portsmouth on the Ohio River north to the city of Cleveland on Lake Erie. Once it was in operation, the Ohio and Erie Canal permitted efficient, bulk shipment of goods from New York City up the Hudson River and through the Erie Canal to Lake Erie, across Lake Erie to Cleveland, down the Ohio and Erie Canal to Portsmouth on the Ohio River, and then down the Ohio River to the Mississippi River and down the Mississippi to New Orleans. As a result of the canal's construction, Ohio farmers were able to ship their crops either to Atlantic coast cities or to the Gulf Coast.

Oil. *See* Petroleum

Oil Well

Although **coal** fueled the first stage of the Industrial Revolution, **petroleum** became increasingly important in the late nineteenth and early twentieth centuries. In 1857, Edwin L. Drake, a former railway conductor living in Titusville, Pennsylvania, decided that oil could be obtained by drilling for it much as people drilled for salt water. Oil could be used for lighting lamps and as a lubricant for industrial machinery. Until Drake began his work, oil was simply gathered from places where it oozed from the ground. He bought up some farm land where oil pooled in puddles on the surface, constructed a drill derrick, and attached a **steam engine** to power a drill bit. On August 27, 1859, his drill bit reached just over seventy feet in depth, and oil slowly began flowing up the shaft. Drake then attached a hand pump and began pulling up oil. An oil boom hit Titusville, and the modern era of petroleum production began.

Otis, Elisha Graves

One element in stimulating the Industrial Revolution was demand for structural **steel**, and the inventive work of Elisha Otis provided a new market for the product. Otis was born in Halifax, Vermont, on August 3, 1811. After finishing school, he went to work in the construction business and eventually began manufacturing carriages and wagons. In his machine shop, he also tinkered and invented. His first successful invention was a turbine waterwheel. Late in the 1840s, Otis moved to Yonkers, New York, where he became supervisor of construction for a **factory** that would manufacture bedsteads. While he was building the factory, he developed several automatic safety devices for the elevator that prevented its fall in the event of a chain or rope snapping. These inventions provided Otis with the opportunity that eventually changed his life and career.

Otis went into the business of manufacturing freight elevators, and in 1854, his elevators were displayed in New York City at the Crystal Palace Exposition. The ability to safely move passengers and freight up and down multistory buildings transformed construction in New York City. Otis built his first passenger elevator in 1857 and installed it in the Haughwout Department Store in New York City. He constructed another one in 1859 for the Fifth Avenue Hotel. His elevator safety devices made it possible to construct ever-taller buildings, which brought about a real-estate boom in Manhattan. Many people consider Otis the individual who made skyscrapers possible. Because it was impossible, however, to build tall, structurally stable buildings out of wood, demand for structural steel boomed as well, and steel manufacturers like **Andrew Carnegie** had a new market for their products.

In addition to elevator safety devices, Otis invented **railroad**-car trucks and brakes (1852), a steam plow (1857), a rotary oven for bread (1858), an automatic wood-turning machine (1859), and a steam elevator (1861). He died in Yonkers, New York, on April 9, 1861.

P

Panic of 1819

The panic of 1819 was a severe, if relatively brief, downturn in the U.S. economy. The dislocation was precipitated by land speculation in western states and the decision of the Second Bank of the United States to end it. Between 1815 and 1819, the American economy had boomed, but it had also stimulated a period of frantic land speculation and the establishment of hundreds of banks, many of which were undercapitalized and unregulated. Many were known as "wildcat banks" because they were located in places where only wildcats lived. Bankers recklessly issued paper banknotes, redeemable only at those single institutions, and the money supply was soon flooded with hundreds of different types of currency. It became all but impossible to determine the value of most of these currencies. On the eve of the panic, a total of 419 banks existed in the United States, each printing its own money without control or any semblance of centralized regulation.

President James Monroe and other members of his cabinet became increasingly alarmed about the proliferation of banks and the issuance of increasing volumes of banknotes, and in 1819, the Second Bank of the United States began calling in all of its loans and insisting that they be paid in gold and silver. The bank also insisted that the state banks redeem their bank notes in gold and silver. The directors of the Second Bank of the United States knew that the wildcat banks had printed bank notes far in excess of their gold and silver reserves and hoped that the new regulations would stem the tide of speculation and make bankers throughout America more cautious and prudent.

But the Monroe administration did not anticipate the economic panic that ensued. Unable to redeem their notes in hard currency, hundreds of banks failed, and with them went thousands of businesses and tens of thousands of small farms. In the years since 1815, hundreds of thousands of farmers in the South and the West had gone deeply into debt to finance land purchases and production increases, and they found themselves bankrupt and without their land. The panic of 1819 stimulated viscerally negative feelings about the Second Bank of the United States, and politicians in the Democratic Party went after the institution. The economy slowly recovered in the early 1820s. Eventually, President Andrew Jackson oversaw the bank's demise in the 1830s.

Panic of 1837

Like its counterpart in 1819, the panic of 1837 emerged out of a period of reckless land speculation and financial irresponsibility in the western states. The economy was booming in the early 1830s, with foreign trade at unprecedented levels and the federal government able to pay all of its bills out of customs duties and income from the sale of public-domain lands. Unfortunately, when President Andrew Jackson decided in 1833 to withdraw federal money from the Second Bank of the United States and deposit those funds in so-called pet state banks, he prompted a speculative boom in which the recipient banks issued huge volumes of paper currency and expanded loans on easy terms, and states chartered hundreds of new, undercapitalized banks. The U.S. Treasury was soon flooded with banknotes because farmers in the western states were purchasing land with them. In 1836, the federal government distributed another $36 million to the state banks, and the speculative mania assumed even greater proportions. When the Second Bank of the United States closed its doors in 1836, the economy lost the only existing check on the speculation. The total volume of banknotes in circulation expanded from $48 million in 1829 to more than $150 million in 1837.

President Jackson decided to rein in the speculation by issuing his Specie Circular in 1836, in which he required that all future purchases of public-domain lands be paid for in gold or silver bullion or with paper currency backed by bullion. The Specie Circular was issued just when an economic downturn in Great Britain dried up the flow of investment capital into the United States. The economy went into a sharp tailspin, with bank insolvencies proliferating, business failures rising, cotton prices falling precipitously, and unemployment hitting unprecedented levels. The economy remained in its stall for four years, finally emerging from its doldrums in 1841.

Panic of 1857

During the early nineteenth century, the American economy fluctuated through the ups and downs of common business cycles. The so-called

panic of 1819 and the **panic of 1837** had been rooted in land speculation and faulty federal government economic policies, but the panic of 1857 was the first downturn that economists attribute to the effects of the Industrial Revolution. During the late 1840s and early 1850s, **railroad** construction boomed in the United States and soon outpaced demand for freight traffic. Since the railroads had gone heavily into debt to generate funding for capital-intensive track and bridge construction, large numbers of banks had their fortunes tied to the railroad economy.

Just how precarious their situation was became abundantly clear on August 24, 1857, when the New York City branch of the Ohio Life Insurance Company declared bankruptcy and closed its doors, prompting a financial panic throughout the Northeast. Hundreds of banks failed, and most other financial institutions suspended specie (gold and silver) payments. Unemployment skyrocketed, and in a society with millions of urban residents, poverty and suffering increased.

The panic of 1857 also had widespread political consequences. At the time, a ferocious sectional debate over the merits of slavery was raging between the North and the South, with northerners proclaiming the superiority of free labor and southerners hailing the advantages of slavery and a plantation economy. The panic of 1857 supplied southerners with ammunition. The plantation economy possessed little industry, few banks, and relatively few railroads, and the panic of 1857 all but passed the South by. Southern apologists gloated over the North's plight, and southerners grew even more convinced of the superiority of a slave-based economy and the Southern lifestyle. A boom in railroad construction in the late 1850s ended the effects of the panic.

Panic of 1873

Economic historians still debate whether the economic downturn of 1873 was a panic or a depression. Traditionally, the term *panic* is used to describe an economic dislocation that was primarily financial in its scope, such as the **panic of 1819**, the **panic of 1837**, and the **panic of 1857**, while the term *depression* is used to describe an economic event that produced widespread unemployment and economic suffering among the middle classes and the working poor. The depression of 1893 and the Great Depression of the 1930s fall into that category.

Actually, the economic dislocation of 1873 was both panic and depression and signified the transition of the American economy to a new industrial base. After the Civil War, a binge of railroad construction caused the economy to boom, with more than 30,000 miles being built.

The railroads went heavily into debt to finance the construction, but they overextended themselves, taking on too many obligations and building excess capacity. Cutthroat railroad competition led to falling freight rates, and many roads could not repay their debts. In September 1873, the firm of Jay Cooke & Company, which had financed the construction of the Northern Pacific Railway, declared bankruptcy. A financial panic swept through the Northeast, and bankruptcies of banks and brokerage firms skyrocketed. Stock prices collapsed. In this regard, the downturn resembled a traditional financial panic.

But because increasing numbers of Americans were living in cities and working in small and large business concerns, the decline also assumed the dimensions of an economic depression. The economy fell into a deflationary spiral, with prices falling rapidly and discouraging business investment. Thousands of firms declared bankruptcy and laid off hundreds of thousands of workers. With unemployment rates rising and consumer spending falling, the downturn only grew worse. The panic of 1873 launched an era of economic instability in the United States that persisted for more than twenty years.

Panic of 1907

In 1907, the money markets in the United States experienced a severe, if brief, period of instability. Financial panics had occurred in the past—1819, 1837, 1857, 1873, and 1893—but the panic of 1907 proved to be particularly significant in American financial history. The panic began in March when prices on the New York Stock Exchange entered a precipitous decline, which prompted a run on banks by panic-stricken depositors. Hundreds of banks failed, as did thousands of businesses, and the panic exposed a critical weakness in the nation's financial system—the inability of bankers to secure liquid reserves during periods of economic emergency. In 1908, Congress responded with the Aldrich-Vreeland Act, which authorized national banks to issue notes backed by state, county, and municipal bonds. Banks could issue such notes for six years, and the notes could circulate freely as currency in the money markets. The legislation provided a measure of elasticity to the money supply, allowing banks to locate additional financial reserves during economic downturns. In addition, the legislation established a National Monetary Commission, headed by Senator Nelson Aldrich, to analyze problems with the national currency system and to suggest remedies. The National Monetary Commission reported its findings in 1912, and in 1913 Congress acted on them and established the Federal Reserve System.

Patent. *See* Intellectual Property Rights

Pennsylvania Railroad

The Pennsylvania Railroad (PR) was perhaps the nation's most important transportation system during the decades of the Industrial Revolution. First chartered by the state legislature in 1846, the PR by 1854 connected Philadelphia with Pittsburgh. Subsequent additions to the line extended the PR's reach from Harrisburg north to Erie, Pennsylvania, and Buffalo, New York; south to Baltimore, Maryland; and northeast to Jersey City, New Jersey, and to New York City. Through purchase and leasing arrangements, the PR expanded even further, and by 1900, it consisted of 265,000 employees working on more than 10,000 miles of track stretching through thirteen states. Until World War II, it enjoyed a reputation as one of the country's most financially stable lines. The PR was also the key railroad through industrial America. It was connected to the coal mines of Pennsylvania, West Virginia, and Ohio; the steel mills of Ohio and western Pennsylvania; and the Great Lakes barge traffic. The iron ore and coal pouring into Andrew Carnegie's steel mills, as well as the finished steel coming out, traveled via the PR.

Petroleum

If coal fueled the first stages of the Industrial Revolution, petroleum products derived from oil became the primary energy source of subsequent stages. The Industrial Revolution's emphasis on factory-based mass production triggered a huge demand for machine tools, and machine tools needed lubricants to reduce friction and overheating. In 1859, the commercial production of oil began in the United States when Edwin L. Drake drilled the world's first successful oil well in Titusville, Pennsylvania. That year, U.S. oil production totaled just over 2,000 barrels, with one barrel consisting of forty-two gallons. Within a year, the Pennsylvania fields were producing 500,000 barrels a year. Eventually, prominent oil fields in the United States were classified as follows: the Eastern field, largely consisting of the Pennsylvania deposits; the Mid-Continent field, primarily Oklahoma, Arkansas, Kansas, northern Louisiana, and northern Texas; the California field; the

Rocky Mountain field, primarily Wyoming but also including Montana and Colorado; and the Gulf Coast field—southern Louisiana and southern Texas.

The discovery of new fields coincided with the development of new uses for petroleum. By the 1880s, machine-tool lubricants no longer consumed most oil. Refineries developed kerosene, which became widely used in lamps to illuminate homes and businesses, and oil products to heat indoor spaces. With the development of the internal-combustion engine in the 1890s, demand for gasoline, a petroleum distillate, increased rapidly, and when Henry Ford began mass-producing automobiles, demand jumped geometrically. Oil production in the United States skyrocketed from 500,000 barrels a year in 1860 to 5.261 million in 1870; 26.286 million in 1880; 45.824 million in 1890; 63.621 million in 1900; 209.557 million in 1910; 442.929 million in 1920; and 1.07 billion in 1930.

Pollock v. Farmer's Loan and Trust Company. See Sixteenth Amendment

Pool

A pool was a business arrangement of the late nineteenth and early twentieth centuries in which businessmen tried to skirt the Sherman Antitrust Act. Growing concern about the rise of corporate monopolies had inspired the legislation, but businessmen could technically avoid the Sherman Act's reach by establishing informal agreements between chief executive officers of competing companies to set prices, allocate markets, or limit production. Pools were used particularly in the railroad industry of the 1890s and early 1900s because the industry had become badly overbuilt, with significant excess capacity. Such an environment created zealous, cutthroat competition that drove down prices. By forming pools, railroad executives could keep freight rates up. Congress attacked pooling arrangements, in one way or another, in the following legislation: the Interstate Commerce Act of 1887, the Sherman Antitrust Act of 1890, the Federal Trade Commission Act of 1914, and the Clayton Antitrust Act of 1914.

Populists

The Populists were a third-party political movement that appeared during the farm crisis of the 1880s and 1890s. During the 1890s, the Populists staged the first major assault on the notion that laissez-faire should dominate public policy in an industrial economy. The Populists ultimately failed because they could not broaden their base of support to include industrial workers, but their vision of an activist federal government regularly intervening in the private economy in order to eliminate gross corporate abuses and to maintain a competitive environment eventually prevailed.

Most American farmers, particularly in the West and the South, were in desperate circumstances in the 1880s. The westward movement had brought tens of millions of new acres into production, while new technologies had greatly increased yields per acre. Gross overproduction soon flooded the markets with every variety of food and fiber, and commodity prices fell steadily. At the same time, railroad freight rates and bank interest rates climbed, squeezing farmers in the trap of rising costs and declining incomes. What they could not solve economically, they tried to do politically.

Farmers developed a political consciousness at meetings of the Grange, a farmer organization founded in 1867 to deal with the isolation of farm life by providing social activities—dances, picnics, lectures, and fairs—for farm families. But at the Grange meetings, talk inevitably drifted to economics and politics and how to solve the farm dilemma. The Grange movement soon turned political, and some state legislatures passed so-called Granger laws regulating railroads and the rates of grain-storage elevators. Railroad and grain-elevator owners sued, and at first the Supreme Court was sympathetic with farmers. In the 1877 case of *Munn v. Illinois*, the Supreme Court upheld the Illinois Warehouse Act of 1871, which regulated the rates grain elevators charged customers. But the Court eventually changed its mind and in the 1886 case of *Wabash, St. Louis & Pacific Railroad Co. v. Illinois* declared unconstitutional a state law regulating railroad rates.

The demise of state laws regulating railroads forced farmer activists to look toward the federal government for assistance, since the Supreme Court had declared Congress exclusively sovereign over interstate commerce. They also organized politically in formal ways. The farmers' alliance movement began in Texas in 1877 and spread throughout the South, becoming known as the Southern Farmers' Alliance, boasting a membership of 1.5 million people by 1890. African American farmers formed the Colored Farmers' Alliance as an auxiliary organization. In 1882, the Northern Farmers' Alliance was established in Chicago, Illinois. The farmers' alliances met in Ocala, Florida, in 1890 and proclaimed the Ocala Platform, which became the political platform of the Populist Party.

The Populist Party was founded in 1891 in Cincinnati, Ohio. It offered a dramatic alternative to the Democratic and Republican parties. The

Populists called for free and unlimited coinage of silver in order to inflate prices; a graduated income tax to force the wealthy to carry a fair share of the burden of the government; federal government ownership of the telephone, telegraph, and railroad industries in order to guarantee fair prices for workers and farmers; establishment of a federal civil service to eliminate political corruption; and creation of a subtreasury plan, which envisioned a series of government-owned warehouses and grain elevators where farmers could store their crops until ideal market conditions would get them top dollar.

In the election of 1892, the Populist Party nominated James Weaver for president, and Weaver managed to secure 1,041,028 popular votes and 22 electoral votes. The Populists then gained momentum because of the depression of 1893, which threw millions of people out of work. The congressional elections of 1894 proved to be the high-water mark of the Populists. They elected six U.S. senators and seven members of the House of Representatives.

The Populists hoped that the presidential election of 1896 would give them control of the White House. The Republicans nominated William McKinley for president, and the Democrats nominated William Jennings Bryan. But when the Democrats endorsed free coinage of silver in their platform, the Populists decided to endorse Bryan as well. In the election, however, McKinley won 7.036 million votes to Bryan's 6.468 million. The Populists had been unable to broaden their support sufficiently beyond the farm belt. Their hope that free coinage of silver would inflate commodity prices sent shivers of fear through eastern workers, who spent most of their meager incomes on food. Also, their Republican-leaning employers convinced them that free coinage of silver would undermine the gold standard, ruin the economy, and throw them out of work. The Populist Party ran a slate of candidates in 1900 and 1904 and then disintegrated.

Powderly, Terence Vincent. *See* Knights of Labor

Precision Lathe

The invention of the precision lathe was a key step in developing modern industrial machinery and in achieving standardization of parts. Before the appearance of the precision lathe, machine parts had to be hand-tooled, and tolerances were never consistent. The lathe is a simple tool that turns components steadily while other tools work on them. Foot-operated wooden lathes have been used since the Middle Ages. In the late eighteenth century, John Harrison in England began using a small precision lathe to manufacture parts for his chronometers, but it was not until 1810 that Henry Maudslay launched the modern era of the precision lathe when he began mass-producing nuts and bolts on his precision screw-cutting lathe. The nuts and bolts came out with perfectly consistent threading. Maudslay managed to turn metal components on the lathe at high speeds and to reduce heat and friction with the use of water and oil lubricants.

The precision lathe was extraordinarily important, an essential element to mass production. As long as parts were hand-tooled, they did not have the consistency necessary to be employed in the mass assembly of finished products or to serve as replacement parts in broken-down machines or products. Precision lathing allowed for the mass production of the internal components of machinery. Today, precision lathes are still used in the manufacture of all metal products.

Printing Press

Until the early nineteenth century, printing technology had not progressed much beyond Johannes Gutenberg's fifteenth-century innovations because printers still had to remove by hand a platen from the type. Even the best presses could not exceed 250 sheets an hour. Friedrich Koenig, a German living in London, invented the first cylinder press in 1810. The cylinder press eliminated the need to manually lift the platen from the type by employing a heavy rotating cylinder that applied pressure to type fixed on a flat bed. Koenig's design increased productivity to 1,100 sheets per hour. In 1846, Richard Hoe of the United States designed the rotary press, in which paper passed between two curved surfaces. One large cylinder contained the embedded type, while several smaller cylinders brought the large cylinder and sheets of paper into contact with one another. Hoe's invention paved the way for modern mass-production newspaper printing. In 1865, William Bullock invented the first rotary web press, in which a continuous roll of paper, which was known as the web, was fed into two type-embedded cylinders, allowing for simultaneous printing on both sides of the paper. The work of Hoe and Bullock became the foundation of the modern printing industry.

Progressive Movement

The Progressive movement of the late nineteenth and early twentieth centuries altered forever the political economy and the nature of public policy in the United States. It was a broad-based movement that transcended both political parties and possessed social, political, and economic agendas, but at its heart was a desire to address some of the Industrial Revolution's more controversial effects on American life. The Industrial Revolution had produced permanent changes in the economy. The world of small, local business enterprises had given way to massive corporations operating in national and international markets. In some cases, like those of the Standard Oil Company of New Jersey and the United States Steel Corporation, business enterprises became large enough to threaten the establishment of monopolistic control, which subverted the workings of the market. Also, relationships between employers and employees had changed permanently. In the preindustrial economy, when businesses had been small and local, employers had often exercised a paternalistic relationship with employees. Workers who had complaints or who needed a pay raise had immediate access to decision makers. But the advent of large corporations created new levels of management between workers and owners, bureaucratizing relationships and leaving employees with a sense of loss of power. In addition, small businesses had functioned in community environments where local leaders held them accountable for their actions, but in the world of the Industrial Revolution, with large corporations operating in communities throughout the country and boards of directors in distant places making all major decisions, businessmen became more powerful and less accountable to local communities. Finally, the Industrial Revolution appeared to have created a new class of urban poor who suffered with barely subsistence-level wages and lived miserable lives of poverty and illness.

For all of these reasons, diverse interests in the United States began contemplating the use of state and federal governments to address the problems created by the Industrial Revolution. In the heartland, farmers complained that they were being squeezed between falling incomes and rising prices, and they held railroads and banks responsible for much of their plight. Many railroads, argued farmers, functioned in monopolistic environments, and freight rates had risen so much that farmers often found themselves facing rates and prices that did not even allow them to recover the costs of production. Small businessmen argued that large corporations were squeezing them out of the marketplace and creating monopolies. Because of their economies of scale, large enterprises could buy wholesale supplies at prices well below those available to smaller businesses, rendering small businessmen unable to compete. Workers, now represented by labor unions, claimed that the new big businesses were no longer accountable to anyone, that they had become the most powerful force in the economy, and that only government possessed the resources to deal with them. Finally, a new generation of social workers insisted that something needed to be done to improve the lives of America's most vulnerable citizens—poor, working women and their children.

At the same time that farmers, small businessmen, and workers were looking critically at the new industrial economy, a generation of intellectuals had developed new ideas about the functioning of the political economy. Ever Adam Smith's *The Wealth of Nations* (1776), the prevailing intellectual consensus had held that the economy operated according to the immutable economic laws of competition and supply and demand, which guaranteed low prices and high-quality goods and services. Because of the reality of competition, there was no need for government intervention. The economy was governed by the "invisible hand" of market forces, Smith argued, and laissez-faire, or "hands off," was the proper ideology for government. Such economic wisdom had been used throughout the nineteenth century to mute calls for government regulation of the economy.

But new voices were now being heard. Such economists as Henry George, Edward Bellamy, Thorstein Veblen, and Herbert Croly argued in the late 1800s and early 1900s that the economy did not operate according to natural law but was actually a complicated social and cultural mechanism subject to human manipulation. If big businessmen were able to exercise enough power to subvert the market, then government could counter their efforts. What one set of human beings could do, they argued, others could undo. The world could be made a better place.

To preserve competition in an economy where the advent of very large corporations threatened monopoly, the federal government became involved in the antitrust movement. Beginning with the Sherman Antitrust Act of 1890 and continuing with the Federal Trade Commission Act of 1914 and the Clayton Antitrust Act of 1914, the Justice Department was authorized to file federal lawsuits against companies guilty of restraining trade. In many cases, support for antitrust action came from small and medium-sized businessmen who feared being squeezed out of the market by their larger rivals. The "New Freedom" of Louis Brandeis and President Woodrow Wilson envisioned a completely competitive business environment in which the federal government policed corporations to prevent restraint of trade.

Other Progressive reformers were not as obsessed with breaking up monopolies as they were with regulating businesses to prevent abuses. In the **New Nationalism** of Herbert Croly and former president Theodore Roosevelt, large enterprises were not inherently bad because of their size. After all, large companies, benefiting from economies of scale, could actually sell goods at lower prices, sustain better research and development efforts, and provide consumers with high-quality manufactured goods. Support for federal regulation came from a variety of sources. In 1887, Congress created the Interstate Commerce Commission to regulate the railroads; the legislation pleased farmers and merchants, who had been complaining about high freight rates, but even some overbuilt railroads backed the measure, hoping that federal regulation of rates would bring an end to the cutthroat competition that had come to characterize the industry. Subsequent federal legislation to regulate railroads, such as the Hepburn Act of 1906 or the Mann-Elkins Act of 1910, generated similar support from diverse sources.

Other influential Progressive reforms in the economy emerged from diverse interests as well. In 1906, Congress passed the **Meat Inspection Act** to regulate the meat-processing industry. The legislation provided for higher federal standards for meat processing and federal inspection of those processes to make sure that consumers were able to purchase high-quality, safe products. The legislation was jump-started by the publication of Upton Sinclair's best-selling novel *The Jungle* (1906), which, although it was a piece of fiction about the plight of immigrant families, portrayed the meat-packing industry's scandalous record in matters of health and sanitation. But in addition to consumers, the country's largest meat packers supported the legislation as well, hoping that the large capital investments required to bring factories up to the federal standards would price smaller concerns out of business. The Pure Food and Drug Act of 1906 had support not only from consumers but also from large, reputable food processors and pharmaceutical companies anxious to make life more difficult for some of their smaller rivals.

Finally, the most important financial reform of the Progressive Era, the Federal Reserve Act of 1913, enjoyed the support of major banking houses that wanted to avoid the financial panics of the past by imposing some government regulation on the money markets. Only with the assistance of the federal government could some elasticity be built into the monetary system and prevent, or at least lessen the impact of, previous financial dislocations. The Federal Reserve Act provided the federal government a small measure of influence over interest rates and the money supply, which reformers hoped would eliminate such financial debacles as the panic of 1819, the panic of 1837, the panic of 1857, the panic of 1873, the depression of 1893, and the panic of 1907.

The Progressive movement had a profound impact on public policy in the United States. No longer would large business enterprises be able to function without worrying about public attitudes and the possibility of government intervention. Although the Progressive movement petered out during and after World War I, its impact had been made permanent. The federal government was now very active in antitrust activities and regulation of railroads, money markets, food processing, and pharmaceuticals.

Pujo Committee

The so-called Pujo Committee was a landmark legal and political event in the history of the Industrial Revolution because it brought much attention to the structure of the credit markets. In the 1880s, various reformers began expressing concern about the development of monopolies in America's major industries and complained about the rise of the "Meat Trust," the "Whiskey Trust," the "Tobacco Trust," the "Steel Trust," and the "Oil Trust." Such laws as the Interstate Commerce Act of 1887 and the Sherman Antitrust Act of 1890 were targeted at these trusts, but their impact seemed limited. Also, when the panic of 1907 did great damage to the credit and stock markets, many reformers became convinced that there was a "Money Trust" at work in the United States.

In 1912, to address those concerns, the House Committee on Banking and Currency opened a formal investigation of the banking industry. It became known as the "Pujo Committee" because Arsène Pujo, Democratic congressman from Louisiana, headed up the investigation. Pujo subpoenaed the nation's leading bankers, and their testimony became fodder for muckraking journalists. The Pujo Committee made it clear that the financial industry had become dangerously concentrated because of a decade of mergers, leveraged buyouts, and widespread employment of interlocking directorates. The Pujo Committee was a key event leading to the creation of the Federal Reserve Act of 1913.

Members of the Pujo Committee in 1912. (Library of Congress)

Pullman, George Mortimer

George Mortimer Pullman, a railroad innovator and industrialist whose policies became synonymous in American history with the exploitation of workers, was born in Brocton, New York, on March 3, 1831. He quit school in 1845 and apprenticed out as a cabinetmaker, learning the trade and becoming regionally known for his skills. In 1855, Pullman moved to Chicago and opened his own construction business. He began specializing in remodeling railroad sleeping cars to make long-distance travel less arduous. Business was so slow at first that in 1859 he moved to Colorado and opened several general stores in mining towns, but the boom-and-bust economy there did not suit him. Pullman returned to Chicago in 1863. In 1864, he tried his hand again at railroad sleeping cars, building a car he named *Pioneer*. With a folding upper berth and extendable seat cushions in the lower berth, the car proved popular with passengers, and because of the Civil War, railroad travel was booming. In 1867, Pullman founded the Pullman Palace Car Company to manufacture his cars. He soon developed a dining car and a vestibule car, and over time, his luxury coaches became more and more elaborate, making Pullman a multimillionaire.

In 1881, Pullman established the town of Pullman, Illinois, where he built his factory and required employees to live. Workers were forced to live in apartments and shop in stores owned by Pullman, and they were paid below-subsistence wages in Pullman scrip, not in real money. Worker resentment steadily increased, and when Pullman cut wages during the depression of 1893, without cutting rent and prices in company housing and company stores, labor-management relations broke down completely. In 1894, Eugene V. Debs, head of the American Railway Union, launched a nationwide strike of Pullman cars. Workers refused to handle trains pulling Pullman cars, bringing railroad traffic and the U.S. mail to a halt. President Grover Cleveland sided with the company and used federal troops to crush the Pullman strike. In the process, Pullman's reputation was destroyed, and he died a broken man on October 19, 1897.

Pullman Strike

The so-called Pullman strike was one of the most notorious and influential labor-union strikes during the era of the Industrial Revolution. George Pullman's Pullman Company on the outskirts of Chicago manufactured railroad sleeping cars, especially those designed to satisfy the tastes and comforts of the rich and powerful. In contrast, Pullman workers labored for subsistence wages in a company town where they had to rent company-owned housing, buy food and clothing in company-owned stores, and receive their pay in Pullman Company scrip. Not only was their pay small, but they were gouged in their purchases of company-supplied products. When the country slipped into the depression of 1893, Pullman cut pay without cutting rent and company-store prices, rendering workers' lives even more miserable.

In unmistakable terms, desperate workers could see their standard of living falling even further, and they bitterly protested the wage cuts. Eugene V. Debs of the American Railway Union (ARU), seeing a perfect opportunity to promote the union and genuinely sympathizing with the Pullman workers, backed them and announced that union members would refuse to handle any railroad trains pulling Pullman cars. Debs's decision to boycott these trains brought railroad traffic throughout the Midwest to a halt, enraging railway executives and other merchants and businessmen dependent upon the railroads for shipping their raw materials and their finished products. Business executives appealed to the federal government for assistance in breaking the strike, and Attorney General Richard Olney, a former corporate attorney sympathetic with business concerns, sided with them. So did President Grover Cleveland. The Pullman Company was able to secure a federal court injunction outlawing the strike and prohibiting Debs and other executives of the ARU from invoking any labor actions that interfered with railroad business. The fact that the railroads were carrying the U.S. mail was used to justify the injunction. Debs refused to obey the injunction, and the strike continued until President Cleveland deployed 2,000 federal troops to Chicago to enforce the injunction. ARU workers resisted them, and a violent riot erupted that left twelve workers dead. The actions of the Cleveland administration had broken the strike.

The outcome of the strike also broke the back of the ARU. Debs was sent to prison for contempt of court and for conspiring to block the U.S. mail. The strike also convinced him that only a radical approach to the nation's labor-management relations could improve the lot of industrial workers. Debs decided that only a government seizure of the railroads and other major corporations could bring about economic justice, and he converted to socialism. Other labor leaders like Samuel Gompers of the American Federation of Labor became even more convinced that the time was not yet ripe in the United States for industrial unionism and that only the organization of skilled craft workers could succeed.

Pure Food and Drug Act of 1906

During the late nineteenth and early twentieth centuries, the rise of large, powerful business enterprises inspired demands from some Americans for government regulation of the economy. At its earliest stages, the demands for federal government intervention revolved around preservation of a competitive economic environment and protection of consumers. The desire to guarantee the survival of industrial competition led to such legislation as the Interstate Commerce Act of 1887, the Sherman Antitrust Act of 1890, the Federal Trade Commission Act of 1914, and the Clayton Antitrust Act of 1914. The need to protect consumers led to such early progressive laws as the Meat Inspection Act of 1906 and the Pure Food and Drug Act of 1906.

Increasingly large numbers of Americans, particularly those who lived in cities and had to depend on commercially processed products, had become concerned about the safety of foods and drugs marketed in the United States. Sickness and death from salmonella, botulism, and *E. coli* in processed meat and canned goods were common, as were reactions to and side effects of pharmaceutical products. Dr. Harvey Wiley, head of the Bureau of Chemistry in the Department of Agriculture, played a leading role in the movement for government regulation. Wiley had grown alarmed about the chemicals that food processors used for preserving meat and dairy products and about the standards used—cooking temperatures, storage temperatures, and packaging quality—in the production of canned goods.

At the same time, Wiley had become concerned about the extent to which pharmaceutical manufacturers exaggerated the health benefits of their products, since few Americans could tell the difference between fraudulent patent medicines and scientifically tested drugs. Most drug manufacturers employed scandalously inaccurate advertising techniques to market their products, making claims of effectiveness that had no basis in fact. A well-known scientist dedicated to the scientific method, Wiley resented the hype. At the same time, as the American medical establishment became more powerful and increasingly emphasized scientific accuracy in diagnosis, its own demands for reliable, scientifically tested pharmaceutical products escalated. Demands for government regulation also came from such groups as the National Consumer Federation, which felt that consumers were often victimized by unscrupulous manufacturers more interested in the financial bottom line than in customer safety. Finally, a number of largest meat and food processors began calling for government regulation of food and drug manufacturing. With enough capital to invest in the most advanced production technologies, they saw government regulation and higher safety standards as a means of driving small, less capitalized producers out of business.

The momentum for government regulation became irresistible in 1906 after publication of Upton Sinclair's novel *The Jungle*—ostensibly a novel about the perils and poverty of immigrant life in Chicago. *The Jungle* included descriptions of the filth in the meat-packing industry that raised the ire of influential Americans, particularly President Theodore Roosevelt. With the backing of the president, who had already been sympathetic to the idea of government regulation, legislation moved successfully through Congress. On June 30, 1906, the Pure Food and Drug Act became law, prohibiting the sale, manufacture, and transportation of adulterated food, drug, or liquor products and requiring that the labels on drug products specifically describe the ingredients. Historians look back on the Pure Food and Drug Act and its companion legislation, the Meat Inspection Act, as the birth of consumer regulatory legislation in the United States.

R

Railroad Brotherhoods

The first major new industry to emerge during the Industrial Revolution was railroads, and, not surprisingly, successful labor unions first appeared there as well. Throughout the nineteenth and twentieth centuries, the railroad industry has been the most organized, in terms of labor unions, of any sector of the economy. The railroad unions began as fraternal organizations for workers but gradually evolved into collective-bargaining agents. They were organized along craft lines, with unskilled workers largely excluded from membership. The major railroad unions, often referred to as *brotherhoods*, were the most thoroughly unionized industry in U.S. labor history.

Railroad Strike of 1877

The so-called great railroad strike of 1877 was the bloodiest labor-management confrontation in U.S. history. The **railroad** industry exploded in growth during the nineteenth century, and railroad unions grew just as exponentially, making the railroad industry the most thoroughly unionized in the United States. Because of the **panic of 1873** and a new sharp downturn in the economy in 1877, a number of railroad executives decided to cut wages for employees. In July 1877, the **Baltimore & Ohio Railroad** (B&O) imposed an additional 10 percent wage cut, and outraged B&O workers went on strike and blocked railway traffic in Martinsburg, West Virginia. The strike resonated with railroad workers everywhere, and work stoppages soon erupted elsewhere. At the request of railroad executives, President Rutherford B. Hayes deployed 200 federal troops to West Virginia to reopen the line. The workers fought back, and in a pitched battle, the troops killed nine strikers.

The strike then spread to Chicago, St. Louis, Pittsburgh, and Buffalo. Rioting workers in Pittsburgh destroyed railroad property by setting fire to machine shops and boxcars and tearing up track. Hayes sent in more troops, and twenty-six strikers died in a series of firefights that looked more like warfare than work stoppage. By the end of July 1877, the strike had largely run its course, but in the process, the **railroad brotherhoods** had become convinced that management had the federal government on its side and that workers, if they were ever to enjoy economic justice, would have to become politically active.

 # Railroads

Historians identify the railroad as the driving force behind the Industrial Revolution during the nineteenth century. Railroads not only became the country's first corporate giants but also stimulated the **coal**, iron, and **steel** industries and linked the different regions of the country into a single national market that provided new opportunities for manufacturers. Few other technologies in the history of the world have had as dramatic an impact on society as the railroad.

Railroad historians trace the beginnings back to sixteenth-century England, where wooden tramways were constructed over which coal-and ore-filled wagons carried freight from mines to port cities and rivers. From there, the ore could be sent in ships and boats to distant sites. The first "wagonways" or "tramways" consisted of little more than parallel wooden planks over which draft animals pulled wagons. By the early 1700s, the wooden planks were lined with strips of iron, which dramatically increased longevity. The addition of crossties then stabilized the parallel planks. The first cast-iron rails were introduced in 1767 in England. These rails, which could carry very heavy loads, were built over the crosstied wooden planks. The first known tramway in the United States was constructed in Boston in 1795 to haul brick. The first true railway—raised track on wooden ties and cars with flanged wheels—was the Granite Line in Massachusetts in 1826, which hauled granite for the Bunker Hill Monument.

New Jersey awarded the first railroad charter in the United States in 1815 to John Stevens, but Stevens could not arrange the financing. The first railroad built in the United States was a thirteen-mile section of the **Baltimore & Ohio Railroad**, which was begun in 1828 and completed in 1830. By the end of 1830, a total of 23 miles of railroad track were in operation. That number jumped to 1,098 miles in 1835 and 5,996 miles in 1848. During the 1850s, more than 10,000 miles of new track were constructed, linking together all of the cities of the United States east of the Mississippi River.

Early in the 1800s, several technological developments gave rise to the modern railroad. Railroads in northern England pioneered the edge rail, in which wagons being hauled had flanged wheels that extended downward over the inside of the cast-iron rail, helping hold the wagon in place.

In 1830, **Robert Livingston Stevens**, an American, invented the flatfooted T-rail for his fledgling Camden & Amboy Railroad. At its base, the T-rail was broader than the top of the T, which allowed builders to nail down the rail with spikes. After 1829, the locomotive driven by a **steam engine** made horses, mules, and oxen obsolete in hauling freight wagons. Finally, cast-iron rails gave way to wrought-iron rails in England beginning in 1820, and late in the 1850s, steel rails began replacing wrought-iron rails.

In the late nineteenth century, an important development in railroad engineering was the advent of standard track gauges. A gauge is the distance separating the two rails, and 4 feet, 8.5 inches, became standard. For years, different railroads built different track gauges, which required all freight to be unloaded and reloaded at the point the track gauge changed. By the late 1880s, virtually all railroads in the United States had adopted the standard gauge, which translated into dramatic improvements in efficiency.

During the 1890s, a major technological innovation was the use of electrical power to drive railroads. Electric traction had been introduced in street railways as early as the 1880s, and in 1895, the New York, New Haven, and Hartford Railroad began using electric traction on some of its shorter sections. Urban residents much preferred the electric traction because it eliminated smoke and steam pollution. The Chicago, Milwaukee, Saint Paul, and Pacific Railroad introduced electrical power in the mountainous sections of Montana because electric power generated more power on steep mountain grades than steam could. The **Pennsylvania Railroad** then constructed about 2,500 miles of electrified track between New York City, Philadelphia, Washington, D.C., and Harrisburg, Pennsylvania, because electric traction allowed greater acceleration and increased carrying capacity, which proved advantageous in urban areas.

The capital requirements of railroad construction were so enormous that state and federal governments frequently became involved. Land donations were the most common way of helping lines with construction costs. The practice began in 1830 when state governments first began making these grants, and the last federal land grant for railroad construction costs came in 1871 for the Texas & Pacific Railroad. A total of 179 million acres were eventually donated to seventy railroads, with the bulk of the contribution—130 million acres—going to just three lines: the **Union Pacific**, the Southern Pacific, and the Atchison, Topeka, and Santa Fe.

After the **Civil War**, the railroad-construction boom continued. In 1870, the United States had a total of 52,922 miles of track, but the construction had become frenzied. Between 1867 and 1873, more than 30,000 miles of track were laid. Total mileage reached 93,261 in 1880; 167,191 in 1890; 198,964 in 1900; and 263,821 in 1920. Between 1860 and 1875, the great **transcontinental railroads** were constructed—the Union Pacific–**Central**

Pacific (1869), the **Northern Pacific** (1883), the Atchison, Topeka, and Santa Fe (1884), and the **Great Northern** (1888). Between 1860 and 1875, four large railroads completed construction projects linking the Atlantic coast with Chicago—the **New York Central Railroad**, the **Pennsylvania Railroad**, the **Baltimore & Ohio Railroad**, and the Grand Trunk Railroad.

Railroad construction had a dramatic impact on the U.S. economy. Because of its all-but-insatiable demand for coal to run its steam engines and for iron and steel to lay track, the railroad became the primary stimulus to the Industrial Revolution. The expense of laying new railroad track required huge amounts of capital, which gave birth to the investment banking industry. The railroads issued bonds that investors took up. To raise capital, business enterprises also incorporated, selling stock rather than borrowing money and therefore relieving themselves of the burden of paying back principal plus interest. More than any other factor, the railroad gave rise to the **corporation** as the most common form of big-business enterprise. As more and more track crisscrossed the country, the nation was integrated into a single national market, allowing manufacturers to sell their goods competitively in distant places. Such booming opportunities to sell stimulated the need for, and therefore the development of, **mass-production** technologies and monumental increases in the size of business enterprises.

But the boom in railroad construction sometimes had a deleterious effect on the economy by making swings in the business cycle more severe. What frequently happened in the nineteenth century was that railroad entrepreneurs borrowed heavily to finance railroad construction and tied themselves into long-term debt obligations. But they soon overbuilt, and with excess capacity, railroad freight rates declined, which made it difficult to pay off the maturing bonds. In 1857, 1873, and 1893, the economy went into tailspins when railroads defaulted on their obligations because the country's money markets were intricately involved in the problem.

The railroads, along with the general economy, recovered in the late 1890s, but technological change was about to send them into a long economic tailspin. During the boom years of the late nineteenth century, railroad management borrowed heavily to raise the capital needed to construct tens of thousands of miles of new track. The railroads assumed heavy, long-term debts. But in the twentieth century, the advent of the internal combustion engine—first automobiles and then trucks—stole freight revenues from the railroads. Although trucks could not carry freight on the same scale as railroads, they could deliver products from the point of production to the point of consumption, which gave them a unique efficiency railroads would never have. By the 1920s, most U.S. railroads were in deep financial trouble, unable to earn enough from freight revenues to meet their long-term debt payments. Economic historians look to that problem to explain much of the chaos in the money markets during the 1920s and early 1930s. Banks, insurance companies, and savings and loan institutions had invested heavily in railroad bonds, and when the railroads defaulted, thousands of financial institutions found themselves in serious trouble as well. The plight of the railroads and the financial institutions holding their bonds was one cause of the Great Depression.

Reaper. *See* McCormick, Cyrus Hall

Rebate

During the late 1870s and 1880s, the **railroad** rebate became a controversial issue of public policy in the United States. The rebate was a private arrangement between a railroad and a shipper to reward a company that did a large volume of business with the railroad. Essentially, the railroad gave a kickback to a privileged shipper for doing exclusive business with one railroad. The results were obvious: large-scale shippers ended up paying freight rates considerably below those offered to others and well below scheduled and published rates, putting small farmers and small businesses at a competitive disadvantage. A variety of interest groups, including small businessmen, farmers, and **Populists** and **Progressives**, called for a ban on rebates, and a succession of federal laws did just that—the Interstate Commerce Act of 1887, the Elkins Act of 1903, and the Hepburn Act of 1906.

Refrigeration

Refrigeration eventually revolutionized food processing in the United States and throughout the world. The principle of refrigeration had been known for centuries. Human beings cool their own bodies by sweating, since the evaporation of water cools surface temperatures. As fluids evaporate, the molecules escaping from a surface take heat with them. Wrapping a damp cloth around a bottle of milk, for example, will keep the milk cool for as long as moisture is evaporating from the cloth, but the cooling process cannot last any longer than the moisture in the cloth.

In 1834, Jacob Perkins, an American living in London, began working on a mechanical cooling system. He filled pipes with volatile fluids known for their rapid evaporating characteristics. By forcing the evaporating molecules back into a compressor, Perkins returned them to a liquid state, which allowed the cooling process to continue indefinitely. In doing so, Perkins created the first refrigerator.

But Perkins was more of an inventor than a businessman and never pursued the commercial possibilities of his invention. He left that to others. In 1856, Alexander Twining in Great Britain began marketing ice in huge quantities, and in 1880, the first shipment of refrigerated meat reached London from Australia. In the United States, meat-packing entrepreneurs like **Gustavus Swift** and **Philip Armour** realized the great potential of refrigeration. Instead of moving live cattle great distances, they could be slaughtered in Chicago and the beef shipped by rail to markets all over the country. Refrigeration gave birth to the modern meat-packing industry.

In the 1920s, Clarence Birdseye developed a technique for the rapid freezing and refrigeration of foods. He founded the General Seafoods Company in 1924 after developing a technique for packing fish, meat, and vegetables into cartons composed of waxed cardboard and then flash-freezing them under high pressure between refrigerated metal plates. The freezing process took place so quickly that ice crystals did not form and ruin the cellular structures of the product. When the food was thawed, it tasted almost as good as fresh, giving birth to the frozen-food industry.

Robber Barons

The term *robber barons* was used widely by muckraking journalists in the 1880s, 1890s, and early 1900s and was made famous by Matthew Josephson's best-selling book *The Robber Barons: The Great American Capitalists, 1861–1901* (1934). As a synonym, journalists and **Progressive** reformers used the term *plutocrats* to describe the generation of super-rich industrialists and financiers who had transformed the American economy in the nineteenth and early twentieth centuries. The advance agents of the Industrial Revolution, the so-called robber barons included people like **John D. Rockefeller, Andrew Carnegie, J. P. Morgan, Jay Gould, Cornelius Vanderbilt**, and **Edward Harriman.**

The term was a pejorative reference to the fabulous sums of money these men accumulated. In best-selling books like Henry Demarest Lloyd's *Wealth against Commonwealth* (1894), Ida M. Tarbell's *History of the Standard Oil Company* (1904), John Moody's *The Truth about the Trusts* (1904), and Upton Sinclair's *The Jungle* (1906), the robber barons were portrayed in the worst possible light. According to critics, the robber barons had made millions of dollars, even billions, by exploiting poor workers and driving smaller, legitimate competitors out of business. They engaged in cutthroat business practices, brooked no opposition, and used whatever legal, financial, and political techniques were necessary to achieve their ends, which amounted to nothing more than money and more money. Critics charged the robber barons with condemning millions of Americans to lives of poverty and exploitation. The Industrial Revolution, which the robber barons had brought to pass, had created an America of two classes—the "haves" and the "have-nots."

The robber-baron image grew and thrived during the Progressive Era and during the Great Depression of the 1930s, when businessmen in general were held in extremely low esteem, but during the 1940s and 1950s, a generation of revisionist historians cast the robber barons in a new light. They were seen as social revolutionaries who created enormous wealth, transformed the structure of society, and led the United States into the modern world. By implementing vast increases in industrial production and productivity and building a modern transportation and communications **infrastructure**, they brought about an economy of rapidly falling prices and greater access to consumption by all Americans. The rise and fall of the reputations of the "robber barons" reflect America's ongoing love-hate relationship with business and businessmen.

Rockefeller, John Davison

John D. Rockefeller was the Bill Gates of the early twentieth century, a man whose name became synonymous with the industry he established and the fortune he accumulated. He was born in Richford, New York, on July 8, 1839, and grew up in Cleveland, Ohio. After graduating from high school and taking a business course, Rockefeller went to work as a clerk and bookkeeper for a produce-commission concern. Consistent with his strict Baptist upbringing, which imbued him with a sense of religious stewardship and a personal loathing of alcohol, tobacco, and gambling, Rockefeller was also a thrifty man, so thrifty that his friends labeled him a "penny-pincher." But those saved pennies turned into dollars and then into hundreds and thousands of dollars, providing him with a small base of capital he used to build America's greatest industrial enterprise.

Rockefeller was only twenty years old in 1859 when Edwin L. Drake drilled the world's first successful **oil well** in Titusville, Pennsylvania. Astute and shrewd, Rockefeller determined that oil would fuel the Industrial Revolution, and he talked his employer into investing in oil refining—converting crude oil into the kerosene used to fire oil lamps. His employer agreed. Within eight years, Rockefeller had become the major owner of the firm known as Rockefeller, Andrews, and Flagler. There he was poised to become the world's richest man, the beneficiary of a modern economy's insatiable demand for refined oil products to lubricate machinery, fire oil lamps, and fuel **railroads**, ships, and **automobiles**. In 1870, the business was incorporated in Ohio as the **Standard Oil Company**.

During the 1870s and 1880s, exploiting ruthlessly competitive techniques, Rockefeller built Standard Oil Company into the world's largest industrial concern, driving independent producers out of business by building huge refineries, which dramatically cut production costs for refining crude oil, or by merging with effective competitors whose physical plants he wanted. Rockefeller also helped pioneer the principle of **vertical integration**, in which a businessman tried to further cut costs and enhance profit margins by asserting control over suppliers, shippers, and distributors. **Standard Oil Company** purchased leases on oil-rich properties, manufactured its own drilling equipment, and acquired controlling interests in railroads and pipelines so that shipping charges could be cut. By pioneering the **trust** and **holding-company** techniques of corporate organization, Rockefeller established centralized control of hundreds of formerly independent refining concerns. In 1890, Standard Oil Company controlled more than 70 percent of all petroleum-refining capacity in the United States. In the process, John D. Rockefeller became a billionaire.

But his success and power also generated considerable animosity. In an age when America suffered much poverty, Rockefeller's fortune seemed obscene to many, and he acquired a reputation as a "**robber baron**," an industrialist or financier guilty of building a personal fortune at the expense of the poor and the downtrodden. In 1890, Congress passed the **Sherman Antitrust Act**, outlawing industrial **monopolies**, and Standard Oil Company began a long battle with the federal government. Eventually, the federal government won. In 1911, in the case of *Standard Oil Co. of New Jersey et al. v. United States*, the Supreme Court upheld the lower court dissolution of the Standard Oil Company. The company was broken up into independent subsidiaries, which eventually evolved into such oil giants as Exxon, Mobil, Esso, and Sohio. Rockefeller later joked, "I got the last laugh."

By that time, Rockefeller was no longer directly involved in company affairs. Beginning in the mid-1890s, he handed day-to-day operations over to associates and diverted Standard Oil's profits into mining and banking. Because of his religious belief that God expected the rich to use their wealth to benefit mankind, Rockefeller spent his later years in philanthropy. He endowed the University of Chicago with millions, spent millions more improving black education in the South, and established the Rockefeller Foundation, which specialized in education and medical and scientific research.

Eventually, Rockefeller outlived his image as a robber baron and tycoon. In the 1930s, he gave witty interviews and was frequently photographed handing out shiny new dimes to small children. The hundreds of millions of dollars he had donated to charitable causes, as well as his own spartan lifestyle, ultimately endeared him to a public that had once feared him. While on vacation in Ormond Beach, Florida, on May 23, 1937, John D. Rockefeller died in his sleep at the age of ninety-seven.

Roosevelt, Theodore

Theodore Roosevelt was the first president to confront the negative side effects of the Industrial Revolution and to try to deal with them through the regulatory powers of the federal government. As such, he remains highly respected by academic historians for his role in bringing about a modern political economy in the United States.

Roosevelt was born in New York City on October 27, 1858, and graduated from Harvard in 1880. He then spent several months reading law privately and several years writing as a historian, producing such well-known works as *The Naval War of 1812* (1882) and the multivolume *The Winning of the West* (1889–1896). After a stint as a Republican in the New York state legislature (1882–1884), Roosevelt headed west for a life of adventure, working on a ranch in North Dakota. His well-to-do family had strong political connections in New York, and in 1889, President Benjamin Harrison appointed him civil service commissioner for the United States. Roosevelt brought dignity and honesty to the task and earned a well-deserved reputation for insulating the civil service from too much political and corporate influence. In 1895, he returned to New York City as police commissioner and earned reformist credentials for his attacks on graft and vice. In 1897, President William McKinley named him assistant secretary of the navy. Roosevelt resigned this post in 1898 when war broke out between the United States and Spain, and he organized the Rough Riders, a voluntary cavalry unit that won fame for bravery in Cuba.

In 1898, Roosevelt returned to the United States as a war hero and promptly won the governorship of New York. Young, charismatic, and energetic, he made a perfect politician, and in 1900, President William McKinley named him as his vice presidential running mate. They won the election handily and were both inaugurated in March 1901. McKinley's subsequent assassination then put Roosevelt in the White House. He was reelected in 1904.

Roosevelt proved to be a highly activist president who was extremely suspicious of the power wielded by the new industrial **corporations** of the

United States. He was especially concerned about the possibility of monopolistic companies restraining trade and destroying competition, which would inevitably produce, he concluded, higher prices and lower quality for manufactured goods. Businessmen got their first taste of his inclinations in 1902 when **coal** miners went on strike. Roosevelt personally intervened to try to negotiate a settlement, but he found the coal operators to be insensitive, stubborn, and unwilling to listen to reason. Frustrated at their arrogance and recalcitrance, he finally ordered the mine owners to settle with the workers, or he would deploy federal troops to take over the mines. The owners then caved in, and the strike ended. It was the first time that the federal government had played such a role in labor-management relations.

Roosevelt was also vigorous in his attacks on **monopolies** or **trusts** which he believed undermined competition in the economy and kept prices artificially high. Under his instigation, the Justice Department launched dozens of **antitrust** suits, the most successful of which broke up the Northern Securities Company in 1904. Roosevelt also helped pioneer the field of federal government consumer protection, which first found expression in the **Meat Inspection Act of 1906** and the **Pure Food and Drug Act of 1906**. Because of both laws, the Department of Agriculture and the Food and Drug Administration brought food processing and drug manufacturing under the umbrella of government oversight.

Roosevelt retired from active political life in 1909, but he was only fifty years old and was not ready to confine himself exclusively to private interests. Over time, however, his thinking evolved, and he came to distinguish between what he labeled "bad trusts" versus "good trusts." Frustrated with the leadership of President **William Howard Taft**, Roosevelt tried to wrest the Republican nomination from him in the **election of 1912**. When he failed, he launched a third-party presidential campaign as the candidate of the Progressive Party, nicknamed the "Bull Moose" Party, and announced the "**New Nationalism**" philosophy, which offered federal regulation and monitoring of "good trusts"—so that consumers would enjoy the benefits of economies of scale that large enterprises could provide—and breaking up "bad trusts" that intentionally undermined competition. His campaign essentially guaranteed the election to Democratic candidate **Woodrow Wilson**, since Roosevelt and Taft split the Republican vote. Theodore Roosevelt died on January 6, 1919. Historians remember him as the first of the modern presidents who believed that the federal government had a key role to play in the management and regulation of the economy.

Rosenwald, Julius. *See* Sears, Roebuck and Company

S

Sachs, Samuel

Samuel Sachs was a pioneer in what became known as investment banking. The Industrial Revolution gave rise to a new generation of corporate enterprises, and their capital needs—to construct **railroads**, **steel** mills, **coal** and iron-ore mines, and new buildings—were huge. By selling shares to investors, these enterprises could raise the capital needed to expand. The appearance of dozens and then hundreds and thousands of **corporations** created the need for a new financial service—underwriting the issue of new securities.

Sachs was born in Baltimore, Maryland, on July 28, 1851. After spending a few years working for several dry-goods businesses, he joined his uncle, Marcus Goldman, in the banking business, and in 1882, they formed a partnership known as Goldman, Sachs and Company. Until Goldman died in 1904, the company concentrated its business on supplying short-term credit, backed by commercial paper assets, to a wide range of businesses. After Goldman died, Sachs changed course and transformed Goldman, Sachs into an international financial institution underwriting new corporate initial public offerings (IPOs). He teamed up with the Lehman Brothers investment banking firm, and together they began underwriting the IPOs of hundreds of new firms, including those not associated with railroads and heavy industry. Since many businesses went public in the late 1800s and early 1900s, Goldman, Sachs had positioned itself for a dominant place in the new financial markets. Goldman, Sachs and Company became one of the most powerful and influential banking firms in the world. Samuel Sachs died on March 2, 1935.

Schwab, Charles

During the course of his life, Charles Schwab became a leading figure in the history of the Industrial Revolution because of the power he exerted in the **steel** industry. Schwab was born in Williamsburg, Pennsylvania, on February 18, 1862. A graduate of St. Francis College, Schwab went to work in 1880 for a grocery store near **Andrew Carnegie**'s steel plant in Homestead, Pennsylvania. In a fortuitous encounter, he became friends with William R. Jones, the general manager of the Edgar Thompson Steel Works, a Carnegie subsidiary, and Jones hired him as an engineer's helper. Jones was as lucky as Schwab, since Schwab proved to be a scientific and managerial genius. Within a year, Schwab was chief engineer at Thompson Steel Works. When Jones died in 1889, Schwab was his natural successor, and at the age of twenty-seven, he was named general superintendent of the plant.

The controversial **Homestead strike** of 1892 provided Schwab with a new opportunity. **Henry Frick**, Carnegie's assistant, had handled the strike so poorly and had so tarnished Carnegie's reputation that the multimillionaire named Schwab general superintendent of Carnegie's main steel plant at Homestead. Five years later, Carnegie rewarded Schwab with the presidency of Carnegie Steel and an annual salary of $1 million. When financier **J. P. Morgan** reorganized Carnegie Steel into **United States Steel Corporation** in 1901, Schwab became president of the new industrial behemoth. Morgan doubled his salary. With his newfound wealth, Schwab went into business for himself as well, purchasing in 1904 a controlling interest in Bethlehem Steel. By that time, he was one of the leading industrialists in the United States. Schwab died on September 18, 1939.

Scientific Management

The leading efficiency engineer of the Industrial Revolution in the United States was Frederick Winslow Taylor, who was essential to the productivity gains in industry during the later nineteenth century. Any technology or system for reallocating assets that increased output without concomitant increases in input led to increased productivity, lower prices to consumers, and higher profits for businessmen. Although most of the great productivity gains came from technological advances, some were simply the result of using employees in different ways.

Taylor was born in Germantown, Pennsylvania, on March 20, 1856. He graduated from Phillips Exeter Academy in 1874 and became a machinist with the Enterprise Hydraulic Workers. In 1878, he took a job as a low-paid laborer at the Midvale Steel Company, but he soon impressed his superiors with his keen eye for detail and mechanical genius. By 1884, he was Midvale's chief engineer. At the same time, he studied engineering in night school at the Stevens Institute of Technology.

During his years with Midvale (1878–1890), Taylor developed what became known as his "scientific management" system. He focused his attention on the interactions between workers and productive machinery and made a science of maximizing the reasonable production capacity of that relationship. Taylor was committed to improving productivity without alienating workers and creating problems for management. He oversaw the development of ever more powerful machinery, and in 1890, he secured a patent on his invention of a large steel hammer. Taylor carefully examined the amount of time it took each worker to perform each task and to move from one task to another. Every operation at Midvale came under Taylor's scrutiny, and no operation was too small to be improved. The results were extraordinary. Under Taylor's tutelage, Midvale's productivity soared, increasing in eight years by more than 300 percent, with an increase in worker wages from 25 to 100 percent.

Taylor's reputation grew along with Midvale's profits, and he eventually embarked on his own as a business consultant, perhaps the first one in American history. At first he specialized in the steel industry and signed Bethlehem Steel as his first big client. Other clients signed on, and within ten years, Taylor was independently wealthy. Convinced that excessive wealth was a detriment to individual character, in 1900, Taylor stopped selling his services for profit and simply became a volunteer efficiency expert. Among his best-known publications was the 1911 book *Principles of Scientific Management*. Frederick Taylor died on March 21, 1915.

Sears, Roebuck and Company

Julius Rosenwald was a pioneer in mass retail marketing in the United States. The Industrial Revolution had given the economy massive productive capacity, but efficient and profitable means of distributing large volumes of consumer goods had to be developed, and Rosenwald did this better than anyone else.

Julius Rosenwald was born to German Jewish immigrant parents in Springfield, Illinois, on August 12, 1862. After finishing high school, he went into the dry-goods business, wholesaling clothes to a variety of small family concerns. During his travels, he concluded that rural areas and small towns were underserved in their access to manufactured goods, and in 1895, he bought a one-quarter interest in a mail-order firm known as Sears, Roebuck and Company. At first, Sears only sold watches and jewelry, but Rosenwald immediately began expanding its product line and was soon made vice president. By exploiting the demand for manufactured goods in rural America and opening offices in railroad stations and in offices near downtown squares all over America, Rosenwald saw Sears's

An advertisement for women's shoes in a Sears, Roebuck and Co. catalog, around 1923. (*Sears, Roebuck and Co., Dallas, Texas, 1923*)

sales leap from $1 million in 1896 to $443 million in 1929.

In 1925, Rosenwald also decided to push Sears into direct retailing. He hired Robert E. Wood away from Montgomery Ward and placed him in charge of retail sales, and Wood opened Sears stores all over the country. In 1926, Wood launched eight stores, and in 1927, he opened sixteen more. Because of the name loyalty Sears had generated during its thirty years of business, the stores succeeded. In 1928, Wood opened 168 new retail stores. By 1929, when the onset of the Great Depression dramatically reduced opportunities for expansion, Sears had 324 operating retail stores. When he died on January 6, 1932, Rosenwald was widely regarded, and has been regarded since then, as America's most successful retailer.

Second Bank of the United States. *See* Bank of the United States

Separate Spheres

The ideology of separate spheres for men and women between public and private life occurred in the mid-nineteenth century as a result of the transformation of the economy during the Industrial Revolution. Whereas prior to industrialization labor largely occurred in the home and involved the entire family, the rise of factory production resulted in a shift to wage-based labor which required men to work long hours outside of the home while women stayed home to care for the family and attend to household matters. Culture and society subsequently supported the establishment of gendered boundaries relegating women to the private sphere dedicated to the home and family, while men inhabited the public sphere focused on work. The shift from family economy to wage economy contributed to a decline in the economic status of women's labor as domestic labor was not considered as contributing to the economy in a manner equal to work for wages. Women who did work for wages did so at a disadvantage, for less pay and less stability in more transient, "temporary" jobs.

Sewing Machine

The invention of the sewing machine was one of the Industrial Revolution's most important technological developments and gave rise to **mass-production** techniques in the ready-to-wear clothing industry. The key figure in the development of the technology was Isaac Singer, who built a sewing industry that came to be synonymous with his name. In 1856, Singer managed to pool a series of patent claims and design a hybrid sewing machine using Walter Hunt's lock stitch, **Elias Howe**'s grooved, eye-pointed needle and second-thread shuttle, and Allen Wilson's four-motion cloth-feeding mechanism. To these Singer added his own designs of a presser-foot pedal, needlecam-bar patents, and straight vertical needles. Singer then steadily improved the technology, and through a vigorous marketing and advertising campaign, his company became the premier organization in the sewing-machine industry. Singer also went beyond the industrial use of sewing machines. Through the use of what he called "Singer emporiums"—clean, cheery storefronts for women—Singer convinced millions of American women that they needed a sewing machine for their homes. Singer retired in 1863 and moved abroad. In 1873, his company introduced his "Family Model," and by 1880, he was selling 500,000 of them a year.

The sewing machine revolutionized the ready-to-wear clothing industry. The rise of the **textile industry** had made cotton and woolen cloth relatively inexpensive, but retail clothing costs were still quite high because workers had to sew patterned cloth together by hand. The introduction of sewing machines to the assembly line led to geometric increases in worker productivity, higher corporate profits, and lower clothing prices for consumers, which greatly enhanced demand.

Sherman Antitrust Act of 1890

The Sherman Antitrust Act of 1890 was the first federal **antitrust** law. Because of the extraordinary development in U.S. transportation **infrastructure** during the nineteenth century, a national market emerged in which goods could be manufactured, distributed, and sold over vast territories. To take advantage of such vastly expanded marketing opportunities, larger and larger **corporations** appeared, especially in the steel, petroleum, beef, railroad, and sugar industries. Critics charged that monopolistic conditions were emerging in these industries, that single companies or consortiums had become so powerful that they could undermine competition and elevate prices beyond normal levels. Support for government intervention began to develop among farmers, workers, and small businessmen.

In 1889, Kansas passed the first state antitrust law, but it soon became obvious that legislation by individual states could not adequately address the power of national corporations. Demands for federal legislation began to mount in the 1880s. The first federal legislation, the Interstate Commerce Act, made its way through Congress in 1887. It outlawed pools among railroads operating in interstate commerce and established the Interstate Commerce Commission to monitor compliance. In 1890, Senator George Hoar of Massachusetts drafted legislation outlawing monopolies in manufacturing industries. Senator John Sherman of Ohio shepherded the legislation through Congress, and it became known as the Sherman Antitrust Act of 1890. The law empowered the Department of Justice of the federal government to employ the federal courts to dissolve monopolies in manufacturing enterprises.

During the 1890s, the Sherman Antitrust Act had little impact because conservative presidents Benjamin Harrison, Grover Cleveland, and William McKinley refused to enforce it. But in 1901, when Theodore Roosevelt became president, the Sherman Antitrust Act acquired teeth, and the president enforced it. He became known as a "trustbuster" because of his vigorous support of antitrust activity, and his greatest success came in 1904 when the Supreme Court upheld the dissolution of the Northern Securities Company, a large holding company that monopolized railroad traffic in the northwest. Roosevelt's successors—Republican William Howard Taft and Democrat Woodrow Wilson—were even more vigorous, and the Clayton Antitrust Act of 1914 strengthened the Sherman Antitrust Act. Today, federal government antitrust action, including the recent lawsuit against Microsoft Corporation, is still conducted under the authority of the Sherman Antitrust Act.

Sinclair, Upton Beall

Although Upton Sinclair was never a government official or labor leader, he played a leading role in bringing about a modern political economy in which large economic institutions became subject to federal government regulation. Sinclair was born on September 20, 1878, in Baltimore, Maryland. In 1897, he graduated from the City College of New York. He spent his life as a highly influential novelist and social critic. A confirmed socialist who believed that social justice would not come to America's working people until the government had assumed control of the means of production and distribution, Sinclair wrote hundreds of articles in newspapers and magazines promoting his views. He became a household word in the United States, however, with the publication of his 1906 novel *The Jungle*. Although Sinclair intended the novel to generate sympathy for the suffering of working-class immigrants and to promote socialism, *The Jungle* became a best seller because of its detailed, sickening descriptions of meat production in Chicago packing houses. Consumers, including President Theodore Roosevelt, were aghast, and demands for federal regulation of meat packing and food processing intensified. Not long after the publication of *The Jungle*, Congress passed the Meat Inspection Act of 1906 and the Pure Food and Drug Act of 1906, both of which marked the beginning of consumer-protection legislation in the United States.

None of Sinclair's subsequent novels had such an impact, but their themes were consistent. In *King Coal* (1917), *Oil!* (1927), and *Boston* (1928), he described how big business exploited workers and consumers and bought out politicians to perpetuate its power. In 1934, at the height of the Great Depression, Sinclair ran for governor of California on a socialist platform he labeled "End Poverty in California." He proved to be quite popular, and only a vicious, mudslinging campaign by Republican Frank Merriam led to Sinclair's defeat. In 1943, Sinclair won the Pulitzer Prize for his novel *Dragon's Teeth*, a visceral attack on world fascism. Sinclair died on November 25, 1968.

Singer, Isaac. *See* Sewing Machine

Single-Tax Movement. *See* George, Henry

Sixteenth Amendment

The Sixteenth Amendment to the U.S. Constitution authorized the federal income tax. One of the most visible outcomes of the Industrial Revolution was the vastly increased gap between the rich and the poor in the United States. The irony of so few people making so much money struck many Americans as immoral, and demands for a progressive federal income tax, in which the rich would pay a higher percentage of their annual income in taxes than the middle and lower classes, gained ground. In 1894, Congress passed the Wilson-Gorman Tariff, which lowered tariff rates substantially, and to make up for the lost income, Congress passed a federal income tax. A number of well-heeled individuals and companies appealed the tax as an unconstitutional violation of their rights to private property, and in the 1895 case of *Pollock v. Farmer's Loan and Trust Company*, the U.S. Supreme Court ruled the federal income tax unconstitutional.

But the movement for a federal income tax was hardly dead, even if the federal courts consistently opposed the tax. In 1910, reformers began promoting an amendment to the U.S. Constitution that would legalize the federal income tax, and the movement quickly gained momentum. In 1913, the requisite number of states had ratified it, and the Sixteenth Amendment became part of the Constitution. The wording of the amendment was quite simple: "The Congress shall have power to lay and collect taxes on incomes, from whatever source derived, without apportionment among the several States, and without regard to any census or enumeration."

Slater, Samuel

Samuel Slater, a merchant and businessman, is widely regarded by most economic historians as the founder of the cotton textile industry in the United States. Until Samuel Slater appeared on the economic scene, American participation in the cotton textile industry, except for small-scale production of finished products, was primarily confined to supplying British textile manufacturers with the raw cotton they needed to process into cloth.

Slater was born in Belper, Derbyshire, England, on June 9, 1768. When he was a child, his father apprenticed him out to a textile-factory owner, where he gradually learned the ins and outs of the business. He soon found himself being trained by Jedediah Strutt, a partner of Richard Arkwright, an inventor whose fertile mind produced a variety of inventions to spin and weave cloth. An excellent student with pragmatic, mechanical aptitudes,

Slater studied carefully, learned his craft, and became good enough at his work to add several improvements to Arkwright's inventions.

Arkwright's invention of spinning and carding machines revolutionized the business of textile manufacturing and led to geometric increases in textile production and productivity and concomitant falls in prices. Hand spinning and loom machines were rendered completely noncompetitive, and in the United States, textile manufacturers began offering a reward to anyone who could reproduce Arkwright's technology. Slater learned of the bounty and immigrated to the United States.

To protect England's burgeoning, state-of-the-art textile industry, English law prohibited the export of any technical drawings or models of Arkwright's inventions, but Slater's fertile mind and rich experience in the British textile industry equipped him to play a key role in the development of the American textile industry. In 1789, when he arrived in Boston, he was ready to revolutionize American textile manufacturing. He settled in Providence, Rhode Island, where the firm of Almy and Brown put him to work. They built a factory at Pawtucket, Rhode Island, and filled it with the spinners and carding machines that Slater reconstructed from memory. Slater remained with Almy and Brown for nearly a decade, making it the first American firm to be able to compete successfully with British textile mills.

In 1798, Slater went out on his own, founding Samuel Slater and Company. He constructed new mills throughout New England, making the region the center of the industry in the United States. With state-of-the-art technology, American textile manufacturers had one competitive advantage over their British counterparts because they did not have to transport raw cotton over such distances. Samuel Slater died on April 21, 1835.

Slaughterhouse Cases

How corporations were perceived under the law played an important role in promoting the Industrial Revolution in the United States. The so-called *Slaughterhouse Cases* marked a key point in the evolution of corporate law. The cases also represented the U.S. Supreme Court's first ruling concerning the Fourteenth Amendment. The Fourteenth Amendment, ratified in 1868, extended citizenship and civil rights to recently emancipated slaves and extended the due-process clause of the Fifth Amendment, as well as other elements of the Bill of Rights, to state governments.

The cases emerged from legislation in Louisiana in 1869 in which the state legislature awarded a monopoly over the slaughtering of cattle, pigs, and sheep to one company, the Crescent City Live Stock Landing and

Slaughterhouse Company. The state did so on health grounds, since it would be easier to monitor the activities of one company. Other butchers sued, arguing that the legislation violated their Fourteenth Amendment property rights by preventing them from competing. In essence, the butchers were claiming that a corporation, not just individuals, enjoyed rights under the Constitution.

The U.S. Supreme Court in 1873 decided against the butchers, claiming that the Louisiana legislation could not be considered a deprivation of property rights. But in stating the decision in that way, the Supreme Court essentially upheld the notion that corporations did enjoy the same constitutional rights as individuals. The application of these constitutional rights to corporations helped create a legal environment in which businessmen and investors could thrive. As a result, more capital became available to fuel economic growth.

Slavery

The role slavery played in the Industrial Revolution has long been a point of political and scholarly debate, especially the issue of whether the institution of slavery retarded and postponed industrial development in the Southern states. The debate commenced in 1857 when Hinton Rowan Helper wrote *The Impending Crisis of the South*. A native of North Carolina, Helper amassed a huge volume of economic data to prove, in his own mind at least, that slavery had retarded the Southern economy and doomed millions of white people to poverty. Unless the South moved beyond slavery into the era of a modern political economy, the region was destined to become a colony of Northern industrial interests. Southerners labeled Helper a traitor, and Southern state legislatures banned the book. In federal post offices throughout the South, clerks refused to distribute it. "Helperism," Southern apologists argued, amounted to nothing more than a weapon of insurrection for Northern extremists. Northern Republicans lived up to that fear. Republican congressmen endorsed "Helperism" and, looking forward to the election of 1860, distributed more than 100,000 copies of the book as political propaganda, contributing to the worsening crisis. Although a subsequent generation of historians debated the issue, the consensus today is that slavery did indeed retard the Southern economy. Because slave labor was so cheap, Southern planters had no incentive to move to labor-saving machinery, which was the backbone of the Industrial Revolution. Also, because Southern planters refused to teach slaves to read and write, the Southern labor force was uneducated and unable to adapt to economic change. Finally, the institution of slavery kept immigrants out of the South, which robbed the region of an economic dynamic that helped transform the North.

Social Darwinism

In the minds of many Americans, the idea or philosophy of Social Darwinism became closely associated with the Industrial Revolution and its impact on society and the economy. In 1859, Charles Darwin, a British biologist, published his book *On the Origin of Species* and revolutionized science, giving birth to modern biology. At the heart of Darwin's theory was the concept of evolution—that life on earth had evolved from simpler forms over the course of millions of years according to what he called the law of natural selection, or "survival of the fittest." Those species that could adapt to changes in their environment survived and passed on to their offspring those same survival qualities, while species that could not adapt became extinct. Such was the law of natural selection.

Darwin's unique theory prompted a bitter debate that still continues in the United States. From most corners of the religious community, attacks on Darwin became intense and shrill. The theory of evolution, many argued, undermined the biblical story of creation and implied, directly or indirectly, that human beings did not have divine origins. Darwin realized that his theories contradicted the seven-day creation story, but he was not an atheist who denied the existence of God. Nevertheless, he became persona non grata among fundamentalist Christians. At the same time, his theories became the building block of modern biological sciences. The theory of evolution became as central to biology as gravity and thermodynamics are to physics.

While debate over the religious legitimacy of evolution was raging, others took the theory of natural selection and applied it to the human social structure. In Great Britain, sociologist Herbert Spencer had actually coined the term *survival of the fittest* in 1852, seven years before Darwin employed it, but Spencer used the term to describe social history. Spencer was engaged in an elegant but ultimately futile task of integrating all fields of human knowledge into a single "synthetic philosophy," everything from physics and biology to psychology and history. Spencer argued that human beings had evolved, or were at least evolving, from a predatory, vicious species to an advanced civilization where peace, prosperity, and altruism prevailed, and that evolution explained the entire process. Spencer also argued, however, that social evolution was a fixed process that could not be tampered with by government, and he opposed government legislation assisting the poor, providing public schools, and mandating sanitary standards. Such legislation, he claimed, only perpetuated social weaknesses by allowing the weak and unfit to survive and reproduce. Reformers who advocated such schemes would only weaken society and the economy. The business of government, according to

Spencer, was only to maintain order, enforce contracts, and provide a reliable monetary system.

Spencer's books proved to be extremely popular in the United States and in Great Britain, selling more than 350,000 copies between 1860 and 1900. At Yale University, political scientist William Graham Sumner took Spencer's ideas and fashioned what he called "Social Darwinism." All social institutions, Sumner claimed, emerged from the human struggle for survival. All existing institutions had evolved rationally from their predecessors according to natural selection. He also claimed that "from the first step that man made above the brute the thing which made his civilization possible was capital." Capitalists had built modern society, and laissez-faire was the only rational public policy. We "must minimize to the utmost the relations of the state to industry. . . . The state cannot get a cent for any man without taking it from some other man, and this latter must be a man who has produced and saved." Sumner labeled him the "Forgotten Man" (Sumner, 1883, 1913).

Sumner was also convinced that the lower classes existed at the bottom of the social pyramid for good reason. They were lazy and/or dumb, either of which was capable of dooming them to the lower class. They were, in a word, "unfit" and incapable of winning the struggle for survival of the fittest. All attempts to lift them would only lower the more talented, hardworking elements of society. Progress depended upon the leadership of a talented elite and the hard work of everyone else. Any public policy that inhibited the elites would undermine social progress. "Let it be understood," Sumner wrote, "that we cannot go outside this alternative: liberty, inequality, survival of the fittest; not liberty, equality, and the survival of the unfittest. The former carries society forward and favors all its best members; the latter carries society downwards and favors all its worst elements" (Sumner, 1963).

Social Darwinism, as Sumner's ideas came to be known, found its way into arguments opposing social reform and the use of government to ameliorate the suffering of the poor. Social Darwinism became, in the minds and rhetoric of many Americans, a companion of laissez-faire economics, a rationale for limiting the role and scope of government in addressing some of the problems created by the Industrial Revolution.

Social Gospel

Throughout the seventeenth, eighteenth, and early nineteenth centuries, most Americans believed that the poor were poor because of their own inadequacies, that either laziness, stupidity, or a combination of the two explained their circumstances in life and the nature of the social structure. Most

Christian ministers and intellectuals sustained that point of view and believed that the only role for the church in society was to evangelize and to establish moral values. All other endeavors they left to other sectors of society.

But the Industrial Revolution posed a challenge to such convenient suppositions about society and the economy. The vast gap between the rich and the poor grew ever larger and ever more visible during the nineteenth century, and exploitation of factory workers appeared to become steadily more severe. Critics began to reject the notion that the victims of poverty were exclusively responsible for their plight and started searching for other culprits. Before long they identified industrial corporations and their super-rich managers and owners as the source of much of the problem. Much poverty, they concluded, originated not in the personality of individuals but in the social and economic structure.

The Social Gospel movement emerged among Christian critics of the new industrial social order. Churches, they argued, should not confine themselves to preaching moral homilies and evangelizing but should exercise their power and moral authority to reform society and the economy, in particular, to support government efforts at the federal, state, and local levels to ameliorate the suffering of the poor. Social Gospel advocates rejected the notions of laissez-faire and Social Darwinism, which worked to limit government interference in social and economic affairs.

One leading Social Gospel crusader was Washington Gladden, a Congregational minister in Cleveland, Ohio. Between 1882 and 1918, the years of his ministry, Gladden observed the arrival of hundreds of thousands of immigrants in Cleveland and witnessed the expansion of urban poverty. For Gladden, an economy based on competition, particularly wage competition, contradicted the teachings of Jesus Christ, and he argued that the federal government should use its authority to protect the weak against exploitation by the strong. When **John D. Rockefeller**, chairman of **Standard Oil Company** and one of the richest men in the world, made a charitable contribution to the Congregational church, Gladden repudiated and condemned it, calling it "tainted money" and accusing those who did accept such contributions of signing a "partnership with the devil." To put it mildly, Gladden was not very popular among most of his ministerial colleagues.

Far more influential was Walter Rauschenbusch, who from 1886 to 1897 served as a Baptist minister in the slum of Hell's Kitchen, New York City. While he was reading the works of Edward Bellamy and Henry George, he noted the severe poverty of Hell's Kitchen and knew that except for a small minority, the individuals themselves were not responsible for their difficulties. He argued that Jesus Christ had taught individuals to work for a better world, not simply acquiesce in the status quo. He expressed his point of view in such books as *Christianity and the Social Crisis* (1907), *Christianizing the Social Order* (1912), and *A Theology for the Social Gospel* (1917).

Throughout history, Rauschenbusch claimed, Christianity had ignored its duty to condemn the exploitation of the weak and the poor. Any economic system that elevated competition above cooperation violated the will of God and trafficked in the worst kind of immorality by demonizing the poor and exalting the rich.

Rauschenbusch's solutions for the problems of the poor went against the grain of American capitalism. He became a committed socialist who advocated highly progressive income and inheritance taxes, pensions for the elderly; subsidized public housing for the poor; minimum-wage laws; recognition of labor unions; and government ownership of the railroads, the telephone and telegraph lines, and the major extractive industries, including coal, iron ore, and petroleum.

Rauschenbusch, however, was not a Marxian socialist. In fact, he condemned Marxists because they replaced the competitive business model of capitalism with a competitive class struggle in which violence and revolution were possible and probable. He called instead for Christian socialism based on a social cooperation mediated by enlightened government. Marxists condemned Christian socialism as hopelessly naïve and unrealistic. Rauschenbusch's beliefs were expressed in his book *Christianity and the Social Crisis* (1907).

Although the Social Gospel has been described as primarily a social movement among Protestants, it also found expression among a number of prominent Roman Catholic priests and intellectuals. While most late-nineteenth-century Protestants had a large middle-class constituency, the Roman Catholic church was overwhelmingly a working-class organization and had to take note of the economic circumstances of its members. The most prominent Catholic reformer was Father John Ryan, who led the National Catholic Welfare Council and wrote such books as *A Living Wage* (1906), *Distributive Justice* (1916), and *A Better Economic Order* (1935). Like most Roman Catholic prelates, Ryan rejected socialism, but he just as vehemently rejected laissez-faire and called on state and federal governments to construct a social-welfare safety net for the poor and unemployed. He endorsed labor unions and collective bargaining, condemned the nasty determinism of social Darwinism, asked government to "compel all employers to pay a living wage," called on government to enforce an eight-hour workday for workers, advocated firm prohibitions of child labor, and promoted progressive income and inheritance taxes, public housing, and old-age pensions. Although the Social Gospel was far more progressive than most Americans who were not ready for government to assume such responsibilities, it nevertheless helped create a moral and intellectual climate that made some forms of government intervention more acceptable to the general public.

Socialism

Socialism is a form of political economy that rejects capitalistic notions of private property in favor of government ownership of the means of production and distribution. Socialist theory emerged in the nineteenth century from the fertile mind of Karl Marx, who argued that there would always be a struggle between capitalists and workers that would eventually culminate in revolution and a workers' state. Such radical political movements, however, always had a difficult time taking root in the United States. The abundant availability of land during the seventeenth, eighteenth, and nineteenth centuries made most Americans property owners, and schemes to solve America's economic problems by seizing private property and awarding its ownership and administration to the federal government never found many adherents. Also, a near cult of individual opportunity infected the entire popular culture, and radical schemes to provide equality of condition, not equality of opportunity, alienated the vast majority of Americans.

The most successful socialist organization in U.S. history was the Socialist Party of America, led by **Eugene V. Debs**. The leader of the American Railway Union, Debs had converted to socialism after the Pullman strike of 1894, when federal troops were called out to crush the strike. In 1901, Debs founded the Socialist Party of America. Unlike Karl Marx, however, Debs believed that socialism could only come peacefully, not through violent revolution, so he dedicated himself to the political process, running for president a number of times. His campaign platform was actually quite modest—women's suffrage, an end to child labor; a minimum wage for workers; prohibition of the use of force to end labor-union work stoppages; a shorter workweek; unemployment compensation; federal old-age pensions; and government ownership of the transportation, communications, and banking systems. Most of his proposals eventually became law. But Debs was always ahead of his time. In his most successful presidential campaign, the election of 1912, he secured just over 6 percent of the vote. Americans simply never warmed to his vision of a land of equality of condition.

Specie Circular (Soft Money)

The term *specie circular*, also referred as *soft money*, first emerged during the late eighteenth century and throughout the nineteenth century to describe paper currency that was not backed by gold or silver. During the American Revolution, a cash-strapped Congress printed millions of dollars of paper "Continental currency," which was not backed by gold or silver, and the result was a high rate of inflation. Another form of soft money was the banknotes issued by hundreds of state banks during the 1820s and 1830s. Those notes became part of the money supply, but because many of them were not backed by bullion, inflation hit the economy. The result was the same during the **Civil War**. Congress had millions of dollars of "greenbacks" (paper currency) printed, as did the Confederacy. Neither forms of paper money were backed by silver or gold. Not surprisingly, economists made a connection between inflation and "soft money," and during the late nineteenth century, when the economy experienced a deflationary cycle, many Americans saw a solution in the issuance of "soft money."

 # Spindletop

The term *Spindletop* refers to a huge salt dome in eastern Jefferson County, Texas, south of the city of Beaumont, where the modern petroleum industry had its beginnings. Late in 1900, at a place called Spindletop Hill, the Gladys City Oil, Gas, and Manufacturing Company began drilling for oil. It was a difficult place to drill for oil given the technology of the day because

Spindletop, the most famous of the Texas oil fields, was discovered in 1901. (Bettmann/Corbis)

of the sands in the salt dome. On January 10, 1901, on land adjacent to the Gladys City holdings, mud began seeping up through a well drilled by some rivals. Later in the day, a geyser of oil spewed forth and reached a height of more than 100 feet. It took the roughnecks (oil rig workers) nine full days to cap the well, by which time nearly 1 million barrels of oil had pooled on the ground. The oil age was born.

Oil wells sprouted throughout the area of the salt dome, and land values skyrocketed south of Beaumont. By the end of 1901, more than $235 million had been invested in the oil fields, and in 1902, production exceeded 17.5 million barrels. Production peaked in 1902 and then declined to 3.6 million barrels in 1904. In subsequent years, however, other fields were found bordering Spindletop, and in 1927, production exceeded 21 million barrels. By 1985, more than 153 million barrels of oil had been recovered from the Spindletop field.

The Texas economy boomed with Spindletop, which inspired massive capital investments in wells, storage facilities, refineries, and pipelines. Houston, Texas, became the oil capital of the country. Several major world companies had their beginnings at Spindletop, including the Texas Company (Texaco), Gulf Oil Corporation, Sun Oil Corporation, and Humble Oil Company (later Exxon). The fact that Spindletop came just when the internal-combustion engine gave rise to automobiles and trucks only underscored its significance to American economic history.

Spinning

Beginning in the mid-eighteenth century, new technologies for spinning cloth revolutionized the textile industry, helped launch the Industrial Revolution, and planted the seeds for the rise of a factory culture in modern economies. The technological revolution began in 1733 when John Kay of Lancashire, England, invented the flying shuttle. The flying shuttle became the first step in the eventual development of an automated loom. Before the flying shuttle, weavers had to pull the shuttle manually through the loom, a time-consuming process. On especially wide pieces of cloth, it required two workers to return the shuttle. But the flying shuttle returned the shuttle automatically and allowed one weaver to work faster than two workers had previously worked.

That innovation created the need for a new spinning technology, since one spinner could no longer keep up with one weaver. In 1764, Englishman James Hargreaves invented the spinning jenny, a mechanical spinning machine composed of several vertical, side-by-side spindles and a clamp that allowed rapid feeding of yarn onto the spindle. One man working a spinning jenny could do the work of four men or women on an old spinning wheel. The invention of the spinning jenny posed a great threat and generated extreme resistance from hand spinners.

In 1769, Richard Arkwright patented a new rotating-flyer spinning wheel, which revolutionized the spinning of flax. Arkwright replaced spinsters, who manually fed fibers through a rotating flyer that twisted the fibers into yarn, with a series of roller pairs that could twist fibers more rapidly and spin several yarns simultaneously. Arkwright eventually made his machine even more sophisticated and powered it by a waterwheel, which resulted in exponential increases in productivity. Arkwright's invention was expensive and inappropriate for home use, which led to the rise of factories where dozens of spinning machines were grouped together. He would bring large cotton bales into the factory and, using flying shuttles, spinning jennies, and his roller-pair rotating flyers, would spin yarn and weave it into finished cloth.

The third major technological innovation in spinning was Samuel Crompton's invention of the "mule" in 1779, which combined the inventions of John Hargreaves and Richard Arkwright into a single machine. Powered by waterwheel technology, the mule did not need skilled workers for its operation and was capable of spinning exceedingly fine fibers into expensive yarns.

The new spinning and weaving technologies gave rise to the British textile industry and then to the American textile industry. In 1751, exports of British cotton products totaled £46,000, but they jumped to £5.4 million in 1800 and £46.8 million in 1861. Because of the extension of the British Empire into East Asia and South Asia, these exports found their way into the undeveloped world. British textile goods, manufactured in England and then shipped across the world, could be sold at far cheaper prices in China and India than those fashioned locally by hand.

Although the major technologies driving the cotton textile industry were invented in Great Britain and transplanted to the United States, the industry soon became central to the Industrial Revolution in America. Because American textile manufacturers could use cotton produced in the Southern states, they soon came to enjoy a slight price advantage over British producers, and by the 1910s, more cotton textiles were produced in the United States than in Great Britain.

Spinning Jenny. *See* Spinning

Standard Oil Company

The Standard Oil Company of New Jersey was the product of John D. Rockefeller's business genius. A devout Baptist committed to God and money, Rockefeller did for oil refining what Andrew Carnegie did for steel. Oil was used for lighting lamps and for lubricants, and the Industrial Revolution created huge demand. Rockefeller went into the oil-refining business and expanded horizontally, purchasing oil refiners or driving them out of business. Acquiring oil supplies, constructing barrel factories and storage tanks, and building pipelines, he achieved a vertical integration that cut his costs. In 1870, Rockefeller formed the Standard Oil Company.

In 1882, he developed the trust, a legal device essentially creating a monopoly. Several companies surrendered voting rights to a trust board, which made important decisions. The trust limited competition by setting prices or allocating specific markets to single companies, which charged whatever the market could bear. In return, companies received trust certificates entitling them to a share of profits. Within a few years, Standard Oil controlled the industry, crushing rivals, fixing prices, and earning millions, chiefly from the world's demand for kerosene. When the internal-combustion engine created a huge demand for gasoline, Rockefeller was positioned to become a billionaire. Trusts proliferated. In 1890, an attorney for the Department of Justice wrote, "Trusts are becoming as common in industry as furnaces and smokestacks. The corporate landscape is littered with them, and they are as powerful as any emperor or potentate in the world."

Resentment of such power and wealth steadily accumulated in American politics, and John D. Rockefeller and Standard Oil became targets of the antitrust movement. The Sherman Antitrust Act of 1890 had outlawed monopolies in manufacturing, and since Standard Oil controlled more than 70 percent of U.S. oil-refining capacity, it constituted a monopoly. During the presidency of Theodore Roosevelt, the attorney general of the United States filed an antitrust suit against Standard Oil. The case wound its way through the federal courts for several years, but in 1911, the U.S. Supreme Court ordered the dissolution of the Standard Oil Company of New Jersey. The shares of thirty-three subsidiaries were then distributed to stockholders.

Stanford, Leland

Development of a nationwide transportation network was a key factor in making the Industrial Revolution possible, and Leland Stanford had much to do with that transportation network. He was born in Watervliet, New York, on March 9, 1824, and was educated at the Clinton Liberal Institute and then at the Cazenovia Seminary in New York before settling in Port

Washington, Wisconsin, where he opened a law practice. In 1852, a fire destroyed his office and library, and Stanford used the accident to reinvent himself. He followed his brothers to California, where mass immigration inspired by the discovery of gold had created new business opportunities. He opened a business supplying gold miners with food, clothing, and supplies.

Stanford also became active in politics, joining the fledgling Republican Party, where he opposed the expansion of slavery, called for high tariffs on manufactured goods, proposed a transcontinental railroad to link the West Coast with the East Coast, and praised the idea of free public-domain land to farmers who would settle and improve it. In 1861, Stanford was elected governor of California. He used his office to make sure that California remained in the Union and to push through the state legislature a series of appropriations to build the Central Pacific Railroad, of which he was president, from San Francisco to Truckee, California. He served only one term, leaving office in 1863.

Stanford then became involved in the railroad business, particularly the construction of the transcontinental line, which Congress had authorized and for which it had offered lucrative construction subsidies and land grants. The Central Pacific Railroad was designated the western branch of the transcontinental railroad, and Stanford constructed it from west to east, taking it over the Sierra Nevada, while the Union Pacific Railroad was built from east to west. The two lines linked up at Promontory Summit, Utah, on May 10, 1869.

The Central Pacific Railroad made Stanford fabulously wealthy, primarily because of the enormous land grants Congress had given to the railroad for each mile of track constructed. Stanford sold much of the land and reinvested the money back into the railroad business. He became president of the Southern Pacific Railroad from 1885 to 1890. Elected and reelected to the U.S. Senate in 1885 and 1891, Stanford died on June 21, 1893. He is primarily remembered today for endowing Stanford University in Palo Alto, California, but economic historians remember Stanford for helping create the economic infrastructure that made the Industrial Revolution possible.

 # Steam Engine

Perhaps the one invention central to the rise and success of the Industrial Revolution was the steam engine, which revolutionized the transportation system through its use on steamboats and railroads and mechanized American factories. Until the appearance of the internal-combustion engine at the end of the nineteenth century, the steam engine powered the

Industrial Revolution. The principle behind the steam engine was simple: water heated to a boil in an enclosed space produces steam, which increases pressure and produces power. The steam engine then transforms steam's heat energy into mechanical energy. That process takes place by forcing steam to expand and cool within a cylinder that is equipped with a movable piston. Denis Papin, a French physicist and inventor, produced the first steam engine in 1690 and used it to pump water. In 1712, Thomas Newcomen installed a working steam engine in a coal mine in Dudley Castle, England. The modern steam engine, however, came from the inventions of British engineer James Watt. Watt patented his steam engine in 1769. Watt's invention was the first truly efficient steam engine. He insulated the cylinder and left it at a constant state of steam temperature. He added a separate water-cooled condenser chamber that he equipped with a vacuum-producing pump. The vacuum allowed the movement of steam from the cylinder to the condenser. In Watt's steam engine, the steam itself, not atmospheric pressure, did the work of moving the piston. Watt eventually fine-tuned his steam engine with other improvements.

Around 1800, British inventor Richard Trevithick and American engineer Oliver Evans simultaneously but independently invented the non-condensing, high-pressure steam engine. That engine was used in the first railroad locomotive. Trevithick and Evans also adapted their steam engine to the first horseless carriages. In 1846, American inventor George H. Corliss made the steam engine more sophisticated by developing a cylinder-shaped valve that completely closed the piston, a process that reduced condensation and friction and vastly improved operating efficiency.

The major problem with the steam engine, however, was that the technology had inherent limits. For each succeeding generation of steam engines to become more powerful, they had to be constructed on a larger scale. The steam engine, therefore, was not suited to massive projects, such as generating electrical energy for very large factories or for towns. Big steam-power installations, such as those in electrical-generating plants or large ships, needed a new technology. That technology would be provided by the steam turbine.

Steam Turbine

Although the steam engine powered the initial stages of the Industrial Revolution, the technology proved to be inefficient for large-scale projects. The steam engine relied on the principle of steam pressure, but to power larger projects, steam engines had to be constructed on an impractical, massive scale. The next generation of steam technology needed to be smaller, lighter, and cheaper. The steam turbine had all those advantages. In the 1870s, English engineer Charles Parsons began building a rotary steam-turbine engine. Instead of using steam pressure, the steam turbine employed the kinetic energy of steam movement to push curved blades, often called wings, which were attached to a wheel. The moving steam turned the wheel and generated electricity. Turbines could be built smaller, lighter, and cheaper than steam engines. Parsons patented the technology in 1884, and in 1887, at Newcastle upon Tyne, England, the Forth Banks Power Station installed four Parsons engines, and the modern era of steam-turbine electricity generation was born. Throughout the industrial world, the steam turbine became the technology of choice in power generation.

 # Steel

Steel, a metal alloy of iron and carbon infinitely superior to iron, is harder and more durable and less likely to flake, bend, or break. Smelting iron ore into usable metal goes back thousands of years in human history, but after the fourteenth century, when smelting furnaces grew in size and increased volumes of air draft were used, the iron took on more of the carbon from charcoal and hardened into pig iron. The basic ingredients of pig iron were iron ore, coke, and limestone. Coke was burned to heat the furnace, and the burning coke gave off carbon monoxide, which combined chemically with the iron oxides in iron ore, resulting in metallic iron. In the process, the heated limestone combined with the iron ore's infusible silicate to produce fusible calcium silicate. Without limestone, iron silicate would form, corrupt the process, and weaken the final product.

During the mid-nineteenth century, two technological innovations gave rise to the modern steel industry. In 1851, William Kelly, an iron master in Kentucky, developed a process for converting pig iron into steel. He did so by blowing a concentrated current of air through the molten iron. Independently of Kelly, British inventor Henry Bessemer developed the technique and perfected it by 1856; it became known as the "Bessemer process." The second innovation was the open-hearth process of production, introduced to the United States in 1868 by Abraham Hewitt. Converting pig iron into steel required burning the excess carbon out of the iron, but the melting point of steel is approximately 2,500°F, which is difficult to achieve. Development of the open-hearth process made temperatures of up to 3,000°F possible. At these levels of heat, the carbon content of the iron is lowered and impurities of manganese, silicon, sulfur, and phosphorus are removed.

The Bessemer process and open-hearth furnaces appeared just when a mania of railroad construction created huge demand for steel. By 1873, a total of 115,000 tons of Bessemer rails were produced, but iron rails still dominated with more than 800,000 tons. These numbers gradually reversed themselves over the course of the next twenty years. Coal production doubled between 1855 and 1875, with bituminous coal becoming more important than anthracite coal. To feed the new steel furnaces, iron ore was needed in massive amounts. In 1866, government surveyors had discovered large ore deposits in northern Michigan and Minnesota, and by 1873, more than 1 million tons of ore a year were being shipped. Because of access to coal mines and iron-ore deposits, the home of the steel industry came to be concentrated in an area near the Great Lakes, from Pittsburgh in the east to Chicago in the west.

Because of the country's huge deposits of iron ore and coal and the ability to move large volumes of these commodities very efficiently by railroad or Great Lakes barges, the American steel industry soon became the most productive in the world. In 1850, British production of pig iron nearly quadrupled that of the United States—2.25 million tons annually to 630,000 tons. By 1870, the ratio had been reduced somewhat, with British mills putting out 5.96 million tons to America's 1.67 million tons. Ten years later, British production was only double that of the United States, and by 1890, the United States surpassed Great Britain in pig-iron production—9.2 million tons to 7.9 million tons. By 1915, American production swamped that of Great Britain—29.92 million tons to 8.79 million tons. Steel production followed a similar path. The total volume of steel ingots and castings produced in 1870 in Great Britain and the United States, respectively, was 220,000 tons and 40,000 tons. In 1890, it was 3.58 million tons for the British compared to 4.28 million tons for the Americans. In 1915, it was 8.55 million tons for Great Britain compared to 32.15 million tons in the United States. By 1895, the United States accounted for nearly half of the steel ingots and castings produced in the world, and its industry dwarfed that of Great Britain.

Stevens, Robert Livingston

Robert Livingston Stevens is widely regarded by American economic historians as the father of the modern railroad, and as such, he played a seminal role in the emergence of a national market. Stevens was born in Hoboken, New Jersey, on October 18, 1787. His father was a well-to-do engineer and businessman, and the younger Stevens was educated privately at home by tutors. Like his father, he developed a fascination for engineering. His first significant work came in maritime fields, where he helped build in 1808 the *Phoenix*, a steamboat that he sailed on the Delaware River. With his father, he built a steam ferry service across the East River between Hoboken and Manhattan. Stevens made the docking of ships in New York much easier by inventing special aprons to deal with changing tides and special docking slips. Historians also believe that Stevens was instrumental in the development of the clipper ships because of his new designs for shipping in general, which included stronger hulls, sleeker lines, and special trusses to reduce stress on ships' keels. During the War of 1812, Stevens worked on developing elongated, high-angle shells and tinkered with armored plating for ships.

In 1830, Stevens received a charter from the New Jersey state legislature for the Camden & Amboy Railroad and Transportation Company, becoming its president and chief engineer of the railroad. He then traveled extensively in Great Britain to learn more about railroad design. He developed the T-rail, a T-shaped track with fish joints and held in place by spikes driven into wooden ties, and he purchased a steam locomotive from Robert and George Stephenson and brought it to the United States. The locomotive, nicknamed the *John Bull*, went into operation on the Camden & Amboy in 1831. Stevens subsequently designed a number of other locomotives, all capable of hauling great freight loads and reaching unprecedented speeds. Stevens spent the last year of his life tinkering with the development of armored steamships driven by screw propellers. He died on April 20, 1856.

Sumner, William Graham. *See* Social Darwinism

Sweatshops

The term *sweatshop* appeared during the late nineteenth century to describe a work environment in which employees suffered from extremely low wages, unsafe working conditions, long hours, and job insecurity. The ready-to-wear clothing industry was characterized most often as a sweatshop industry because employees performed piecework (being paid not by the hour but by the number of items produced) in crowded, damp, and dark factories, where they hunched over sewing machines for fourteen- to sixteen-hour days. Sweatshop labor also characterized the cigar-rolling industry. Large numbers of immigrant workers, especially in New York, made for poor wages. Manufacturers used sweatshops because they kept labor costs to a minimum. The new immigrants from eastern and southern

Europe had few job skills, did not speak English, and were desperate for work. The needle and tobacco trades frequently hired immigrant women and children and paid them even less than what they paid male workers.

Conditions in the sweatshops prompted the formation of such labor unions as the Amalgamated Clothing Workers and the International Ladies' Garment Workers Union, which crusaded for better wages, safer working conditions, and shorter hours. In 1884, New York State passed the first legislation trying to ameliorate sweatshop conditions. The law prohibited the production of tobacco products in individual homes. It was not until the Great Depression of the 1930s and the advent of the New Deal that the federal government made a concerted effort to eliminate sweatshops.

Swift, Gustavus Franklin

Gustavus Swift was born on June 24, 1839, in Sandwich, Massachusetts. Soon after leaving high school, Swift began brokering cattle there and running a meat market. The business, though small-time, was successful and provided Swift the apprenticeship he needed to pursue even more success. Virtually all of the cattle he purchased came live by railroad car from Chicago and were slaughtered after arriving at eastern markets. Sensing a business opportunity, Swift moved to Chicago in 1875 and established Swift & Company. The opportunity was obvious: moving live cattle by rail was quite expensive. In order to keep the animals alive, they could not be crowded too closely together, which limited the maximum capacity of boxcar storage space. Since not all of the animal could be harvested and sold, moving cattle guaranteed wasted freight costs. Finally, scattering live animals all over eastern markets prevented the application of mass production to the slaughtering and butchering process.

Swift concluded that slaughtering and butchering the cattle in Chicago and then shipping them by refrigerated rail car would greatly eliminate waste. He hired engineers to build a railroad car cooled by ice and then constructed the cars at his own expense. The idea encountered bitter resistance from eastern butchers who worried that the application of mass-production techniques to meat packing would cost them their jobs, but Swift persisted and became one of the leading lights in the beef industry, an innovative entrepreneur who became fabulously wealthy. In 1902, he joined forces with the Armour Meat Packing Company to form the National Packing Company, which exercised near-monopolistic power over the industry. Critics accused Swift and Armour of creating the "Beef Trust" and artificially jacking up the cost of meat. Actually, Swift's innovations had lowered the real cost of beef to consumers. Nevertheless, the federal government filed an antitrust suit against the National Packing Company, and Swift countered. His case, *Swift & Co. v. United States*, failed when the Supreme Court in 1905 ruled in favor of the government. While the case was in litigation, Swift died on March 29, 1903.

Swift & Co. v. United States (1905)

The case of *Swift & Co. v. United States* was one of the most important in the history of antitrust action in the United States. During the course of the Industrial Revolution, as factory production multiplied geometrically, corporate size increased concurrently, until fewer and fewer firms controlled more and more of the marketplace. Progressive reformers, concerned about the ability of a few large corporations to control the market by eliminating competition, pushed for government regulation and breakup of monopolies, and the result was the **Sherman Antitrust Act of 1890**. At first, the federal courts interpreted the law very narrowly. In *United States v. E.C. Knight Co.* (1895), the U.S. Supreme Court made a sharp distinction between manufacturing and commerce and insisted that a manufacturing entity's intention to distribute its products across state lines did not open its activities up to federal regulation. That decision greatly limited congressional authority over manufacturing entities.

But *Swift & Co. v. United States* reversed that. The Justice Department had filed suit under the Sherman Antitrust Act to break up the so-called Beef Trust, a virtual monopoly enjoyed by Swift & Company and closely related firms over the beef-processing industry. Citing the *E.C. Knight* case, Swift & Company argued that the company's activities were intrastate, not interstate, and therefore were not subject to federal regulation. The case reached the Supreme Court and was decided unanimously on January 30, 1905. The Court reversed itself and concluded that although Swift's meat-processing plants were indeed intrastate, the company had nevertheless intended to wipe out all competition and establish a monopoly. Justice Oliver Wendell Holmes, in his majority opinion, established the idea of "stream of commerce"—the Beef Trust, by the way in which it processed and then shipped processed beef, had virtually created an interstate business that was under congressional jurisdiction. The federal government's case against the Beef Trust survived, and Swift & Company was broken up.

Sylvis, William. *See* National Labor Union

Taft, William Howard

A corporate attorney who made his living in business law, William Howard Taft ironically became the most enthusiastic trustbusting president in U.S. history. He was born in Cincinnati, Ohio, on September 15, 1857. Taft graduated from Yale in 1878 and the University of Cincinnati in 1880. He was very active in state Republican Party activities, and for a brief period he served as collector of internal revenue of Ohio. Taft practiced law privately between 1883 and 1887, and in 1887, he became a justice for the superior court of Ohio. In 1889, President Benjamin Harrison appointed Taft to be solicitor general of the United States. He became a federal circuit-court judge in 1892.

In 1900, after the United States had acquired the Philippine Islands as part of the Treaty of Paris of 1898 ending the Spanish-American War, President William McKinley needed an individual of great administrative ability to govern the new colony. Taft accepted appointment as head of the Philippines Commission and served as governor-general of the Philippines until 1904. In that year, Taft returned to the United States as secretary of war under President Theodore Roosevelt, who had a great impact on Taft, particularly in convincing Taft that the federal government had a key role in maintaining a competitive environment in the economy. Taft received the 1908 Republican nomination for president. With the force of Roosevelt's endorsement, Taft defeated Democratic candidate William Jennings Bryan 7,676,258 to 6,406,801.

Influenced by his association with corporate attorneys and Republican conservatives, Taft argued, "The lesson must be learned that there is only a limited zone within which legislation and governments can accomplish good." Unfortunately for big business, however, Taft believed that antitrust and railroad regulation fell within that zone. He considered the Sherman Antitrust Act "a good law." During his presidency, he initiated ninety antitrust suits, including cases against United States Steel and International Harvester. He supported the Mann-Elkins Act of 1910, which let the **Interstate Commerce Commission** suspend railroad rates it deemed unfair and brought telephone, telegraph, cable, and wireless companies under its authority. The law prohibited railroads from charging more for short hauls than for long ones and from purchasing competitive lines. Finally, against strong opposition from big business, Taft backed the Sixteenth Amendment legalizing a federal income tax, which Congress passed in July 1909 and the needed number of states had ratified by 1913. He also backed the Seventeenth Amendment to take the election of U.S. senators out of the hands of state legislatures in favor of popular election. It too was ratified in 1913.

But Taft had also managed to alienate progressive Republicans. In the election of 1908, Republicans had promised to reduce the Dingley Tariff of 1897, the highest in American history and a burden on working families. Taft called Congress into special session in March 1909 to cut rates, yet he managed the debate poorly, and it spun out of control. Lobbyists persuaded Congress to add 847 amendments, most of them calling for rate increases. Congress passed the Payne-Aldrich Tariff, and Taft signed it, but to a chorus of public indignation.

Former president Theodore Roosevelt was especially frustrated with Taft's leadership and in 1912 contested Taft's renomination for a second term. When he failed to get the nomination, Roosevelt launched a third-party candidacy for the presidency, casting Taft as a conservative politician dominated by business interests. The split in the Republican Party guaranteed that Democratic candidate Woodrow Wilson would come out on top, and he did. Taft then retired to private life. In 1921, President Warren Harding appointed Taft chief justice of the U.S. Supreme Court, a post Taft held until his death on March 8, 1930.

Taylor, Frederick Winslow. *See* Scientific Management

 ## Telegraph

The telegraph was a key technological development in the Industrial Revolution. In order for a national market to emerge, which could give rise to large **corporations** mass-producing products for sale throughout the country, an efficient transportation and communication system needed to be developed, and the telegraph was a critical step in providing such a system. Until the advent of the telegraph, information could be shipped no faster than the fastest transportation system because it had to be carried by horseback, wagon, **canal**, or **railroad**. The telegraph provided essentially instantaneous communication over long distances, which allowed businesses, especially railroads, to synchronize their operations, solve problems quickly, and prevent many problems from ever occurring.

The man who first achieved single-circuit telegraphs successful in long-distance transmission was **Samuel F. B. Morse**. He first developed a code system for transmitting messages in which each letter was characterized by a series of spaces and teeth. When letters were arranged on composing sticks and pulled past a contact, an electrical circuit opened at spaces and closed at teeth, sending letters and words as a series of dots and dashes. He had difficulty producing a working telegraph line until he learned that long-distance electromagnetic transmission was only possible through high-voltage energy supplied by powerful electromagnets and multiple battery cells connected together. By then employing distant electromagnets as relay devices, Morse could send messages over long distances. In 1843, Congress appropriated $30,000 to finance an experimental line, and Morse built it along the **Baltimore & Ohio Railroad** line between Baltimore and Washington, D.C. Morse's demonstration of the telegraph's ability was a success.

The telegraph's implications immediately dawned on railroads, newspapers, business, and the postal service. By September 1846, telegraph lines had been installed between New York, Boston, and Harrisburg, Pennsylvania, and from Washington, D.C., to Mobile, Alabama. Buffalo, New York, and Cleveland, Ohio, were added into the system in 1847, and New Orleans in 1848. In each case, the telegraph lines were strung along railroad lines. Between 1852 and 1860, another 23,000 miles of telegraph lines were constructed. In 1866, Congress passed the Pacific Telegraph Act to subsidize the construction of a transcontinental line. The Western Union Telegraph Company began commercial operations in 1856, and by 1866, it had emerged as the largest company in the telegraph business. That year the Atlantic telegraph cable provided instantaneous communication with Europe. When the transcontinental railroads were constructed in the 1870s, 1880s, and 1890s, the entire country became linked together in an efficient communication system.

Telephone

For all the success of the **telegraph**, it had a disadvantage in that messages had to be coded, decoded, and transmitted by technicians trained in the technology and familiar with Morse code. **Alexander Graham Bell**, a Scottish-born professor of vocal physiology at Boston University, began tinkering with a way to have speech vibrate a membrane, convert those vibrations into electric impulses, send them along a telegraph line, and then have another membrane reconvert the impulses back into speech. In 1875, with the help of Thomas Watson, a mechanic, Bell developed an iron-plate diaphragm. Sound waves from speech vibrated the diaphragm and triggered electromagnetic currents in copper induction coils connected to permanent magnets. The electromagnetic impulses were transmitted through wires, received by another diaphragm, and converted back into sound waves. Bell filed his patent application in 1876. Western Union, recognizing the threat that the telephone posed to the telegraph, contested the patent, and it took two years to settle the dispute.

The telephone's appeal to consumers was huge. In July 1877, there were 230 telephones operating in the United States. By 1879, there were more than 56,000 in use. Demand soon outpaced the existing technologies, and Bell Telephone went to the use of powerful, centralized systems of batteries and switchboards. By 1900, 1.4 million telephones were in use, with more than 6,000 companies supplying the service. Bell Telephone dominated the industry. The need for individuals and businesses to communicate instantaneously seemed insatiable, and by the 1930s, most American homes and businesses had telephones.

Tesla, Nikola

Nikola Tesla, one of the great inventors during the late stages of the Industrial Revolution, was born in Smiljan, Lika, Austria-Hungary, on July 9, 1856. At universities in Karlstadt and Graz, he studied mathematics and physics, and then attended the University of Prague to study philosophy. After finishing his education in Prague, Tesla made his home in Budapest and went to work as an inventor. His first practical invention was the telephone repeater, and he then discovered the principle of rotating magnetic fields. When he immigrated to the United States in 1884, Tesla went to work for George Westinghouse and Thomas Edison. He proved to be a prolific scientist, inventing the alternating-current motor in 1888 and the Tesla transformer in 1891. He was soon recognized around the world for his expertise in alternating electrical currents. Among Tesla's other inventions were the arc-lighting technology (1886), the alternating-current power-transmission system (1888), electrical conversion and distribution using oscillatory discharges (1889), high-frequency-current generators (1889), mechanical oscillators and generators that produced electrical oscillations (1894), and the high-potential magnifying transmitter (1897). In his later years, Tesla devoted his research to wireless communication systems. He died in New York City on January 7, 1943.

Textile Industry

Today, most historians recognize that the Industrial Revolution had its beginnings in the textile industry, where technological innovations made **mass production** a reality. Until the mid-eighteenth century, the textile industry was a home-based, hand-driven system in which cloth was spun on **spinning** wheels and woven by hand shuttles. But in the mid-1700s, such English inventors as John Hargreaves and Richard Arkwright developed a series of new technologies, such as the flying shuttle and the spinning jenny, which vastly improved productivity. These inventions, combined with Eli Whitney's cotton gin, which gave rise to huge increases in cotton production in the American South, set the stage for an unprecedented boom in the textile industry.

The boom began in Great Britain, where the primary technological innovations were made. In 1751, when English textile production was still home based and handcrafted, annual textile exports totaled £46,000, but they increased to £46.8 million by 1861. In the United States, the textile industry remained confined to traditional production systems until late in the nineteenth century. Thread and yarn were produced on traditional spinning wheels in factories that were little more than workhouses or at home through the putting-out system. In 1790, British immigrant Samuel Slater built a textile mill in Pawtucket, Rhode Island, using waterwheels to operate large spinning frames, which mass-produced a tightly woven fiber. Slater's power loom carded the cotton fibers for spinning and then spun the thread. He then distributed the thread to families who in their homes wove it into cloth. Slater eventually established other mills in Rhode Island and Massachusetts.

As a result of these technological innovations, the price of cotton clothing fell drastically. In 1813, after a trip to England, Francis Cabot Lowell of Boston designed a power loom, and with $400,000, he opened the first mill in the United States that integrated all of the processes of textile production under one roof. He located the mill in Waltham, Massachusetts, where a ten-foot waterfall provided free power. Lowell named his company the Boston Manufacturing Company. He later managed to raise large amounts of capital from investors known as the Boston Associates. In the mill, Lowell relied largely on unskilled female labor to run the machines. Most of the workers were single young women who lived in company dormitories and worked fourteen-hour days, six days a week.

With abundant supplies of raw cotton from the South, the American textile mills boomed. The center of the industry became the Connecticut River valley of Vermont, Massachusetts, and Connecticut; the Delaware River valley of Pennsylvania and New Jersey; and throughout Rhode

Island, eastern Massachusetts, and southern New Hampshire. By the time of the Civil War, American textiles were competing successfully in world markets with their British counterparts.

Tractor

The **internal-combustion engine** had a great variety of applications, and few of them were more important than in agriculture. Until then, farmers held plows pulled by horses, cattle, mules, and oxen, and the idea of a gasoline-driven plow, or tractor, quickly caught the imagination of inventors. In 1892, John Froelich, a blacksmith in Iowa, constructed the first tractor driven by an internal-combustion engine. Although well-to-do farmers rapidly adopted Froelich's invention, it did have serious disadvantages, none more significant than its weight. The heavy metal wheels bogged down and got stuck in wet ground. Benjamin Holt in 1904 came up with the answer: replacing heavy metal wheels with "caterpillar tracks," which distributed the weight load over a great area and reduced the problem of getting stuck in the mud. By the early 1900s in the United States, major **automobile** manufacturers were also building tractors, which had become very popular.

Transcontinental Railroad

At the conclusion of the Mexican-American War in 1848, the Treaty of Guadalupe Hidalgo shifted sovereignty over what is today California, Arizona, New Mexico, Nevada, Utah, and parts of Colorado from Mexico to the United States. The acquisition of vast amounts of western territory prompted interest in construction of a transcontinental railroad, and the discovery of gold in California and the rush of prospectors to the territory intensified the interest. Several proposals to construct a transcontinental line surfaced in Congress during the 1850s, but sectional differences between the North and the South always undermined them.

But after the secession of the Southern states in 1860–1861, Republicans dominated Congress, and during the **Civil War**, two Pacific Railway Acts were passed providing for federal subsidies for the construction of a transcontinental line. As soon as the war was over, the **Union Pacific Railroad** began extending its lines west, and the **Central Pacific Railroad** began laying track from San Francisco heading east. The two lines met at Promontory Summit in Utah on May 10, 1869, linking San Francisco with St. Louis and the rest of the eastern seaboard. In 1883, construction was completed on the Northern Pacific Railway, which linked Lake Superior in Minnesota with Puget Sound in what is today Washington State. By 1884, construction on the Atchison, Topeka, and Santa Fe Railroad linked Kansas and Colorado with Texas and Oklahoma and then branched out to Albuquerque, Denver, Los Angeles, and San Francisco. By 1888, the Great Northern Railway connected Minneapolis and Duluth, Minnesota, with Seattle and Vancouver. Finally, by 1900, the Southern Pacific Railroad stretched from Portland, Oregon, to Los Angeles, California, and then east to New Orleans.

Construction of the transcontinental railroads completed dreams of a truly national market in the United States. The Pacific Rim, with its oceanic contacts with Asia, now had efficient access to markets in the eastern United States. Raw materials from the western states and territories began flowing east, and finished products now made their way west in increasing volumes.

Triangle Shirtwaist Fire

More than any other event in the history of the Industrial Revolution, the Triangle Shirtwaist fire galvanized the labor movement and triggered government intervention into labor-management issues. It started innocently enough. On Saturday, March 25, 1911, at 4:45 p.m., a fire broke out at the Triangle Shirtwaist Company, which occupied the top three floors of the ten-floor Asch Building at Washington and Green streets in Manhattan. It was a small fire that few of the fi500 factory workers—most of them young, immigrant Jewish women—even noticed.

In fact, anyone who had considered the threat posed by the fire might have concluded that Triangle Shirtwaist was a safe place, at least on paper. The factory, owners Max Blanck and Isaac Harris insisted, was fireproof. It was not a rickety edifice that an odd spark could destroy; it had fireproof walls, fireproof floors, and fireproof furniture. It had multiple staircases, multiple fire escapes, and plenty of other safety features. Leaders of the Women's Trade Union League (WTUL) disagreed, saying that the factory was dangerous; a wide gulf separated safety regulations and actual conditions. They documented a litany of abuses—rusted windows, locked doors, obstructed fire escapes, and piles of flammable cloth.

The fire confirmed the worst fears of the WTUL. Workers tried to extinguish the blaze, but it spread, jumping from one pile of debris to the next, growing larger and more deadly. Workers rushed for elevators and stairwells. But few elevators worked, and, to keep workers from wandering about the plant, most hallway doors were locked. Hundreds were trapped.

After forcing open windows that had been rusted shut, scores of women clambered down the fire escape, but it collapsed, spilling them to their deaths. Others jumped from window ledges toward nets firemen held floors below. But as the *New York Times* noted, "The catapult force that the bodies gathered in the long plunges made the nets utterly without avail. [They] . . . tore the nets from the grasp of the holders, and bodies struck the sidewalks and lay just as they fell. Some of the bodies ripped big holes through life nets."

Altogether, 146 workers died pointless deaths. Fire codes had been ignored—doors opened in rather than out and were often locked, and the building had too few staircases and elevators and no sprinklers. Blanck and Harris were acquitted of manslaughter, but the negligence was not forgotten. A traumatized Jewish community refused to allow so many mothers, wives, and daughters to die in silence. On a rainy April day, more than 120,000 attended a funeral march that had two purposes: to mourn the dead and to organize workers. Only a strong union, the WTUL announced, could prevent such disasters. At one rally, Rose Schneiderman, a union organizer, told a crowd that the only thing that can save the working people is "a strong working-class movement." Citizens listened, and workers heard. The Triangle Shirtwaist fire increased union membership, reinforced convictions that only government could deal with the nation's malaise, and accelerated the drive for women's right to vote.

Trust

During the late nineteenth and early twentieth centuries, a trust was a legal entity designed to assist in the establishment of a **monopoly** in a particular market. In a trust arrangement, stockholders trade with a board of trustees a controlling interest in their company in return for trust certificates. Competing companies do the same, and the board of trustees then makes corporate decisions for all of them with the aim of creating monopolistic conditions. The **Standard Oil Company** first introduced the concept in 1882, and others soon followed. The Sugar Refineries Company formed the "Sugar Trust" in 1884. The Distillers' and Cattle Feeders' Trust, or "Whiskey Trust," appeared in 1887. Congress reacted to the trust arrangement with the **Sherman Antitrust Act of 1890**, which outlawed monopolies in manufacturing industries. Reformers eventually identified as well a "Beef Trust," a "Money Trust," and a "**Railroad Trust**," all of which eventually became objects of attack for the **antitrust** movement.

Turner, Frederick Jackson. *See* Frontier Thesis

Turnpike

During the late eighteenth and early nineteenth centuries, American cities along the Atlantic seaboard were connected only by the most rudimentary roads, which became all but impassable during inclement weather. The Industrial Revolution depended upon the development of a reliable transportation system that would allow the efficient shipment of goods. Without decent roads, freight rates would have been so high as to condemn the economy to a future of local transactions only.

The first stage in the development of a modern economy in the United States is known today as the "turnpike era," a boom in road construction. Private individuals first organized into groups to finance construction of turnpikes, or toll roads. During the 1790s, a series of turnpikes opened that linked eastern communities with frontier settlements. In 1790, construction began on the first turnpike, from Philadelphia to Lancaster, Pennsylvania, a distance of sixty-six miles. It proved to be a financial success and inspired other projects around the country. The Knoxville Road and the Wilderness Road, both of which were completed in 1795, opened up the Ohio River valley to settlement. The Old Walton Road, also completed in 1795, linked Knoxville and Nashville, Tennessee. Highways soon proliferated in other regions of the country as well, allowing farmers to transcend a subsistence lifestyle by shipping their produce to distant markets. By 1810, more than 300 turnpike companies had been chartered in the United States.

The second stage of the turnpike era involved federal government subsidies for construction of the highways. Secretary of the Treasury Albert Gallatin suggested in 1804 the need for federal capital to accelerate highway development, and although this prompted a vigorous debate over the role of the federal government in American life and the constitutionality of federally financed **internal improvements**, Congress nevertheless authorized in 1806 the construction of what became known as the **Cumberland Road**, also called the Old National Road. The 130-mile stretch of road, from Baltimore, Maryland to Wheeling, Virginia, was not completed until 1818, but it was then extended to Zanesville, Columbus, and Springfield, Ohio; Terre Haute, Indiana; and Vandalia, Illinois.

The so-called turnpike era never completely ended, because construction of roads and highways remains a key program of state and federal governments. But in the 1820s and 1830s, the construction of turnpikes was superseded by the construction of **canals**, and then in the 1840s and 1850s by the construction of **railroads**. In early U.S. history, the turnpike-building boom was the initial stage in the creation of a national market and therefore a critical preliminary stage in the development of the Industrial Revolution.

Typewriter

Invention of the typewriter revolutionized office work in the United States just when the Industrial Revolution had given rise to large business **corporations** and large government bureaucracies. At its most basic level, the typewriter was a machine for printing or impressing characters on paper. As the need for increased speed in the preparation of legal and business documents grew, various inventors tried to develop the technology. In 1814, British inventor Henry Mill took out a patent on a typewriter, and fifteen years later, American inventor William Burt received a patent on a similar machine. But neither of the inventions were simple enough or reliable enough for wide distribution. In 1843, American inventor Charles Thurber came up with a slightly improved model.

In 1868, three American inventors—Christopher Sholes, Carlos Glidden, and Samuel Soulé—put their minds to the task. Sholes was a journalist with the *Milwaukee News* and knew that an invention that made faster writing possible would attract great interest. One problem with existing typewriters, he noticed, was that typists would go too fast and the keys would jam. Sholes then redesigned the keyboard, creating the seemingly irrational "qwerty" system in which typists had to reach greater distances to type frequently occurring letter sequences. This slowed them down and prevented most jamming. Today, that design still dominates keyboards even though electric typewriters and computers have made it an anachronism. Sholes patented a machine two years later and contracted with the E. Remington & Sons Company of Ilion, New York, to manufacture the "typewriter." Remington had been in the business of manufacturing **sewing machines** and bicycles. In September 1873, the first Remington typewriter came off the production line. It proved immediately successful, and Remington soon spun off a separate corporation, Remington Typewriter Company, that eventually pioneered the business of office machines.

E. Remington & Sons, a gun manufacturer, began producing typewriters like this 1873 model, based upon the invention of printer Christopher Latham Sholes. (Time & Life Pictures/Getty Images)

The typewriter soon became known simply as a "Remington." Operators placed a piece of paper in a carriage; the paper was held in place between a rubber platen and a smaller rubber cylinder. The platen and rubber cylinder were parallel to one another. A spring moved the carriage from right to left as each letter was typed. At the end of a line, the operator manually pushed a lever that returned the carriage all the way to the right. At the same time, a ratchet and pawl revolved the platen the height of one line so that a new line could be typed. Between the platen and the keys was an inked cloth ribbon. When the operator struck one letter on a keyboard, it elevated a type bar with the corresponding letter. The various type bars were arranged in a circular setting. The first Remingtons typed only capital letters, but in 1878, Remington invented the carriage shift that allowed for typing upper- and lowercase letters. This also allowed the addition of numbers and other symbols. Early in the 1880s, engineering changes allowed the writer to see the letters strike the ink cloth and paper. The Remington typewriter of the 1870s and 1880s became the prototype for almost all typewriters for nearly a century. The advent of the typewriter revolutionized office work and greatly facilitated the transmission of information in a society that was increasingly bureaucratic. The days of hand copying of documents ended forever with the invention of the typewriter.

U

Union Pacific Railroad

During the years of the Industrial Revolution, the Union Pacific was one of the nation's best-known **railroads** and a key line in creating a truly national market in the United States. Congress passed the Pacific Railway Acts of 1862 and 1864, giving the Union Pacific Railroad a charter and 11 million acres of public-domain land to be used for constructing a **transcontinental railroad** from Omaha, Nebraska, to San Francisco, California. California businessmen then secured a congressional charter to establish the **Central Pacific Railroad** and build a transcontinental railroad east from San Francisco. A race was on, and the two lines met at Promontory Summit, Utah, on May 10, 1869, when a pure-gold spike was driven into the ground to signify the completion of the country's first transcontinental railroad.

Construction of the transcontinental railroad produced the greatest political scandal of the nineteenth century. General Grenville Dodge supervised the construction and established a construction company known as the Crédit Mobilier to handle the project. Because Congress had agreed to huge subsidies for every mile of track construction, a large volume of money was available, and Crédit Mobilier soon became involved in kickbacks and multiple acts of official corruption, bringing in subcontractors in return for under-the-table cash payments. The scandal wrecked the presidential administration of Ulysses S. Grant. Shortly thereafter, the **panic of 1873** sent the Union Pacific into a tailspin; only the intervention of financier **Jay Gould** saved the company from bankruptcy. Gould even managed to expand the Union Pacific trunk lines throughout Utah, Colorado, and Wyoming. He also added the Kansas Pacific Railroad to the Union Pacific.

The Union Pacific fell on hard times again in the 1890s when it went into receivership. It was finally reorganized in 1898 by **E. H. Harriman**, who then brought the Southern Pacific Railroad under Union Pacific control. The Union Pacific also acquired the Los Angeles & Salt Lake Railroad in 1902, which gave it access to Southern California markets. Harriman made the Union Pacific part of his Northern Securities Corporation until 1904, when the federal government's **antitrust** suit against the **holding company** succeeded.

United Mine Workers

The United Mine Workers was the first successful union among **mass-production** workers in the history of the Industrial Revolution. During the 1880s, a variety of labor unions appeared in the **coal**-mining industry, including the Amalgamated Association of Miners, the National Federation of Miners and Mine Laborers, and the National Progressive Union of Miners and Mine Laborers. In 1890, the **American Federation of Labor** reorganized them into the United Mine Workers (UMW), which claimed a membership of more than 100,000 workers. The union survived for only three years, all but dissolving during the **depression of 1893** when one of its strikes failed miserably. By 1895, its membership had fallen to only 10,000 members.

But the UMW then experienced a revival, especially when its 1897 strike against coal operators had some success in improving wages and working conditions. By 1898, its membership exceeded 250,000 workers, and John Mitchell led the union. In 1902, Mitchell proclaimed a nationwide coal strike, demanding an eight-hour workday and higher wages. The coal operators proved to be recalcitrant, even when President **Theodore Roosevelt** tried to arbitrate the strike. It was not until the president threatened to call in federal troops to seize the mines that owners decided to give in to some of the UMW demands. By 1920, when John L. Lewis assumed the presidency, the UMW claimed a membership of more than 300,000 workers.

United States Steel Corporation

The United States Steel Corporation was the first $1-billion company in the history of the Industrial Revolution. In 1901, financier **J. P. Morgan** engineered a merger of the Carnegie Steel Company, the Federal Steel Company, and six other **steel** companies, bringing them together under one board of directors headed by **Elbert H. Gary** of Chicago. The United States Steel Corporation was capitalized at over $1 billion and was the largest steel company in the world. Gary then proceeded to vertically integrate the company, acquiring its own sources for all the raw materials that go into the manufacture of steel. In 1907, United States Steel became even bigger by acquiring the Tennessee Coal and Iron Company, a merger President **Theodore Roosevelt** approved in spite of his antitrust sympathies. Even today, United States Steel, now known as USX Corporation, remains the giant in the industry.

United States v. E. C. Knight Company (1895)

The U.S. Supreme Court decision in *United States v. E. C. Knight Company* restricted the power of Congress to regulate corporations. In 1890, Congress had passed the **Sherman Antitrust Act** outlawing corporate monopolies. Early in 1892, the American Sugar Refining Company purchased all of the outstanding stock of its primary competitors, essentially establishing a monopoly on the processing of refined sugar. The Justice Department filed a lawsuit to suppress the corporate monopoly. Company officials appealed the antitrust suit, and a federal district court dismissed the government's case. The Justice Department then appealed the decision to the U.S. Supreme Court, which heard the case in October 1894 and decided it by an 8–1 vote on January 21, 1895. The arguments revolved around the question of congressional authority over interstate commerce and whether a manufacturing monopoly fell under the jurisdiction of the Sherman Antitrust Act. The real issue, however, was the extent to which a manufacturing entity functioned within the context of interstate commerce. Did the mere act of distributing a finished product across state lines subject it to congressional scrutiny under the commerce clause of the U.S. Constitution? In its decision, the U.S. Supreme Court agreed with the lower court's dismissal of the government's case, making a sharp distinction between manufacturing and commerce and insisting that a manufacturing entity's intention to distribute its products across state lines did not open its activities up to federal regulation. Otherwise, the Court concluded, Congress would enjoy regulatory jurisdiction over every element of a modern economy. *United States v. E. C. Knight Company* had a dampening effect on the ability of the federal government to preserve a competitive economy.

V

Vanderbilt, Cornelius

A key factor in ensuring that the Industrial Revolution could take off and be sustained in its course was the development of a transportation **infrastructure** capable of moving people and products efficiently. Those individuals prescient enough to see the opportunities in transportation positioned themselves to become multimillionaires, and none was more influential in that regard than Cornelius Vanderbilt. He was born on Staten Island, New York City, on May 27, 1794, and quit school at the age of eleven to go to work. Blessed with an enterprising mind and a gift for seeing opportunities, Vanderbilt started his own business at the age of sixteen, purchasing a small boat and ferrying people and goods from Staten Island to Manhattan. When the War of 1812 erupted, he secured a contract from the U.S. government to supply provisions to the forts in New York harbor. Vanderbilt then built a schooner to run passengers and supplies back and forth across Long Island Sound. From 1818 to 1829, Vanderbilt captained a supply ship plying the coast between New York, Boston, and New Brunswick.

Vanderbilt made his fortune, however, with steamboat operations along the Hudson River, ferrying freight and passengers between New York City and New Jersey and between New York City and Albany, New York. By 1834, he had accumulated more than $500,000, which he invested in transportation enterprises. When gold was discovered in California in 1848 and the rush of settlers and miners began, Vanderbilt negotiated and received a charter from the government of Nicaragua to operate a service taking passengers from the Caribbean side of the country to the Pacific side. Vanderbilt established the Accessory Transit Company to run the service, and using boats and wagons, he could deliver passengers from coast to coast in two days less than the isthmus route across Panama. In 1855, Vanderbilt sold the Accessory Transit Company and invested in shipping lines crossing the Atlantic Ocean.

After the **Civil War**, Vanderbilt branched out into **railroads**, which vastly increased his personal wealth. He first secured control of the New York & Harlem Railroad, added the Hudson River Railroad, and acquired control of the **New York Central Railroad**, which became one of the most important roads in the country. When Vanderbilt died in New York City on January 4, 1877, he was worth more than $100 million and was considered the wealthiest man in America.

Veblen, Thorstein

During the nineteenth and early twentieth centuries, the Industrial Revolution developed in an intellectual and scientific atmosphere dominated by classical economic theory. Thorstein Veblen, a brilliant economist and social scientist, was one of the first Americans to call economic orthodoxy into question, and in doing so, he set the stage for vigorous attacks on businessmen, the consumer culture, and **laissez-faire** theories. Veblen's economic ideas laid a foundation for **Progressive** reform and the New Deal in the twentieth century.

Born in Wisconsin to Norwegian immigrant parents in 1857 and raised in Wisconsin, Veblen at first planned a career in the Lutheran ministry, but he was too much of a skeptic and intellectual iconoclast to tolerate a seminary education. He ended up at Johns Hopkins University studying philosophy, and there his intellect flowered under the nurturing of a more tolerant faculty. Veblen went on to Yale for a doctorate, which he finished in 1884. Abrasive and an avowed agnostic, he turned off most people and could not get a college teaching job for years after he returned home to Wisconsin to live with his parents.

Veblen returned to academic life in 1891 when he studied economics at Cornell University, but after a year he accepted a faculty post at the University of Chicago. He remained there for fourteen years before moving to Stanford University for a three-year

As an economist and social critic, Thorstein Veblen was one of the leading figures in the revolt against nineteenth-century social thought in the United States. (Carleton College Archives)

stint. Although his intellect was powerful and incisive, his irascible temperament and boring lectures made him quite unpopular in academe.

But few denied the power and insight of Veblen's fertile mind. In 1899, he wrote *The Theory of the Leisure Class*, which established the foundation of his theory of modern society. According to Veblen, human beings had embedded in their natures a need to engage in purposeful activity and an intense aversion to futile activities. Veblen labeled that inclination the *instinct of workmanship*, and the accumulation of wealth by an individual is a worthy pursuit since it provides visible proof of success.

"In order to gain and to hold the esteem of men, it is not sufficient merely to possess wealth or power. The wealth or power must be put in evidence, for esteem is awarded only on evidence," Veblen wrote. The best evidence of his success a wealthy man can offer is what Veblen termed *conspicuous leisure*, or avoiding useful work in favor of useless activities. Even better than "conspicuous leisure" for displaying wealth, according to Veblen, was "conspicuous consumption." In the long run, such a condition hurt society because it diverted talented people from useful, productive activities. For society as a whole, the drive for conspicuous consumption had affected most forms of human endeavor, including government, education, art, religion, and family relations.

In other books—*The Theory of Business Enterprise* (1904), *The Instinct of Workmanship* (1914), and *Absentee Ownership and Business Enterprise in Recent Times* (1923)—Veblen distinguished clearly between industry and business. Industry for Veblen was a positive social force because it generated work and productivity. Businessmen, on the other hand, possessed an interest only in making money, not necessarily in producing anything. Too often, Veblen claimed, they were given to fraud and useless manipulations of economic forces in order to make more money, which then led to more conspicuous consumption. As a result of their activities, which were in the long term useless, the economy actually became less productive.

Veblen's ideas were quite controversial, particularly his book, *Engineers and the Price System* (1921), which proposed that a huge government bureaucracy of economic engineers assume control over the economy and eliminate all wasteful and fraudulent activities. Most economists took serious exception to such notions, but the rest of Veblen's thinking in the long run stimulated a vigorous debate among businessmen, political reformers, and economists. His most important contribution to modern economic thinking was the proof he offered that the economy was not a self-regulating mechanism operating according to predictable, rational natural laws. Instead, Veblen argued, and most economists came to agree, the economy was a man-made institution subject to irrational individual and group behaviors. When Thorstein Veblen died on August 3, 1929, he was widely considered to be the most important economic thinker in U.S. history.

Vertical Integration

In order to secure a greater market share by ruthlessly cutting costs, industrial entrepreneurs in the late nineteenth and early twentieth centuries turned to an organizational technique known as "vertical integration." Vertical integration involved eliminating middle men by acquiring complete control over the natural resources needed to manufacture products, the transportation systems needed to deliver raw materials to factories and from factories to wholesale and retail outlets, and, where possible, the wholesale and retail outlets themselves. Nobody did it better than **John D. Rockefeller**. After acquiring a near monopoly over petroleum refining in the United States, Rockefeller's Standard Oil Company of New Jersey vertically integrated by signing oil leases to guarantee its reserves; acquiring drilling equipment to bring the oil to the surface; adding railroads, ships, and pipelines to deliver crude oil to refineries and from refineries to Rockefeller-owned wholesalers; and establishing retail outlets to market diesel, gasoline, lubricants, and kerosene.

Vulcanization

Charles Goodyear (1800–1860) is the man who discovered what he called the **vulcanization** of rubber and launched one of the Industrial Revolution's most influential new technologies. His father owned a hardware business, and after finishing school, Charles went to work for him. The younger Goodyear became interested in the industrial possibilities of the so-called India rubber and read everything he could on the topic. Because of rubber's elastic and waterproof qualities, it seemed to have an infinite number of industrial applications. The problem was the impact of high temperatures on rubber, which made it melt and lose its shape, and very low temperatures, which made it brittle and subject to breaking up under pressure.

Goodyear began tinkering with the problem and trying to "cure" rubber, but he had little success for more than fifteen years. In 1837, however, he purchased the rights to Nathaniel Hayward's discoveries of combining rubber and sulfur and soon patented a process for preventing rubber from melting at high temperatures and crumbling at low temperatures. Along with Hayward, Goodyear had learned that adding sulfur to rubber gave it more temperature-resistance qualities. Goodyear tinkered with the process and then made an accidental discovery. One evening in 1839 he inadvertently dropped a mixture of rubber and sulfur onto a burning stove, and the next morning he realized that the rubber had acquired a new firmness and elasticity while retaining its water resistance. What Goodyear eventually learned from what he called the vulcanization process was that a rubber-sulfur mixture, heated to between 120°C and 160°C, became even tougher; more resistant to water, low temperatures, and high temperatures; and insoluble in most typical solvents of the day. In 1844, he was awarded a patent by the U.S. government.

Goodyear tried to capitalize on his discoveries, but he proved to be a poor businessman and failed to secure patents in France and Great Britain, which led to gross violations of his **intellectual property rights** and pirating of his discovery. The American, British, and French companies he established to manufacture rubber all went bankrupt, and in 1856 Goodyear was incarcerated in debtors' prison in France. He died penniless in New York City on July 1, 1860.

W

Wabash, St. Louis & Pacific Railroad Co. v. Illinois (1886)

Ever since the 1850s, the U.S. Supreme Court had held that state legislatures could impose "indirect" but not "direct" burdens on interstate commerce. The Court agreed, for example, that state legislatures could impose safety regulations on railroads operating within state boundaries, and it identified such regulations as an "indirect" burden. But in 1885, the Illinois legislature empowered a state commission to regulate railroad freight rates within the state. The Wabash, St. Louis & Pacific Railroad Company appealed the legislation, arguing that if every state imposed its own regulatory burden, interstate commerce would be seriously compromised. The railway insisted that only Congress had such authority. The case of *Wabash, St. Louis & Pacific Railroad Co.* reached the Supreme Court, where it was argued on April 14–15, 1886. The justices, by a vote of 6–3, rendered their decision on October 25, 1886. They found against the state of Illinois and in favor of the railroad, ruling that state regulation of railroad rates in lines shipping goods across state lines violated the commerce clause of the U.S. Constitution and impinged on Congress's exclusive power over interstate commerce.

The *Wabash* case was a landmark in the history of the Industrial Revolution. The rise of a national market and large, national and international **corporations** created new concerns about consumers, farmers, workers, and small businesses, many of whom wanted to employ government to eliminate serious corporate abuses. But the *Wabash* case essentially shifted the major burden of regulation from the states to the federal government. Congress responded in 1887 by passing the Interstate Commerce Act and creating the **Interstate Commerce Commission** to regulate the railroads. The advent of the modern federal administrative state had begun.

Waltham System

During the last decades of the eighteenth century, a variety of small-scale manufacturing operations appeared in the United States, particularly in the New England states, and the **textile industry** took root there. **Samuel Slater**, an immigrant from England, in 1790 established a cotton textile mill in Pawtucket, Rhode Island, employing technologies he had learned in Great Britain. He had managed to smuggle out of England the textile machinery designs and later helped develop a power loom. Soon a textile industry emerged in New England that was patterned after the English system, with whole families laboring at barely subsistence wage levels. Even children worked full days and were unable to attend school. Some mill owners claimed that they preferred children because their small hands and nimble fingers did better work. The real reason was that the owners could get away with paying children less.

But a new labor system emerged in Lowell, Massachusetts. It was known as the Waltham System and was designed by Nathan Appleton and the Boston Associates, a group of textile industry investors. Wanting to develop an ample source of labor and run mills that did not replicate the squalid conditions in other factories, Appleton recruited young women from local farms. The women lived in clean, company-owned boardinghouses and were watched over by matronly chaperones. They were paid decent wages in cash, could attend school, and published their own magazine, *Lowell Offering*. Mill owners advertised the Waltham System as "industrialism with a human face." Eventually, however, the Waltham System proved to be too expensive in terms of its labor costs. Mill owners could not support the women workers in such a way and still compete with factories employing **child labor**. Gradually, the Waltham System degenerated into an impersonal, regimented pattern resembling other industrial labor systems.

Ward, Aaron Montgomery

Aaron Montgomery Ward is considered by historians of the Industrial Revolution to be one of the founders of the modern retailing industry. The creation of a national market and the advent of **mass-production** techniques made possible a consumer culture in which social life in America revolved largely around the purchase of goods. Manufacturers were capable of producing vast amounts of goods, but these goods also had to be distributed efficiently, on a large scale, to consumers living in a wide variety of circumstances. Ward achieved this.

Ward was born in Chatham, New Jersey, on February 17, 1844, but was raised in Niles, Michigan. He quit school at the age of fourteen for work in a barrel-stave factory, but soon changed jobs for employment in a brickyard. Ambitious and convinced that the brickyard was a dead end for him, he took a job in a general store in St. Joseph, Michigan, and found that he loved merchandising. In 1865, Ward moved to Chicago to work for Marshall Field's mercantile business. The job at Marshall Field's gave him experience in the hub of the business, but he wanted some field experience as well, so he took a job as a traveling salesman, riding the rails throughout the West selling a variety of products for a dry-goods warehouse. It soon became obvious to him that isolated farmers needed a more reliable and competitive source to secure finished goods than the local general store, which essentially exercised a retail **monopoly**.

Ward decided that a mail-order business in which manufacturers sold goods for cash directly to rural consumers could fill a need. In 1872, he printed and mailed a single-page product and price list. It was an immediate hit, with orders pouring in from the hinterland. His next printing was an eight-page pamphlet, and he followed that up with a seventy-two page catalog complete with illustrations. Ward then entered into an agreement with the National Grange to give discounts to farmers, and the business boomed. The 1884 catalog stretched to 240 pages and advertised more than 10,000 products. Sales topped $1 million in 1888, and when Ward died on December 7, 1913, annual sales exceeded $40 million. Ward had pioneered a form of direct marketing that would not find a true successor until Internet buying in the 1990s.

Washington, Booker T. "Atlanta Compromise Speech" (1895)

African American educator and reformer Booker T. Washington's September 18, 1895 speech at the Cotton States and International Exposition in Atlanta outlined his advocacy of blacks improving their social status through obtaining vocational skills and education, rather than through civil rights reform. Washington's address would come to be known as the "Atlanta Compromise" because of its tone of accommodation in race relations during the post–Reconstruction era. Washington suggested blacks could rise in prosperity, and contribute to the New South, by helping as laborers in the growth of industry in the region. While his position was favored among white industrialists in the North and the South, civil rights reformers, particularly W. E. B. Dubois, took issue with Washington's dismissal of political and social reform.

Westinghouse, George

George Westinghouse, an inventor and leading figure in developing the power systems to accelerate the Industrial Revolution, was born in

Central Bridge, New York, on October 6, 1846. He was fourteen years old when the **Civil War** commenced, and he joined the Union army a year later. Westinghouse served for the duration of the war as a naval engineer and then returned home to work in his father's machine shop. He was a mechanical genius and in just two years had patented a rotary **steam engine**, a piece of equipment to replace derailed **railroad** cars on the track, and a railroad frog. His greatest early invention, however, and the one that earned him instant fame, was his 1868 compressed-air brake for railroads. In 1866, he had almost been killed in a railroad accident, and he decided that a market existed for improved braking systems. In 1868, Westinghouse invented an air brake based on compressed-air technology. In September of that year, he founded the Westinghouse Air Brake Company to manufacture the devices, which eventually came to be used on most of the world's railroads. He then turned his attention to other railroad inventions, including railroad signals and interlocking switches. Early in the 1880s, Westinghouse patented a system for safely shipping natural gas over long distances.

But his perfection of alternating-current **electricity** was his greatest contribution to the Industrial Revolution. Direct current could only be transmitted a few miles over wire, but alternating current, Westinghouse perceived, could be distributed far more widely. In 1884, he founded the Westinghouse Electric Company to develop the technology. He came into direct conflict with **Thomas Edison**, whose inventions were built on direct-current systems, but Westinghouse's alternating current eventually prevailed. Westinghouse teamed up with **Nikola Tesla**, the great immigrant inventor, and along with other technicians developed alternating-current motors, machines for distributing high-tension current, and vast municipal lighting systems employing the **hydroelectric power** generated at Niagara Falls. Westinghouse Electric eventually became a key manufacturer of electrical engines and appliances of every type and, along with **General Electric Corporation**, dominated the industry. George Westinghouse eventually patented more than 400 inventions. By the time of his death on March 12, 1914, Westinghouse's various enterprises were valued at more than $170 million, and he employed more than 50,000 workers.

Whitney, Eli

Eli Whitney, an inventor, manufacturer, and businessman, exercised great influence in the implementation of the Industrial Revolution in the United States. He was born in Westborough, Massachusetts, on December 8, 1765. Even as a child he displayed talents that would help him make his mark on the American economy and on American history, constructing a workshop on the family farm and during the American Revolution, while he was still in his young teens, launching a successful business manufacturing nails, hinges, and metal implements, all of which were in short supply during the war years. After the war, Whitney tried to expand the business, but it fell on hard times, and he decided to complete his education, which had been interrupted when he had quit school at the age of twelve. In 1792, Whitney graduated from Yale.

He headed south to Savannah, Georgia, to work as a tutor but soon became intrigued with the great problem faced by cotton planters. The short-staple cotton they produced was loaded with green seeds embedded into the balls of fiber. Before the cotton could be processed, the seeds had to be removed, a labor-intensive process that had to be done by hand, since the seeds clung tightly to the fiber. By 1793, Whitney had a working model of what he called the "cotton gin"—a mechanical device composed of a rotating metal cylinder with teeth—which could be operated by hand or by horsepower. Whitney moved back to New Haven, Connecticut, filed a patent on his new invention in 1794, and went into business manufacturing cotton gins. The business proved to be a financial disaster, primarily because patent law, although already on the books after passage of the first patent legislation in 1790, was unenforceable. Manufacturers throughout the North and South jumped into the gin-making business, and Whitney profited only slightly. One successful lawsuit, which took thirteen years to make its way through the legal system, eventually yielded him a modest settlement.

In 1798, with the Napoleonic Wars well under way in Europe, Whitney went into the gun-manufacturing business, obtaining from the U.S. government a contract to deliver 10,000 muskets. It was an audacious project, since at the time, muskets were manufactured by hand, with each component uniquely hand tooled and hand assembled. The process was extremely laborious, time-consuming, and expensive, and the idea of producing 10,000 muskets proved to be quite daunting. Whitney put his fertile mind to work and decided to develop a technique for speeding up the production process. He concluded that the only way to make the contract profitable was to employ power-driven machine tools to mass-produce each component of a musket and to use such narrow tolerances that the components would be interchangeable. For example, the trigger fitting one musket would be interchangeable with the trigger mechanism on another. The idea of interchangeable parts made the process of assembling muskets and repairing them much simpler, since replacement parts did not have to be retooled by hand grinding or hand filing.

They did not deliver the 10,000 muskets until 1809, nine years late according to the terms of his contract, but his so-called uniformity system of industrial fabrication—power-driven **mass production** of interchangeable parts—became the model for industrial production in the United States. Other individuals were experimenting with such production techniques in the early 1800s, but Whitney deserves much of the credit for revolutionizing manufacturing processes. He died in New Haven, Connecticut, on January 8, 1825.

Wilson, Thomas Woodrow

Woodrow Wilson was elected president at the height of the **Progressive movement**, and as a Democrat who believed in the merits of a free, competitive economy, he became perhaps the most prominent figure, until Franklin D. Roosevelt and the advent of the New Deal, in the creation of a modern political economy. One of the most conspicuous and wide-reaching effects of the Industrial Revolution was the rise of big government, especially at the federal level. As **corporations** grew larger and more powerful and operated in national and international markets, questions arose about the survival of competition in the economy and whether such large companies could be trusted to remember consumer interests as well as their profit margins. The fear of **monopoly** led to the **antitrust** movement and to demands that the federal government assume the role of monopoly breaker and protector of the public interest.

Wilson was born in Staunton, Virginia, on December 28, 1856. His father was a Presbyterian minister, and the younger Wilson grew up with devout religious beliefs that shaped his character and his life. In 1879, he graduated from Princeton (then known as the College of New Jersey) and matriculated at the University of Virginia, where he earned a law degree. But Wilson was more of an academic than a lawyer, and he found the practice of law boring. In 1886, he received a PhD in political science from Johns Hopkins University. There he developed an interest and deep respect for the British system of government and wrote *Congressional Government.*

Wilson began his academic career teaching at Bryn Mawr College and then at Wesleyan University in Middletown, Connecticut. In 1902, he joined the faculty of Princeton, eventually becoming president of the institution. As a political science professor, Wilson had believed in the ability of government to rationally regulate the economy, and in 1910, he won the governorship of New Jersey as a Democrat. He proved to be an activist governor who backed state regulation of public utilities and railroads, a direct primary election, and a corrupt-practices law.

Wilson was a popular governor, and in 1912, the Democratic Party selected him as its presidential nominee. It was an auspicious time for a Democratic candidate because former president **Theodore Roosevelt** had broken with Republican President **William Howard Taft** and had launched a third-party bid for the White House. Roosevelt found Taft too conservative for the post and promoted what he called the "**New Nationalism**." In addition to a series of social-welfare proposals, Roosevelt announced that antitrust action was not always beneficial for the economy. Large companies, because of the benefits of economies of scale and money for research and development, could often deliver better products at cheaper prices to consumers. He called for government monitoring of large companies and monopolies, and he distinguished between "good **trusts**" and "bad trusts." Wilson developed what he called the "**New Freedom**"—unapologetic support for antitrust action against all monopolies. Whether or not trusts were good at first, he argued, they would become bad in the long run and stifle competition. Most Americans voted Republican in 1912, but the vote was split between Taft and Roosevelt, and Wilson won in the electoral college.

During his first term in office, Wilson labored to fulfill the New Freedom's vision. He promoted and Congress passed the **Federal Reserve Act of 1913**, the **Federal Trade Commission Act of 1914**, and the **Clayton Antitrust Act of 1914**. During his first administration, the Justice Department vigorously pursued antitrust cases as the president worked to implement his vision of a competitive economy. Wilson was reelected in 1916, but when the United States entered World War I in April 1917, the New Freedom had to be put on a back burner. In order to pursue the war effort, the federal government entered into a close relationship with the country's largest corporations and scrapped antitrust actions. Such huge government agencies as the War Industries Board, the War Labor Board, and the War Finance Corporation signified that the federal government had become a key player in the private economy, regulating corporations but not breaking them up. In that sense, Wilson's policies during his second term more resembled Theodore Roosevelt's New Nationalism than his own New Freedom.

In 1920, Wilson toyed with the idea of seeking a third term in office, but his health precluded the run. He had suffered a debilitating stroke in 1919, and its effects still lingered with him. He retired to private life in March 1921 and died on February 3, 1924.

Wilson-Gorman Tariff. *See* Sixteenth Amendment

Women in the Workplace

As the United States evolved as a capitalist society, the role of women in the American workplace shifted over time. Moreover, both class and racial factors shaped the workplace experience of women from different social and ethnic groups. Although American women have been denied job opportunities both by law and custom, their protests in the nineteenth and twentieth centuries were instrumental in compelling sexual equality in the workplace.

The rise of industrialization in the nineteenth century drew women into the workforce as never before. New shoe and textile factories at mill towns like Lowell, Massachusetts, employed thousands of eager white farmwomen in the 1830s. They were the first generation of American women to come into contact with class consciousness and the difficult industrial conditions in the northeastern cities. The women were extremely exploited through low wages, poor conditions, and little time off. Most women associated with manufacturing during this time, however, engaged in the putting-out system. Manufacturers would bring unfinished clothing to the homes of women who would finish the garments and return them to the factory for a small sum.

Despite many women's need to work in order to survive, the cult of domesticity of the time held that women should remain in the home to

Women Rivet heaters at Puget Sound Navy Yard in 1919. (National Archives)

provide a refuge for men from the difficulties of the industrial workplace. White, middle-class women in the Victorian Era were surrounded by guidebooks and other self-help literature praising the special qualities of women as mothers, wives, and tenders of the home.

Still, American women could be found in a variety of occupations by the eve of the Civil War. One-fourth of the 100,000 women working in New York City by 1860 worked in the manufacturing sector. Indicating the importance of textile production for female employment, two-thirds of women industrial laborers worked in the clothing trade. Only 10 percent of all white women held paying jobs in 1860, but nearly the majority of black women worked, most of them as involuntary laborers. During the Civil War, American women on both sides of the conflict took on roles that violated traditional notions of female work. Women took on dangerous jobs as spies, like Harriet Tubman, or as nurses and hospital organizers, like Dorothea Dix. Some women even dressed as men, enlisted in the Union and Confederate armies, and fought in combat.

Elite white women made some inroads into traditionally male occupations in the late nineteenth century. Some became doctors and lawyers, while others became writers and essayists, like Harriet Beecher Stowe, the author of *Uncle Tom's Cabin*. The ability of women to attend college by the late nineteenth century enabled them to improve their economic prospects. Female college graduates like Jane Addams, the founder of the immigrant settlement home Hull House, found socially acceptable and meaningful work roles that extended the reach of women into the workforce while keeping them within the accepted bounds of the cult of domesticity.

Between 1880 and World War II, American women entered the workforce in ways unforeseen a generation earlier. Elizabeth Cady Stanton and Susan B. Anthony called for the broadening of women's roles in politics and the workplace. As a movement, women's suffrage helped propel women into prominent and visible organizational roles in self-help groups. More than 16 percent of women could be found in the workplace in 1880. By 1900, that figure had increased to 21 percent.

Most of that participation comprised the work of African American women in the South and immigrant women in Northern cities. Forty percent of African American women were employed in 1890 and forty-four percent in 1920. Yet only 15 percent of native-born white women and 20 percent of foreign-born white women were employed in 1890. Overall, though women were entering new professions, most American women had yet to work predominantly outside the home due to rigid cultural values that reinforced the private and domestic nature of female life.

New opportunities in American cities in the 1900s and 1910s drew thousands of women from all across the United States into new roles in the workplace. African American women migrated to Chicago, New York, and Detroit to take advantage of factory labor, like men, while new female immigrants from Southern Europe sought employment in garment factories in Eastern cities. White native-born women took on new white-collar jobs as typists, stenographers, telephone operators, and department store clerks. Many began to live alone and compile a savings, unthinkable behavior a generation before. The number of women working as domestics dropped from three women in every five in 1870 to one in four in 1910. That decrease represented the white-collar and factory work increasingly taken by women. The latter also became a launching pad for women to enter the ranks of prolabor unionism in the early twentieth century.

Y

Yellow-Dog Contract

With the rise of national labor unions after the **Civil War**, some employers resisted the organization of workers by requiring prospective workers to sign contracts promising not to join a union. Signing the contract was a condition of employment. By the early 1900s, labor-union advocates had labeled such documents "yellow-dog contracts" and began calling for government prohibitions of them. They did not succeed until the Great Depression of the 1930s and the advent of the New Deal. Section 7(a) of the National Industrial Recovery Act of 1933 guaranteed labor's rights of collective bargaining and essentially made yellow-dog contracts illegal. The Fair Labor Standards Act of 1935 outrightly defined yellow-dog contracts as an unfair labor practice.

PRIMARY DOCUMENTS

Engineer Horatio Allen's Description of the First Run (1851)

Horatio Allen was chief engineer of the Delaware & Hudson Canal Company, which ran from Carbondale, Philadelphia, to New York City. In 1828, he traveled to England to purchase locomotives for the company. One of the four locomotives purchased, the Stourbridge Lion, was the first steam locomotive to run in the United States and was first tested on August 8, 1829. His account of the machine's first run, written 22 years later, revealed that many factors—the track, infrastructure, and the locomotive itself—needed to be merged for steam railroads to be practical.

The circumstances which led to my being left alone [on the Lion] were these: The road had been built in the summer, the structure was of hemlock timber, and the rails [hemlock stringers] of large dimensions, notched onto caps placed far apart. The timber had cracked and warped, from exposure to the sun. After about 500 feet of straight line, the road crossed the Lackawaxen creek on a trestle-work about 30 feet high and with a curve of 350 or 400 feet radius. The impression was very general that the iron monster would either break down the road or that it would leave the track at the curve and plunge into the creek. My reply to such apprehension was, that it was too late to consider the probability of such occurrences . . . that I would take the first ride alone. . . . [Placing] my hand on the throttle-valve handle . . . and preferring that if we did go down, to go down handsomely and without any evidence of timidity, I started with considerable velocity, passed the curve in safety, and was soon out of hearing of the large assemblage present. At the end of two or three miles [actually at Seelyville, where a bridge over the track was too low for the 15-foot high smokestack],

I reversed the valves and returned without accident to the place of starting, having thus made the first railroad trip by a locomotive in the Western Hemisphere.

Source: Carter, Charles Fredericks. *When Railroads Were New.* New York: Henry Holt and Company, 1909, 21.

Andrew Carnegie's "Gospel of Wealth," *North American Review* (1889)

Written in 1889, Andrew Carnegie's most famous essay describes the responsibility of the wealthy to contribute to the betterment of society through philanthropy. Carnegie believed that poverty in a capitalist society could be alleviated by wealthy philanthropists. The following is an excerpt from his essay.

This, then, is held to be the duty of the man of wealth: First, to set an example of modest, unostentatious living, shunning display or extravagance; . . . and, after doing so, to consider all surplus revenues which come to him simply as trust funds, which he is called upon to administer . . . to produce the most beneficial results for the community—the man of wealth thus becoming the mere trustee and agent for his poorer brethren, bringing to their service his superior wisdom, experience and ability to administer, doing for them better than they would or could do for themselves.

Source: Carnegie, Andrew. "The Gospel of Wealth." *North American Review* 148, no. 391 (June 1889): 653, 657–62.

Carnegie's Letters to Frick during Homestead Strike (1892)

Andrew Carnegie communicated with the chairman of the Carnegie Steel Company Henry Clay Frick during the 1892 Homestead Strike in Homestead, Pennsylvania. The labor dispute was between the Amalgamated Association of Iron and Steel Workers and the steel company. The letters and telegrams show Carnegie's support for Frick's plans to break the union, despite Carnegie's public support of labor unions and pronounced disapproval of strikebreakers.

May 4 Letter to Frick "One thing we are all sure of: No contest will be entered in that will fail. It will be harder this time at Homestead. . . . On the other hand, your reputation will shorten it, so that I really do not believe it will be much of a struggle. We all approve of anything you do, not stopping short of approval of a contest. We are with you to the end." **June 10 Telegram to Frick** "Of course, you will be asked to confer, and I know you will decline all conferences, as you have taken your stand and have nothing more to say. . . . Of course you will win, and win easier than you suppose, owing to the present condition of the market." **July 6 The battle at Homestead**. **July 7 Telegram to Frick** "Cable received. All anxiety gone since you stand firm. Never employ one of these rioters. Let grass grow over works. Must not fail now. You will win easily next trial." **July 17 Letter to cousin** "Matters at home bad—such a fiasco trying to send guards by Boat and then leaving space between River & fences for the men to get opposite landing and fire. Still we must keep quiet & do all we can to support Frick & those at Seat of War. I have been besieged by interviewing Cables from N York but have not said a word. Silence is best. We shall win, of course, but may have to shut down for months." **November 18 Telegram from Frick at end of lockout** "Victory!" **November 21 Telegram from Frick** "Strike officially declared off yesterday. Our victory is now complete and most gratifying. Do not think we will ever have any serious labor trouble again. . . . Let the Amalgamated still exist and hold full sway at other people's mills. That is no concern of ours." **Late November Telegram to Frick from Italy** "Life is worth living again—Cables received—first happy morning since July— surprising how pretty Italia—congratulate all around—improve works— go ahead—clear track—tariff not in it—shake." **Late December Letter to Frick from Rome** "I am well and able to take an interest in the wonders we see. . . . Shall see you all early after the New Year. Think I'm about ten years older than when with you last. Europe has rung with Homestead, Homestead, until we are sick of the name, but it is all over now—So once again Happy New Year to all. I wish someone would write me about your good self. I cannot believe you can be well. Ever your Pard, A.C."

Source: Carnegie, Andrew to Henry Clay Frick, Homestead Strike Correspondence, 1892. *Available at:* http://www.pbs.org/wgbh/amex/carnegie/sfeature/mh_letters.html.

McClure's Magazine **Muckraking Expose on Standard Oil and Rockefellers by Ida Tarbell**

Ida Minerva Tarbell became one of the leading American muckrakers, bringing her international fame as a journalist. In 1891, she went to Paris to study history and do research on the role of women in the French Revolution. To maintain herself abroad, she earned money writing articles for periodicals in the United States. Soon she would meet Samuel McClure, who would revolutionize the magazine world with his McClure's, a mass-circulation journal with high literary content. For McClure's, Tarbell wrote a series of 19 articles called "The History of the Standard Oil Company." The following is from one of those articles, which exposed the Southern Improvement Company scheme, a plan to benefit certain railroad lines and major oil producers through secret concessions and rebates that were harmful to smaller level businessmen.

For several days an uneasy rumor had been running up and down the Oil Regions. Freights were going up. Now an advance in a man's freight bill may ruin his business; more, it may mean the ruin of a region. . . .

On the morning of February 26, 1872, the oil men read in their morning papers that the rise which had been threatening had come; moreover, that all members of the South Improvement Company were exempt from the advance. At the news all Oildom rushed into the streets. Nobody waited to find out his neighbor's opinion. On every lip there was but one word, and that was "conspiracy.". . .

For weeks the whole body of oil men abandoned regular business and surged from town to town intent on destroying the "Monster," the "Forty Thieves," the "Great Anaconda," as they called the mysterious South Improvement Company. Curiously enough, it was chiefly against the combination which had secured the discrimination from the railroads—not the railroads which had granted it—that their fury was directed. They expected nothing but robbery from the railroads, they said. They were used to that; but they would not endure it from men in their own business.

Source: Tarbell, Ida. "The History of the Standard Oil Company." *McClure's Magazine* Vol. 20, November 1902–April 1903. New York: The S. S. McClure Co., 1903, 248.

Atlantic Monthly Article on Telegraph Technology (1860)

Part of a series, this article appeared between Cyrus Field's first and second attempts to lay a cable in the Atlantic Ocean. It discusses the rapid growth of telegraph technology and notes the problems with laying underwater transmission lines.

The lines of electric telegraph are increasing so rapidly, that the length in actual use cannot be estimated at any moment with accuracy. At the commencement of 1848, it was stated that the length in operation in this country was about 3000 miles. At the end of 1850, the lines in operation, or in progress, in the United States, amounted to 22,000. In 1853, the total number of miles of wire in America amounted to 26,375.

It is but fifteen years since the first line of electric telegraph was constructed in this country; and at the present time there are not less than 50,000 miles in successful operation on this continent, having over 1400 stations, and employing upwards of 10,000 operators and clerks.

The number of messages passing over all the lines in this country annually is estimated at upwards of 5,000,000, producing a revenue of $2,000,000; in addition to which, the press pays $200,000 for public despatches. . . .

The electric telegraph, which has made such rapid strides, is yet in its infancy. The effect of its future extension, and of new applications, cannot be estimated, when, as a means of intercourse at least, its network shall spread through every village, bringing all parts of our republic into the closest and most intimate relations of friendship and interest. In connection with the railroad and the steamboat, it has already achieved one important national result. It has made possible, on this continent, a wide-spread, yet closely linked, empire of States, such as our fathers never imagined. The highest office of the electric telegraph, in the future, is thus to be the promotion of unity, peace, and good-will among men. . . .

No limit has yet been found to aerial telegraphing; for, by inserting transferrers into the more extended circuits, renewed energy can be attained, and lines of several thousands of miles in length can be worked, if properly insulated, as surely as those of a hundred. The lines between New York and New Orleans are frequently connected together by means of transferrers, and direct communication is had over a distance of more than two thousand miles. No perceptible retardation of the current takes place; on the contrary, the lines so connected work as successfully as when divided into shorter circuits.

This is not the case with subaqueous lines. The employment of submarine, as well as of subterranean conductors, occasions a small retardation in the velocity of the transmitted electricity. This retardation is not due to the length of the path which the electric current has to traverse, since it does not take place with a conductor equally long, insulated in the air. It arises, as Faraday has demonstrated, from a static reaction, which is determined by the introduction of a current into a conductor well insulated, but surrounded outside its insulating coating by a conducting body, such as seawater or moist ground, or even simply by the metallic envelope of iron wires placed in communication with the ground. When this conductor is presented to one of the poles of a battery, the other pole of which communicates with the ground, it becomes charged with electricity, like the coating of a Leyden jar,—electricity which is capable of giving rise to a discharge current, even after the voltaic current has ceased to be transmitted. . . .

It was owing to the retardation from this cause that communication through the Atlantic Cable was so exceedingly slow and difficult, and not, as many suppose, because the cable was defective. It is true that there was fault in the cable, discovered by Varley, before it left Queenstown; but it was not of so serious a character as to offer any substantial obstacle to the passage of the electric current. . . .

Everything pertaining to the actual operation of the Atlantic Cable has been studiously withheld from the public, until it has come to be seriously doubted whether any despatches were ever transmitted through it. . . .

Source: "The Progress of the Electric Telegraph." *The Atlantic Monthly: A Magazine of Literature, Art, and Politics* 5, no. 29 (March 1860): 290–97.

Harper's Weekly Report on Construction of the Transcontinental Railroad (July 27, 1867)

The transcontinental railroad was the subject of several reports in Harper's Weekly during its construction. This excerpt from the July 27, 1867, issue, discusses the commercial benefits of the railroad for New York City.

We have also expressed the belief that the constantly changing wants and exigencies of a growing country like ours demand, and will compel, a radical change in our present railway system; that with the completion of the grand arterial road across the continent to the Pacific, all other roads must become tributary and subservient to it—the direction of railway traffic (freights) being traverse to the water communication that cuts the country from north to south. A consolidation of railroad interests will naturally result, as well as a change in the mode of operating and running. The future requirements are already foreseen and felt; the first movement toward the new order of things is the proposed combination of leading railroads to form a great Western route under one management. The parties to the combination are the New York Central, Lake Shore, Cleveland and Toledo, Michigan Southern, and those other roads that constitute the northernmost tier of transverse communication. Another rival organization is promised, to include a more southern route, and will embrace the Pennsylvania Central, Pittsburg, Fort Wayne and Chicago, etc. Their interests will not conflict; on the contrary, the commercial necessities of the country will on the course of time require one or two more routes still further south to convey the produce of the sea-board States to their western destination.

When the Pacific Railroad is completed in 1870, all these gigantic tributaries will converge toward the main stem, like the fingers of a hand. All the immense and richly productive districts of the Atlantic and the East will contribute to supply the vital fluid that courses through them. Even the vast domain of the "New Dominion" (traversed by the long-projected "Intercolonial Railway" and tapped by an absolutely indispensable line extending through Maine from Bangor) will be induced to furnish its quota of subsistence. But the seat of the vital principle will be in the city of New York. There will the mighty beat of its palpitation be heard. Already the commercial centre of America, it will then, by its geographical position, become the commercial centre of the world. We do not assume that the Pacific Railway will supersede vessels in the carrying trade, for that would be impossible; a dozen lines of railroad could not furnish the required transportation, even if it could carry as cheaply. But from its closer relations and proximity to other countries, New York could command the commerce. It would be as nearly united to Asia as it has been to Europe. The distance to

China, now accomplished in forty-three to forty-five days, will be shortened to thirty days. A letter will reach Hong Kong by way of San Francisco much quicker than when it went by way of Liverpool, just as our enterprise had shortened the time of our communication with Brazil. The London banker would no longer pocket the commissions and the exchange on the immense trade carried on between New York and China, as well as South American and the West Indies; but New York would become, to America at least, what London is not to the rest of the world, namely, the place on which exchange is universally drawn. Millions of dollars would thereby be saved to our merchants annually, to say nothing of the difference of time, which is as precious as money.

We have heretofore spoken of the advantages to be obtained by the operation of the Pacific Railroad in developing the treasures of California and the Rocky Mountain region, and the easy access it afford to Asiatic trade. The gains, to be sure, are for the present purely speculative, but it is easy to conjecture the results from past experience. And we are to obtain all this by an estimated outlay of $45,000,000 currency for a road 1565 miles long, while the Intercolonial Railroad of the "New Dominion" of only 480 miles is expected to cost upward of $20,000,000 in gold. It will take rime to overcome the commercial and financial derangement which the late war inflicted upon the court, and to stimulate the productive interests of the several sections to their full capacity; but by the time the Pacific Railroad is completed we hope to lie upon the top wave of prosperity, and to tax our new lines of intercommunication to their utmost limit.

Source: Harper's Weekly Report on the Transcontinental Railroad (July 27, 1867). Available at: http://www.pbs.org/wgbh/americanexperience/features/primary-resources/tcrr-reports/?flavour=mobile.

Chicago Tribune's Coverage of the 1871 Great Fire

Prior to the disastrous Chicago Fire of 1871, the Chicago Tribune had published an editorial on September 10 highlighting the city's many wood buildings, the shoddy construction of its brick and stone buildings, and the city government's unwillingness to institute reforms and building codes. The fire that began on October 8 became unmanageable until two days later, when rainstorms were able to extinguish it. Using a borrowed printing press, publisher Joseph Medill was able to print an issue of the Tribune, and he described the fire in detail and publicized the relief needs of the city.

October 11, 1871

Fire!

Destruction of Chicago! 2,600 Acres of Buildings Destroyed. Eighty-Thousand People Burned Out. All the Hotels, Banks, Public Buildings, Newspaper Offices and Great Business Blocks Swept Away. Over a Hundred Dead Bodies Recovered From Debris. Tens of Thousands of Citizens Without Home, Food, Fuel or Clothing. Eighteen Thousand Buildings Destroyed. Incendiaries and Ruffians Shot and Hanged by Citizens. Fatalities by Fire, Suffocation, and Crushed by Falling Walls. Relief Arriving from Other Cities Hourly. Organization of a Local Relief Committee. List of Names of Over Two Hundred Missing Men, Women, and Children. The City Without Light or Water. Crosby's and Hooley's Opera House, McVicker's and the Dearbers Theatres, Wood's Museum, and all the Art Galleries in Ashes.

During Sunday night, Monday, and Tuesday, this city has been swept by a conflagration which has no parallel in the annals of history, for the quantity of property destroyed, and the utter and almost irremediable ruin which it wrought. A fire in a barn on the West Side was the insignificant cause of a conflagration which has swept out of existence hundreds of millions of property, has reduced to poverty thousands who, the day before, were in a state of opulence, has covered the prairies, now swept with the cold southwest wind, with thousands of homeless unfortunates, which has stripped 3,600 acres of buildings, which has destroyed public improvements that it has taken years of patient labor to build up, and which has set back 100 years the progress of the city, diminished her population, and crushed her resources. But to a blow, no matter how terrible, Chicago will not succumb. Take as it is the season, general as the rule is, the spirit of her citizens has not given way, and before the smoke has cleared away, and the ruins are cold, they are beginning to plan for the future. Though so many have been deprived of homes and sustenance, aid in money and provisions is flowing in from all quarters, and which of the primal distress will be alleviated before another day has gone by.

It is at this moment impossible to give a full account of the losses by the fire, or to state the number of fatal accidents which have occurred. So much confusion prevails, and people are so widely scattered, that we are unable for a day to give absolutely accurate information concerning them. We have, however, given a full account of the fire, from the time of its beginning, reserving for a future day a detailed statement of losses. We would be exceedingly obliged if all persons having any knowledge of accidents, or the names of persons who died during the fire, would report them at this office. We also hope that all will leave with or at No. 15 South Canal Street, a memorandum of their losses and their insurance, giving the names of the companies. . . .

The West Side

At 9:30 a small cow barn attached to a house on the corner of DeKoven and Jefferson streets, one block north of [Twelfth] street, emitted a bright light followed by a blaze, and in a moment the building was hopelessly on fire. Before any aid could be extended the fire had communicated to a number of adjoining sheds, barns and dwellings, and was rapidly carried north and east, despite the efforts of the firemen. The fire seemed to leap over the engines, and commenced far beyond them, and working to the east and west, either surrounded the apparatus or compelled it to move away. In less than ten minutes the fire embraced the area between Jefferson and Clinton for two blocks north, and rapidly pushed eastward to Canal street.

When the fire first engulphed the two blocks, and the efforts of the undaunted engineers became palpably abortive to quench a single building, an effort was made to head it off from the north, but so great was the area that it already covered at 10:30 o'clock, and so rapidly did it march forward, that by the time the engines were at work the flames were ahead of them, and again they moved on north. From the west side of Jefferson street as far as the eye could reach, in an easterly direction—and that space was bounded by the river—a perfect sea of leaping flames covered the ground. The wind increased in fierceness as the flames rose, and the flames walled more hungrily for their prey as the angry gusts impelled them onward. Successively the wooden buildings on Taylor, Forquer, Ewing, and Polk streets became the northern boundary and then fell back to the second place. Meanwhile, the people in the more southern localities bent all their energies to the recovery of such property as they could. With ample time to move all that was movable, and with a foreboding of what was coming in their neighborhood, at least they were out and in safety long before the flames reached their dwellings. They were nearly all poor people, the savings of whose lifetime were represented in the little mass of furniture which blocked the streets, and impeded the firemen. They were principally laborers, most of them Germans or Scandinavians. Though the gaunt phantom of starvation and homelessness for the night, at least, passed over them, it was singular to observe the cheerfulness, not to say merriment that prevailed. Though mothers hugged their little ones to their breasts and shivered with alarm, yet, strange to say, they talked freely and laughed as if realizing the utter uselessness of expressing more dolefully their consciousness of ruin. There were many owners of the buildings who gave themselves up to the consolation of insurance. But even that appeared to weaken as the flames spread, and they gave themselves up to their fate. Many of the victims were stowed away in the houses on the west side of Jefferson street, while those on Clinton caught between two fires had rushed away losing

all but their lives and little ones. How many of these little ones were abandoned, either from terror or in the confusion, it is impossible to guess, buy
every now and then a woman wild with grief would run in and out among
the alleys and cry aloud her loss. . . .

_____

Source: "Fire!" *Chicago Tribune* (October 11, 1871).

Chicago Tribune Article on the Haymarket Riot of 1886

The Haymarket Square riot of May 4, 1896, left seven policemen dead and injured 70 people. The May 6 issue of the Chicago Tribune *reported on plans to indict and prosecute the anarchists considered responsible for the deadly riot.*

Justice May Reach Them Arranging for the Prosecution of Spies et al.

State's-Attorney Grinnell and Chief of Police Ebersold closeted themselves together twice yesterday to consult as to the best course to pursue
in getting together the evidence necessary to convict the murderous Anarchists who perpetrated the atrocious wholesale murder on Desplaines
street Tuesday night. It was suggested that the State's Attorney had in
mind the calling together of a special grand jury for the indicting of the
treacherous rioters, and that all known Anarchists who participated in
the meeting would be indicted by name on all possible charges, and that
the indictments for the unknown rioters would be made to read "a person
unknown by name, to be pointed out." "We will pursue the prosecution
of the men who instigated the riot and helped carry out the murder as far
as the law allows us," said Mr. Grinnell after he came out of the Chief's
office. "We intend and determine to punish these rioters to the fullest extent of the law and for all there is in it," he continued, "and we hope justice will not be cheated this time. We want to look over all the evidence
before declaring on what charge or charges to make and I cannot say now
what the charges will be. I think we will bring the matter before the next
regular grand jury."

It was rumored yesterday that the State's Attorney would present a request in due form to Judge Rogers or Judge Garnett to impanel a special
grand jury to act on the cases of the Socialists Spies and Fielden, their associates, and dupes. The regular grand jury it was thought, would not be
impaneled till Monday week, and would have all it could do to attend to
the ordinary jail cases. Some good citizens suggested a special grand jury,
because they do not like the personnel of the regular one. A few good men

like Murray Nelson, A. J. Grover, and George Adams have been drawn, but the majority are small politicians, saloonkeepers, etc. It might not be safe to instrust them with any business of importance. It is not likely that this will be done. . . .

Source: "Justice May Reach Them Arranging for the Prosecution of Spies et al." *Chicago Tribune* (May 6, 1896).

Jacob Riis's *How the Other Half Lives* (1890)

An extraordinarily gifted photographer, Jacob Riis focused much of his attention on capturing the plight of the country's poor. In a series of publications, but most notably this one of 1890, Riis published photographs and accompanying text showing in what horrible conditions the poor of New York City lived in the tenements. An excerpt of the book, entitled How the Other Half Lives, appears below. Riis's work shocked the nation and led to calls for poor relief, sanitation and health care reform, and greater workers' rights.

1. The dread of advancing cholera, with the guilty knowledge of the harvest field that awaited the plague in New York's slums, pricked the conscience of the community into action soon after the close of the war. A citizens' movement resulted in the organization of a Board of Health and the adoption of the "Tenement-House Act" of 1867, the first step toward remedial legislation. A thorough canvass of the tenements had been begun already in the previous year; but the cholera first, and next a scourge of small-pox, delayed the work, while emphasizing the need of it, so that it was 1869 before it got fairly under way and began to tell. The dark bedroom fell under the ban first. In that year the Board ordered the cutting of more than forty-six thousand windows in interior rooms, chiefly for ventilation—for little or no light was to be had from the dark hallways. Air-shafts were unknown. The saw had a job all that summer; by early fall nearly all the orders had been carried out. Not without opposition; obstacles were thrown in the way of the officials on the one side by the owners of the tenements, who saw in every order to repair or clean up only an item of added expense to diminish their income from the rent; on the other side by the tenants themselves, who had sunk, after a generation of unavailing protest, to the level of their surroundings, and were at last content to remain there. The tenements had bred their Nemesis, a proletariat ready and able to avenge the wrongs of their crowds. Already it taxed the city heavily for the support of its jails and charities. The basis of opposition, curiously enough was the same at both extremes; owner and

tenant alike considered official interference an infringement of personal rights, and a hardship. It took long years of weary labor to make good the claim of the sunlight to such corners of the dens as it could reach at all. Not until five years after did the department succeed at last in ousting the "cave-dwellers" and closing some five hundred and fifty cellars south of Houston Street, many of them below tide-water, that had been used as living apartments. In many instances the police had to drag the tenants out by force.

2. The work went on; but the need of it only grew with the effort. The Sanitarians were following up an evil that grew faster than they went; like a fire, it could only be headed off, not chased, with success. Official reports, read in the churches in 1879, characterized the younger criminals as Victims of low social conditions of life and unhealthy, overcrowded lodgings, brought up in "an atmosphere of actual darkness, moral and physical." This after the saw had been busy in the dark corners ten years! "If we could see the air breathed by these poor creatures in their tenements," said a well-known physician, "it would show itself to be fouler than the mud of the gutters." Little improvement was apparent despite all that had been done. "The new tenements, that have been recently built, have been usually as badly planned as the old, with dark and unhealthy rooms, often over wet cellars, where extreme overcrowding is permitted," was the verdict of one authority. These are the houses that to-day perpetuate the worst traditions of the past, and they are counted by thousands. The Five Points had been cleansed, as far as the immediate neighborhood was concerned, but the Mulberry Street Bend was fast outdoing it in foulness not a stone's throw away, and new centres of corruption were continually springing up and getting the upper hand whenever vigilance was relaxed for ever so short a time. It is one of the curses of the tenement-house system that the worst houses exercise a levelling influence upon all the rest, just as one bad boy in a schoolroom will spoil the whole class. It is one of the ways the evil that was "the result of forgetfulness of the poor," as the Council of Hygiene mildly put it, has of avenging itself.

Source: Riis, Jacob. *How the Other Half Lives: Studies Among the Tenements of New York.* New York: Charles Scribner's Sons, 1890, 15–17.

Booker T. Washington's Atlanta Compromise Speech (1895)

One of the leading African American spokesmen of his day, Booker T. Washington delivered this address on September 18, 1895, at the Cotton States Exposition in Atlanta, Georgia. Washington advocated a policy of separate-but-equal facilities for African Americans, arguing that blacks must elevate themselves through hard work and education in order to enjoy true equality with whites in the United States someday. Although Washington had a large following among some African Americans, his views infuriated others and sparked the early civil rights movement under the direction of W. E. B. Du Bois.

Mr. President and Gentlemen of the Board of Directors and Citizens:

One-third of the population of the South is of the Negro race. No enterprise seeking the material, civil, or moral welfare of this section can disregard this element of our population and reach the highest success. I but convey to you, Mr. President and Directors, the sentiment of the masses of my race when I say that in no way have the value and manhood of the American Negro been more fittingly and generously recognized than by the managers of this magnificent Exposition at every stage of its progress. It is a recognition that will do more to cement the friendship of the two races than any occurrence since the dawn of our freedom.

Not only this, but the opportunity here afforded will awaken among us a new era of industrial progress. Ignorant and inexperienced, it is not strange that in the first years of our new life we began at the top instead of at the bottom; that a seat in Congress or the state legislature was more sought than real estate or industrial skill; that the political convention or stump speaking had more attractions than starting a dairy farm or truck garden.

A ship lost at sea for many days suddenly sighted a friendly vessel. From the mast of the unfortunate vessel was seen a signal, "Water, water; we die of thirst!" The answer from the friendly vessel at once came back, "Cast down your bucket where you are." A second time the signal, "Water, water; send us water!" ran up from the distressed vessel, and was answered, "Cast down your bucket where you are." And a third and fourth signal for water was answered, "Cast down your bucket where you are." The captain of the distressed vessel, at last heeding the injunction, cast down his bucket, and it came up full of fresh, sparkling water from the mouth of the Amazon River. To those of my race who depend on bettering their condition in a foreign land or who underestimate the importance of cultivating friendly relations with the Southern white man, who is their next-door neighbor, I would say: "Cast down your bucket where you are"—cast it down in making friends in every manly way of the people of all races by whom we are surrounded.

Cast it down in agriculture, mechanics, in commerce, in domestic service, and in the professions. And in this connection it is well to bear in mind that whatever other sins the South may be called to bear, when it comes to business, pure and simple, it is in the South that the Negro is given a man's chance in the commercial world, and in nothing is this Exposition more eloquent than in emphasizing this chance. Our greatest danger is that in the great leap from slavery to freedom we may overlook the fact that the masses of us are to live by the productions of our hands, and fail to keep in mind that we shall prosper in proportion as we learn to dignify and glorify common labour, and put brains and skill into the common occupations of life; shall prosper in proportion as we learn to draw the line between the superficial and the substantial, the ornamental gewgaws of life and the useful. No race can prosper till it learns that there is as much dignity in tilling a field as in writing a poem. It is at the bottom of life we must begin, and not at the top. Nor should we permit our grievances to overshadow our opportunities.

To those of the white race who look to the incoming of those of foreign birth and strange tongue and habits for the prosperity of the South, were I permitted I would repeat what I say to my own race, "Cast down your bucket where you are." Cast it down among the eight millions of Negroes whose habits you know, whose fidelity and love you have tested in days when to have proved treacherous meant the ruin of your firesides. Cast down your bucket among these people who have, without strikes and labour wars, tilled your fields, cleared your forests, builded your railroads and cities, and brought forth treasures from the bowels of the earth, and helped make possible this magnificent representation of the progress of the South. Casting down your bucket among my people, helping and encouraging them as you are doing on these grounds, and to education of head, hand, and heart, you will find that they will buy your surplus land, make blossom the waste places in your fields, and run your factories. While doing this, you can be sure in the future, as in the past, that you and your families will be surrounded by the most patient, faithful, law-abiding, and unresentful people that the world has seen. As we have proved our loyalty to you in the past, in nursing your children, watching by the sick-bed of your mothers and fathers, and often following them with tear-dimmed eyes to their graves, so in the future, in our humble way, we shall stand by you with a devotion that no foreigner can approach, ready to lay down our lives, if need be, in defense of yours, interlacing our industrial, commercial, civil, and religious life with yours in a way that shall make the interests of both races one. In all things that are purely social we can be as separate as the fingers, yet one as the hand in all things essential to mutual progress.

There is no defense or security for any of us except in the highest intelligence and development of all. If anywhere there are efforts tending to curtail the fullest growth of the Negro, let these efforts be turned into stimulating, encouraging, and making him the most useful and intelligent citizen. Effort or means so invested will pay a thousand per cent interest. These efforts will be twice blessed—blessing him that gives and him that takes. There is no escape through law of man or God from the inevitable:

The laws of changeless justice bind Oppressor with oppressed;
And close as sin and suffering joined We march to fate abreast. . . .

Nearly sixteen millions of hands will aid you in pulling the load upward, or they will pull against you the load downward. We shall constitute one-third and more of the ignorance and crime of the South, or one-third [of] its intelligence and progress; we shall contribute one-third to the business and industrial prosperity of the South, or we shall prove a veritable body of death, stagnating, depressing, retarding every effort to advance the body politic.

Gentlemen of the Exposition, as we present to you our humble effort at an exhibition of our progress, you must not expect overmuch. Starting thirty years ago with ownership here and there in a few quilts and pump-kins and chickens (gathered from miscellaneous sources), remember the path that has led from these to the inventions and production of agricul-tural implements, buggies, steam-engines, newspapers, books, statuary, carving, paintings, the management of drug stores and banks, has not been trodden without contact with thorns and thistles. While we take pride in what we exhibit as a result of our independent efforts, we do not for a mo-ment forget that our part in this exhibition would fall far short of your expectations but for the constant help that has come to our educational life, not only from the Southern states, but especially from Northern phi-lanthropists, who have made their gifts a constant stream of blessing and encouragement.

The wisest among my race understand that the agitation of questions of social equality is the extremest folly, and that progress in the enjoy-ment of all the privileges that will come to us must be the result of severe and constant struggle rather than of artificial forcing. No race that has anything to contribute to the markets of the world is long in any degree ostracized. It is important and right that all privileges of the law be ours, but it is vastly more important that we be prepared for the exercise of these privileges. The opportunity to earn a dollar in a factory just now is worth infinitely more than the opportunity to spend a dollar in an opera-house.

In conclusion, may I repeat that nothing in thirty years has given us more hope and encouragement, and drawn us so near to you of the white race, as this opportunity offered by the Exposition; and here bending, as it were, over the altar that represents the results of the struggles of your race and mine, both starting practically empty-handed three decades ago, I pledge that in your effort to work out the great and intricate problem which God has laid at the doors of the South, you shall have at all times the patient, sympathetic help of my race; only let this he constantly in mind, that, while from representations in these buildings of the product of field, of forest, of mine, of factory, letters, and art, much good will come, yet far above and beyond material benefits will be that higher good, that, let us pray God, will come, in a blotting out of sectional differences and racial animosities and suspicions, in a determination to administer absolute justice, in a willing obedience among all classes to the mandates of law. This, coupled with our material prosperity, will bring into our beloved South a new heaven and a new earth.

Source: Washington, Booker T. "Atlanta Compromise Speech," 1895. In *Up from Slavery: An Autobiography.* New York: Doubleday, Page & Co., 1901.

Political Cartoon, *"The Little Boy and the Big Boys"* (1901)

Critics dubbed the new class of multimillionaire industrialists "robber barons," and charged them with condemning millions of Americans to lives of poverty and exploitation. The most famous of these 19th century industrialists were John D. Rockefeller of Standard Oil and Andrew Carnegie of US Steel. The Industrial Revolution, which the robber barons had brought to pass, had created an America of two classes—the "haves" and the "have-nots."

Source: Library of Congress.

"Little Boy—*They say that with a little practice at catching hot balls I'll be a wonder.*"

Political Cartoon from *Puck*, *"The Kind of Anti-Trust Legislation That Is Needed"* (1902)

Antitrust legislation had its beginnings in 1890 when Congress passed the Sher-

"Uncle Sam—*You're a powerful big man, and you have your uses. But if you're honest why do you hide in the dark?—Open up those books!*"

man Antitrust Act. Progressive reformers as well as small businessmen worried that the new industrial monopolies had established such control over markets that they had essentially suspended the laws of competition. During the election of 1896, Democratic presidential nominee, William Jennings Bryan, famously stated that it was government's responsibility to put "rings in the noses of hogs"—which was a blatant reference to his party's support for government regulation of the trusts. Antitrust fervor continued to gain momentum and became a defining political issue of the Progressive Era. The Clayton Antitrust Act of 1914 strengthened the provisions of the Sherman Antitrust Act by outlawing monopolistic price discrimination and interlocking directorates. The law also legalized strikes, boycotts, peaceful picketing, and demonstrations.

Source: Library of Congress.

Frederick Jackson Turner's "The Significance of the Frontier in American History" (1893)

Historian Frederick Jackson Turner was the author of several essays on the American frontier, which opened up a new period in the interpretation of American history. In 1920, he published his essays in a compilation, The Frontier in American History. The following is an excerpt from the book's

*first chapter. It is from a paper he read at a meeting of the American Histori-
cal Association in Chicago on July 12, 1893.*

American social development has been continually beginning over again
on the frontier. This perennial rebirth, this fluidity of American life, this
expansion westward with its new opportunities, its continuous touch with
the simplicity of primitive society, furnish the forces dominating American
character. The true point of view in the history of this nation is not the Atlantic Coast, it is the Great West. Even the slavery struggle, which is made
so exclusive an object of attention by writers like Professor von Holst, oc-
cupies its important place in American history because of its relation to
westward expansion.

Source: Turner, Frederick Jackson, "The Significance of the Frontier in American
History, 1893." In *The Frontier in American History.* New York: Henry Holt &
Co., 1921.

 ## Charles Eliot Norton's "True Patriotism" (1898)

*Professor and progressive social reformer Charles Eliot Norton taught art
history at Harvard and was an editor of the North American Review. At the
turn of the twentieth century, the area around Boston was a center of anti-
imperialist activity. The following is an excerpt of a talk Norton delivered to
the Men's Club of the Prospect Street Congregational Church in Cambridge,
Massachusetts, on June 7, 1898. It speaks to perceptions of the shifts in the social order and values in American society during the late nineteenth century.*

And because it is so, and just in proportion to his love of the ideals for
which his country stands, is his hatred of whatever is opposed to them
in private conduct or public policy. Against injustice, against dishonesty,
against lawlessness, against whatever may make for war instead of peace,
the good citizen is always in arms.

No thoughtful American can have watched the course of affairs among
us during the last thirty years without grave anxiety from the apparent decline in power to control the direction of public and private conduct, of the
principles upon regard for which the permanent and progressive welfare
of America depends; and especially the course of events during the last few
months and the actual condition of the country today, should bring home
to every man the question whether or not the nation is true to one of the
chief of the ideals to which it has professed allegiance.

A generation has grown up that has known nothing of war. The blessings
of peace have been poured out upon us. We have congratulated ourselves
that we were free from the misery and the burdens that war and standing

armies have brought upon the nations of the Old World. "Their fires"—I cite a fine phrase of Sir Philip Sidney in a letter to Queen Elizabeth—"Their fires have given us light to see our own quietness."

And now of a sudden, without cool deliberation, without prudent preparation, the nation is hurried into war, and America, she who more than any other land was pledged to peace and good-will on earth, unsheathes her sword, compels a weak and unwilling nation to a fight, rejecting without due consideration her earnest and repeated offers to meet every legitimate demand of the United States. It is a bitter disappointment to the lover of his country; it is a turning-back from the path of civilization to that of barbarism.

Source: Norton, Charles Eliot. "True Patriotism." A speech delivered at the Men's Club of the Prospect Street Congregational Church in Cambridge, Massachusetts, June 7, 1898.

Upton Sinclair's *The Jungle* (1906)

In 1906, author Upton Sinclair published this scathing expose regarding sanitation practices in the meat-packing industry and the brutal condition of the workers' lives who labored in that industry. The Jungle *shocked the American public and led to clamorous calls for federal legislation to protect consumers from such health hazards. Below is an excerpt from the book. It remains the most popular and powerful piece of fiction associated with the Progressive Era.*

There was never the least attention paid to what was cut up for sausage; there would come all the way back from Europe old sausage that had been rejected, and that was mouldy and white—it would be dosed with borax and glycerine, and dumped into the hoppers, and made over again for home consumption. There would be meat that had tumbled out on the floor, in the dirt and sawdust, where the workers had tramped and spit uncounted billions of consumption germs. There would be meat stored in great piles in rooms; and the water from leaky roofs would drip over it, and thousands of rats would race about on it. It was too dark in these storage places to see well, but a man could run his hand over these piles of meat and sweep off handfuls of the dried dung of rats. These rats were nuisances, and the packers would put poisoned bread out for them, they would die, and then rats, bread, and meat would go into the hoppers together. This is no fairy story and no joke; the meat would be shovelled into carts, and the man who did the shoveling would not trouble to lift out a rat even when he saw one—there were things that went into the sausage in comparison with which a poisoned rat was a tidbit. There was no place for the men to wash their hands before they ate their dinner, and so they made a practice of washing them in the water that was to be ladled into the sausage. There were the butt-ends of smoked meat, and the scraps of corned beef, and all the odds and ends of the waste of the plants, that would be dumped into old barrels in the cellar and left there. Under the system of rigid economy which the packers enforced, there were some jobs that it only paid to do once in a long time, and among these was the cleaning out of the waste barrels. Every spring they did it; and in the barrels would be dirt and rust and old nails and stale water—and cart load after cart load of it would be taken up and dumped into the hoppers with fresh meat, and sent out to the public's breakfast. Some of it they would make into "smoked" sausage—but as the smoking took time, and was therefore expensive, they would call upon their chemistry department, and preserve it with borax and color it with gelatine to make it brown. All of their sausage came out of the same bowl, but when they came to wrap it they would stamp some of it "special," and for this they would charge two cents more a pound. . . .

Source: Sinclair, Upton. *The Jungle.* New York: Doubleday, 1906, 135–37.

A critical component of the Advanced Placement Exam in U.S. History is the document-based essay question, also known as the "DBQ." The DBQ requires students to respond to a question by composing a coherent essay that incorporates evidence from their interpretation of several historically relevant documents. The documents provided can include anything from maps and photographs, to newspaper articles and political speeches. In order to achieve a high score, essays must cite key evidence from the student's analysis of the documents provided, and also demonstrate the student's outside knowledge of the period.

SAMPLE DOCUMENT-BASED ESSAY QUESTION (DBQ)

Question

Explain how late-nineteenth-century journalistic portrayals of robber baron industrialists and their business activities inspired the Progressive Movement and its ethos of social reform. Include discussion of specific events and individuals, as well as general themes from the period in your answer. Draw on the following six primary documents and factual evidence from your knowledge of the period to support your argument.

Document 1

Political cartoon, "*The Little Boy and the Big Boys*" (1901)

Document Information

Cartoon depicts a baseball training session with overly large players representing industrial "trusts" assailing a considerably smaller player, "the common people," with baseballs labeled *high prices*, *oppression*, and *low wages*. The subtitle reads, "Little Boy—They say that with a little practice at catching hot balls I'll be a wonder."

Document Inferences

Power and influence of the rich over the poor.
Social inequities between the rich and the poor.
Corporate consolidation and the rise of big business.

Entries Related to the Document

Carnegie, Andrew; Muckrakers; Robber Barons; Rockefeller, John D.; Vanderbilt, Cornelius

Document 2

Political cartoon, "*The Kind of Anti-Trust Legislation That Is Needed*" (1902)

Document Information

Cartoon depicts a bloated "Trusts" king wearing a jeweled crown and ermine robes festooned with dollar signs. He is surrounded by padlocked accounting books and ledgers as he shields the contents of an open ledger book from Uncle Sam's spotlight of "Congressional Legislation." The subtitle reads, "Uncle Sam—You're a powerful big man, and you have your uses. But if you're honest why do you hide in the dark?—Open up those books!"

Document Inferences

Corporate consolidation and the rise of big business.
   Antitrust legislation.

Entries Related to the Document

Bryan, William Jennings; Clayton Antitrust Act of 1914; Election of 1896; Interlocking Directorate; Monopoly; Morgan, John Pierpont; Pool; Sherman Antitrust Act of 1890; Trust; *United States v. E.C. Knight Company* (1895)

Document 3

Jacob Riis's *How the Other Half Lives* (1890)

Document Information

Photojournalist Jacob Riis's depictions of the squalid living conditions the poor endured in the crowded tenements of New York City's slums in the 1880s.

Document Inferences

Reflects common contemporary perceptions of the poor as deserving of their condition.

Entries Related to the Document

Child Labor; Muckrakers; Social Gospel; Triangle Shirtwaist Fire

Document 4

McClure's Magazine muckraking expose on Standard Oil and the Rockefellers by Ida Tarbell

Document Information

Muckraker Ida Tarbell's 1872 article exposed the Southern Improvement Company scheme, a plan to benefit certain railroad lines and major oil producers through secret concessions and rebates that were harmful to smaller level businessmen.

Document Inferences

Reflects emergent social justice concepts exposed in popular journalism about fair business practices and government regulation in a capitalistic economy.

Entries Related to the Document

Monopoly; Muckrakers; Railroads; Rockefeller, John D.; Sherman Antitrust Act of 1890; Standard Oil Company; Trust

Document 5

Carnegie's letters to Frick during the Homestead Strike (1892)

Document Information

Excerpts from the letters exchanged between Andrew Carnegie and his partner in the Carnegie Steel Works, H. C. Frick discussing Frick's handling of the 1892 Homestead Strike at the steel plant in Homestead, Pennsylvania.

Document Inferences

Exposes Carnegie's shrewd recommendation for strict action against the strike, an opinion contrary to what he was communicating to the press at that time.

Entries Related to the Document

Amalgamated Association of Iron, Steel, and Tin Workers of the United States; Carnegie, Andrew; Frick, Henry Clay; Homestead Strike

Document 6

Excerpt from Andrew Carnegie's "Gospel of Wealth," *North American Review* (1889)

Document Information

Industrialist Andrew Carnegie explains that the rich bear the responsibility to give to the poor through philanthropy.

Document Inferences

New conceptions of distribution of wealth
  Perceptions of the poor as weak

Entries Related to the Document

Andrew Carnegie; Capitalism; Laissez-Faire; Social Gospel; Steel

TOP TIPS FOR ANSWERING DOCUMENT-BASED ESSAY QUESTIONS

Reading the Question

First, read the question several times and underline its various parts to make sure you fully understand what the question is asking. Most document-based essay questions have multiple parts to them and one of the most common mistakes students make is to answer only a portion of the question. It is important to spend some time going over each part of the question to make sure your essay will answer the question in full.

Once you have understood the question, noting its key terms and date parameters, it is helpful to make a list of your outside knowledge and facts that you are going to draw on in your essay.

Developing a Thesis Statement

One test for assessing the strength of your thesis statement is to imagine that it is the only sentence in your essay. If your thesis had to stand on its own, would it provide an answer to the question?

It can be helpful to develop a thesis statement after you have read the question and jotted down a list of your outside knowledge, *but before* you examine the documents.

Writing a thesis statement first and then examining the documents can make it easier to see how the documents can be used to support your thesis. Of course, once you examine the documents, they may spark a new idea which will make it necessary to edit your thesis.

Analyzing the Documents

Ask yourself whose point of view is being expressed in the document and consider the document's origins and the context in which it was created.

You should also consider who the intended audience was and what the document's original purpose may have been. It may be helpful to make notes on the documents as you examine them.

Using the Documents

Your interpretation of the documents should be incorporated into your essay as *evidence* in support of your thesis. Your essay should not simply offer a description or assessment of the documents.

There is no need to cite the documents in the order they were presented in the exam and though you should refer to a majority of the documents in your essay, it is not absolutely necessary to cite each one.

Conclusion

A good conclusion will reiterate your thesis statement from the introductory paragraph and tie together your supporting evidence.

Appendix A: Chronology of the Industrial Revolution in America

1756	The first **coal** mine in America opens in Virginia.
1783	John Stevens files a patent for the first multitubular boiler, making possible the steam engine.
1787	On the Delaware River in New Jersey, John Fitch launches the first steamboat. Later in the year, James Rumsey launches the second steamboat on the Potomac River. The Constitutional Convention meets in Philadelphia.
1790	**Samuel Slater** begins reproducing machinery from the Richard Arkwright textile factories in England. Slater builds the machinery in a mill in Pawtucket, Rhode Island, and operates it with waterpower. Congress passes the first patent law.
1791	Alexander Hamilton presents to Congress his *Report on Manufactures.* Congress establishes the **Bank of the United States**.
1792	The New York Stock Exchange is established.
1793	**Eli Whitney** invents the **cotton gin**.
1794	The first major American **turnpike** connects Philadelphia and Lancaster, Pennsylvania.
1800	Congress passes the first bankruptcy law. Oliver Evans invents the first noncondensing high-pressure steam engine.
1807	Robert Fulton invents the first commercially successful steamboat, which he runs on the Hudson River between New York City and Albany.
1810	The U.S. Supreme Court decides *Fletcher v. Peck.* Henry Maudslay invents the **precision lathe**.

	1811	The Bank of the United States is not rechartered. Construction of the **Cumberland Road** begins.
	1816	Congress establishes the Second Bank of the United States.
	1819	The U.S. Supreme Court decides *Dartmouth College v. Woodward*. The U.S. Supreme Court decides *M'Culloch v. Maryland*. The **panic of 1819** erupts.
	1824	The U.S. Supreme Court decides **Gibbons v. Ogden.**
	1825	The **Erie Canal** opens.
	1827	The **Baltimore & Ohio Railroad** is chartered.
	1829	The Chesapeake and Delaware Canal opens. Peter Cooper builds the first American locomotive.
	1830	**Robert Stevens** designs the T-rail.
	1831	**Cyrus McCormick** invents the reaper.
	1832	The first phase of the **Ohio and Erie Canal** opens.
	1833	President Andrew Jackson withdraws government funds from the Second Bank of the United States.
	1836	President Andrew Jackson issues the **specie circular (soft money)**.
	1837	**John Deere** introduces the first steel plow in the United States. The U.S. Supreme Court decides *Charles River Bridge v. Warren Bridge*. The **panic of 1837** erupts.
	1839	Charles Goodyear develops the process of **vulcanization**.
	1841	Congress passes a new federal bankruptcy law.
	1843	Charles Thurber invents the **typewriter**.
	1844	**Samuel F. B. Morse** develops the first functional **telegraph**.
	1846	George H. Corliss invents the valve-gear and drop-cutoff systems, which make possible the four-valve steam-engine control system, which reduces condensation and greatly improves engine efficiency. **Elias Howe** patents the first practical **sewing machine**. **Richard M. Hoe** invents the first rotating **printing press**.
	1851	William Kelly develops a system for converting pig iron into **steel** by applying air currents to molten metal.
	1856	In England, Henry Bessemer perfects the **Bessemer Process**, a technique for converting pig iron into steel. The Western Union Telegraph service is established.

1857	The **panic of 1857** occurs.
1859	Edwin L. Drake develops the first successful oil-drilling machine at Titusville, Pennsylvania. Etienne Lenoir invents the first internal-combustion engine.
1861	The **Civil War** begins.
1862	Congress passes the Morrill Act. Congress passes the Pacific Railway Act to fund a transcontinental railroad.
	The American Tobacco Company is founded.
	Congress passes the **Sherman Antitrust Act**.
	Congress passes the Sherman Silver Purchase Act.
1864	**George Pullman** develops the first railroad sleeping car.
	Congress passes a second Pacific Railway Act.
1865	William Bullock invents the first web printing press.
	The Civil War ends.
1866	Congress passes the Pacific Telegraph Act to build a transcontinental telegraph system.
	The transatlantic telegraph cable is completed.
	The **National Labor Union** is formed.
1867	The Granger movement is established.
	Congress passes a new federal bankruptcy law.
1868	**George Westinghouse** invents the first air brake for railroads.
	Abraham Hewitt introduces to the United States the open-hearth process for manufacturing steel.
1869	The **Union Pacific Railroad** and the **Central Pacific Railroad** link up at
	Promontory Summit, Utah, completing the first **transcontinental railroad**.
1870	The **Great Atlantic and Pacific Tea Company** is renamed.
	Armour Meat Packing Company is incorporated.
	The **Standard Oil Company** of New Jersey is incorporated in Ohio.
1873	The U.S. Supreme Court decides the *Slaughterhouse Cases*.
	The **panic of 1873** occurs.
1875	William A. Anthony builds the first electric dynamo.

1876	**Alexander Graham Bell** invents the **telephone**.
1877	The U.S. Supreme Court decides *Munn v. Illinois*.
	The great **railroad strike of 1877** erupts.
1879	**Thomas Edison** invents the incandescent **light bulb**.
1881	Edison Machine Works in New Jersey builds the first successful operating electric dynamo.
1882	Thomas Edison's system of centralized electric power production is introduced in New York.
1886	The U.S. Supreme Court decides *Santa Clara County v. Southern Pacific Railroad*.
	The U.S. Supreme Court decides *Wabash, St. Louis & Pacific Railroad Co. v. Illinois*.
	The **American Federation of Labor** is established.
	The **Haymarket riot** occurs.
1887	Congress passes the **Interstate Commerce Act**.
	The Whiskey Trust is formed.
1890	The U.S. Supreme Court decides *Chicago, Milwaukee & St. Paul Railroad Co. v. Minnesota*.
1892	The General Electric Company is formed.
	The **Homestead strike** occurs.
	John Froelich builds the first **tractor**.
1893	The **depression of 1893** begins.
	The **Duryea brothers** build the first gasoline-powered automobile.
1894	The **Pullman strike** occurs.
	Jacob Coxey leads "**Coxey's Army**" in a protest march of unemployed workers in Washington, D.C.
1895	The U.S. Supreme Court decides *United States v. E. C. Knight Company*.
	The U.S. Supreme Court decides *In re Debs*.
	At Niagara Falls, New York, the era of modern hydroelectric power is inaugurated.
1898	Congress passes a new federal bankruptcy law. Adolphus Busch builds the first diesel engine.

1900	Congress passes the **Gold Standard Act**.
1901	**United States Steel Corporation** is formed.
	Northern Securities Company is formed.
1902	The great anthracite coal strike by the **United Mine Workers** occurs.
1903	The **Ford Motor Company** is formed.
1904	The U.S. Supreme Court decides *Northern Securities Company v. United States.*
1905	The U.S. Supreme Court decides *Swift & Company v. United States.*
	The U.S. Supreme Court decides *Lochner v. New York.*
1907	The **panic of 1907** occurs.
1908	The U.S. Supreme Court decides *Muller v. Oregon.*
	General Motors Corporation is founded.
1909	Ford Motor Company introduces the Model T Ford.
1911	The U.S. Supreme Court decides *Standard Oil Company of New Jersey et al. v. United States.*
	The U.S. Supreme Court decides *United States v. American Tobacco Company.*
1912	In the presidential election, **Woodrow Wilson** wins the presidency, but
	Socialist candidate **Eugene V. Debs** manages to secure more than 6 percent of the popular vote.
1913	The **Sixteenth Amendment** to the Constitution is ratified, legalizing the federal income tax.
	Congress passes the **Federal Reserve Act**. Congress creates the **Federal Trade Commission**.
1914	Congress passes the **Clayton Antitrust Act**.
1918	The U.S. Supreme Court decides
	Hammer v. Dagenhart.
	The U.S. Supreme Court decides **1922** *Bailey v. Drexel Furniture Co.*

APPENDIX B: PERIOD LEARNING OBJECTIVES FOR STUDENTS

A review of the events, movements, people, and inventions highlighted in this book should help enhance a student's period knowledge of the Industrial Revolution that occurred in the United States during the late nineteenth century. Specific period knowledge, coupled with an understanding of the themes that emerge from the overarching narrative of this chapter in American history, should leave students well positioned to thoughtfully consider and intellectually engage with the following broader objectives.

Students should be able to:

- Explain the ways in which changes in transportation and technology transformed the U.S. economy in the late nineteenth century.
- Explain how the Industrial Revolution shaped American society and the lives of workers.
- Analyze how public discourse on capitalism and corporate power influenced U.S. economic policy during the late nineteenth century.
- Compare and contrast the ideologies and goals of the Organized Labor, Populist, and Progressive movements, in their campaign for changes to the American economic system during the late nineteenth century.
- Explain how reform movements affected changes in government policy and society.
- Analyze the ways in which scientific theories were adapted and applied to both challenge and defend prevailing economic policies and social ideologies in the late nineteenth century.
- Explain how changes in immigration from abroad, as well as internal migrations like urbanization and the Great Migration, altered ethnic and social demographics in American life.

APPENDIX C: LISTING OF BIOGRAPHICAL ENTRIES

Armour, Philip Danforth
Bell, Alexander Graham
Bellamy, Edward
Bryan, William Jennings
Carnegie, Andrew
Chrysler, Walter Percy
Clay, Henry
Cooper, Peter
Crocker, Charles
Croly, Herbert David
Debs, Eugene Victor
Deere, John
Donnelly, Ignatius
Duke, James Buchanan
Du Pont, Pierre
Durant, William Crapo
Eastman, George
Edison, Thomas Alva
Ely, Richard T.
Field, Cyrus West
Firestone, Harvey Samuel
Ford, Henry
Frick, Henry Clay
George, Henry
Gompers, Samuel
Gould, Jay
Harriman, Edward Henry
Hill, James Jerome

Hoe, Richard March
Hopkins, Mark
Howe, Elias
Jones, Mary Harris ("Mother Jones")
Marshall, John
McCormick, Cyrus Hall
Morgan, John Pierpont
Morse, Samuel Finley Breese
Otis, Elisha Graves
Pullman, George Mortimer
Rockefeller, John Davison
Roosevelt, Theodore
Sachs, Samuel
Schwab, Charles
Sinclair, Upton Beall
Slater, Samuel
Stanford, Leland
Stevens, Robert Livingston
Swift, Gustavus Franklin
Taft, William Howard
Taylor, Frederick Winslow
Tesla, Nikola
Vanderbilt, Cornelius
Veblen, Thorstein
Ward, Aaron Montgomery
Westinghouse, George
Whitney, Eli
Wilson, Woodrow

Appendix D: Listing of Entries Related to Supreme Court Cases and Acts of Congress

Supreme Court Cases

Bailey v. Drexel Furniture Co. (1922)
Chicago, Milwaukee & St. Paul Railroad Company v. Minnesota (1890)
Gibbons v. Ogden (1824)
Hammer v. Dagenhart (1918)
Inre Debs (1895)
Lochner v. New York (1905)
Muller v. Oregon (1908)
Munn v. Illinois (1877)
Swift & Co. v. United States (1905)
United States v. E. C. Knight Company (1895)
Wabash, St. Louis & Pacific Railroad Co. v. Illinois (1886)

Acts of Congress

Clayton Antitrust Act of 1914
Federal Reserve Act of 1913
Federal Trade Commission Act of 1914
Gold Standard Act of 1900
Interstate Commerce Act of 1887
Meat Inspection Act of 1906
National Banking Act of 1864
Sherman Antitrust Act of 1890

Bibliography

Agriculture and Food Industry

Adams, Jane. *Fighting for the Farm: Rural America Transformed*. Philadelphia: University of Pennsylvania Press, 2003.

Bogue, Allan G. *From Prairie to Corn Belt: Farming on the Illinois and Iowa Prairies in the Nineteenth Century*, 2nd ed. Chicago: Ivan R. Dee, 2011.

Jensen, Joan M. *Loosening the Bonds: Mid-Atlantic Farm Women, 1750–1850*. New Haven: Yale University Press, 1986.

Nestle, Marion. *Food Politics: How the Food Industry Influences Nutrition and Health*. Berkeley: University of California Press, 2013.

Yafa, Stephen. *Big Cotton: How a Humble Fiber Created Fortunes, Wrecked Civilizations, and Put America on the Map*. New York: Viking, 2005.

Young, James Harvey. *Pure Food: Securing the Federal Food and Drug Act of 1906*. Princeton, NJ: Princeton University Press, 1989.

Biography

Bak, Richard. *Henry and Edsel: The Creation of the Ford Empire*. Hoboken, NJ: Wiley, 2003.

Chernow, Ron. *Titan: The Life of John D. Rockefeller, Sr*. New York: Random House, 1998.

Klein, Maury. *The Life and Legend of Jay Gould*. Baltimore: Johns Hopkins University Press, 1986.

Krass, Peter. *Carnegie*. Hoboken, NJ: John Wiley & Sons, 2002.

Mackay, James A. *Alexander Graham Bell: A Life*. New York: Wiley, 1997.

Renehan, Edward. *Dark Genius of Wall Street: The Misunderstood Life of Jay Gould, King of the Robber Barons*. New York: Basic Books, 2005.

Sale, Kirkpatrick. *The Fire of His Genius: Robert Fulton and the American Dream*. New York: Free Press, 2001.

Business

Barrett, James R. *Work and Community in the Jungle: Chicago's Packinghouse Workers, 1894–1922*. Urbana, University of Illinois Press, 1987.

Beatty, Jack, ed. *Colossus: How the Corporation Changed America*. New York: Broadway Books, 2001.

Blackford, Mansel G. *The Rise of Modern Business in Great Britain, the United States, and Japan*. Chapel Hill: University of North Carolina Press, 1988.

Blackford, Mansel G., and K. Austin Kerr. *Business Enterprise in American History*. Boston, MA: Wadsworth, Cengage Learning, 1994.

Brinkley, Douglas. *Wheels for the World: Henry Ford, His Company and a Century of Progress*. New York: Viking, 2003.

Galambos, Louis, and Joseph Pratt. *The Rise of the Corporate Commonwealth: U.S. Business and Public Policy in the Twentieth Century*. New York: Basic Books, 1988.

Haeger, John Denis. *The Investment Frontier: New York Businessmen and the Economic Development of the Old Northwest*. Albany: State University of New York Press, 1981.

Ingham, John. *The Iron Barons: A Social Analysis of an American Urban Elite, 1874–1965*. Westport, CT: Greenwood Press, 1978.

Jeremy, David J. *Transatlantic Industrial Revolution: The Diffusion of Textile Technologies between Britain and America, 1790–1830s*. Cambridge, MA: MIT Press, 1981.

Klein, Maury. *The Change Makers: From Carnegie to Gates, How the Great Entrepreneurs Transformed Ideas into Industries*. New York: Times Books, 2003.

Lamoreaux, Naomi R. *The Great Merger Movement in American Business, 1895–1904*. New York: Cambridge University Press, 1985.

Lustig, R. Jeffrey. *Corporate Liberalism: The Origins of Modern American Political Theory, 1890–1920*. Berkeley and Los Angeles: University of California Press, 1982.

Micklethwait, John, and Adrian Wooldridge. *The Company: A Short History of a Revolutionary Idea*. New York: Modern Library, 2003.

Nelson, Daniel. *Managers and Workers: Origins of the New Factory System in the United States, 1880–1920*. Madison: University of Wisconsin Press, 1975.

Noble, David F. *America by Design: Science, Technology, and the Rise of Corporate Capitalism*. New York: Knopf, 1977.

Perkins, Edwin J., ed. *Men and Organizations: The American Economy in the Twentieth Century*. New York: G. P. Putnam's Sons, 1977.

Seely, Bruce E., ed. *Encyclopedia of American Business History and Biography: Iron and Steel in the Twentieth Century*. New York: Facts on File, 1994.

Strouse, Jean. *Morgan: American Financier*. New York: Perennial, 2000.

Tucker, Barbara M. *Samuel Slater and the Origins of the American Textile Industry, 1790–1860*. Ithaca, NY: Cornell University Press, 1984.Watts, Sarah Lyons. *Order against Chaos: Business Culture and Labor Ideology in America, 1880–1915*. Westport, CT: Greenwood Press, 1991.

Zunz, Olivier. *Making America Corporate, 1870–1920*. Chicago: University of Chicago Press, 1990.

Communication

Bray, John. *The Communications Miracle: The Telecommunications Pioneers*. New York: Plenum, 1995.

Davies, L. J. *Fleet Fire: Thomas Edison and the Pioneers of the Electric Revolution*. New York: Arcade Publishing, 2003.

Fischer, Claude S. *America Calling: A Social History of the Telephone to 1940*. Berkeley: University of California Press, 1992.

Lebow, Irwin. *Information Highways and Byways: From the Telegraph to the 21st Century*. New York: IEEE Press, 1995.

Economy

Chernow, Ron. *The House of Morgan: An American Banking Dynasty and the Rise of Modern Finance*. New York: Grove/Atlantic, 2010.

Gordon, John Steele. *An Empire of Wealth: The Epic History of American Economic Power*. New York: HarperCollins, 2004.

Lind, Michael. *Land of Promise: An Economic History of the United States*. New York: HarperCollins, 2013.

McGraw, Thomas K. *The Founders and Finance: How Hamilton, Gallatin, and Other Immigrants Forged a New Economy*. Cambridge, MA: Harvard University Press, 2013.

Muir, Diana. *Reflections in Bullough's Pond: Economy and Ecosystem in New England*. Hanover, NH: University Press of New England, 2000.

Environment and Natural Resources

Hahn, Steven, and Jonathan Prude, eds. *The Countryside in the Age of Capitalist Transformation: Essays in the Social History of Rural America*. Chapel Hill: University of North Carolina Press, 1985.

Melosi, Martin V., ed. *Pollution and Reform in American Cities, 1870–1930*. Austin: University of Texas Press, 1980.

Steinberg, Theodore. *Nature Incorporated: Industrialization and the Waters of New England*. Cambridge, England: Cambridge University Press, 1991.

General

Bruchey, Stuart. *Enterprise: The Dynamic Economy of a Free People.* Cambridge: Harvard University Press, 1990.

Dublessis, R. S. *Transformation to Capitalism in Early Modern Europe.* Cambridge: Cambridge University Press, 1997.

Hudson, Pat. *The Industrial Revolution.* New York: Oxford University Press, 2005.

Licht, Walter. *Industrializing America: The Nineteenth Century.* Baltimore: Johns Hopkins University Press, 1995.

Olson, James S. *Dictionary of United States Economic History.* Santa Barbara: ABC-CLIO, 1992.

Industrialism

Boydston, Jeanne. *Home and Work.* New York: Oxford University Press, 1990.

Cochran, Thomas C. *Frontiers of Change: Early Industrialism in America.* New York: Oxford University Press, 1981.

Dalzell, Robert F., Jr. *Enterprising Elite: The Boston Associates and the World They Made.* Cambridge, MA: Harvard University Press, 1987.

Freese, Barbara. *Coal: A Human History.* New York: Perseus, 2003.

Hindle, Brooke, and Steven Lubar. *Engines of Change: The American Industrial Revolution, 1790–1860.* Smithsonian Institution Press, 1986.

Hounshell, David A. *From the American System to Mass Production, 1800–1932: The Development of Manufacturing Technology in the United States.* Baltimore: Johns Hopkins University Press, 1984.

Hunter, Louis C. *A History of Industrial Power in the United States, 1780–1930.* Vol. 1, *Water Power in the Century of the Steam Engine.* Charlottesville: Published for the Eleutherian Mills-Hagley Foundation by the University Press of Virginia, 1979.

Hyde, Charles K. *Riding the Roller Coaster: A History of the Chrysler Corporation.* Detroit: Wayne State University Press, 2003.

Lindstrom, Diane. *Economic Development in the Philadelphia Region, 1810–1850.* New York: Columbia University Press, 1978.

Maynard, Micheline. *The End of Detroit: How the Big Three Lost Their Grip on the American Car Market.* New York: Currency/Doubleday, 2003.

Nelson, Daniel. *Managers and Workers: Origins of the Twentieth-Century Factory System in the United States 1880–1920.* Madison: University of Wisconsin Press, 1995.

Sellers, Charles. *The Market Revolution: Jacksonian America, 1815–1846.* New York: Oxford University Press, 1991.

Siracusa, Carl. *A Mechanical People: Perceptions of the Industrial Order in Massachusetts, 1815–1880.* Middletown, CT: Wesleyan University Press, 1979.

Trachtenberg, Alan. *The Incorporation of America: Culture and Society in the Gilded Age.* New York: Hill and Wang, 1982.

Watts, Sarah Lyons. *Order against Chaos: Business Culture and Labor Ideology in America, 1880–1915.* New York: Greenwood Press, 1991.

Labor

Barrett, James R. *Work and Community in the Jungle: Chicago's Packinghouse Workers, 1894–1922.* Urbana: University of Illinois Press, 1987.

Blewett, Mary H. *Men, Women, and Work: Class, Gender, and Protest in the New England Shoe Industry, 1780–1910.* Urbana: University of Illinois Press, 1988.

Buhle, Paul. *Taking Care of Business: Samuel Gompers, George Meany, Lane Kirkland, and the Tragedy of American Labor.* New York: Monthly Review Press, 1999.

Dublin, Thomas. *Transforming Women's Work: New England Lives in the Industrial Revolution.* Ithaca, NY: Cornell University Press, 1994.

Fine, Lisa M. *The Souls of the Skyscraper: Female Clerical Workers in Chicago, 1870–1930.* Philadelphia: Temple University Press, 1990.

Friedman, Gerald. *State-Making and Labor Movements. The United States and France, 1876–1914.* Ithaca, NY: Cornell University Press, 1998.

Glickstein, Jonathan A. *Concepts of Free Labor in Antebellum America.* New Haven, Yale University Press, 1991.

Hattam, Victoria C. *Labor Visions and State Power.* Princeton, NJ: Princeton University Press, 1993.

Hild, Matthew. *Greenbackers, Knights of Labor, and Populists: Farmer-Labor Insurgency in the Late-Nineteenth-Century South.* Athens: University of Georgia Press, 2007.

Jensen, Joan M. *Loosening the Bonds: Mid-Atlantic Farm Women, 1750–1850.* New Haven: Yale University Press, 1986.

Larkin, Jack. *The Reshaping of Everyday Life, 1790–1840.* New York: Harper & Row, 1988.

Laurie, Bruce. *Artisans into Workers: Labor in Nineteenth-Century America.* New York: Hill and Wang, 1989.

McCormick, Anita L. *The Industrial Revolution in American History.* Springfield, NJ: Enslow Publishers, 1998.

McHugh, Cathy. *Mill Family: The Labor System in the Southern Cotton Textile Industry, 1880–1915.* New York: Oxford University Press, 1988.

Montgomery, David. *The Fall of the House of Labor: The Workplace, the State, and American Labor Activism, 1865–1925.* New York: Cambridge University Press, 1987.

Nasaw, David. *Andrew Carnegie.* New York: The Penguin Press, 2010.

Oestreicher, Richard Jules. *Solidarity and Fragmentation: Working People and Class Consciousness in Detroit, 1875-1900*. Urbana: University of Illinois Press, 1986.

Pacyga, Dominic A. *Polish Immigrants and Industrial Chicago*. Columbus: Ohio State University Press, 1991.

Prude, Jonathan. *The Coming of Industrial Order: Town and Factory Life in Rural Massachusetts, 1810-1860*. New York: Cambridge University Press, 1983.

Reef, Catherine. *Working in America: An Eyewitness History*. New York: Facts on File, 2000.

Rock, Howard. *Artisans of the New Republic: The Tradesmen of New York City in the Age of Jefferson*. New York: New York University Press, 1979.

Rodgers, Daniel T. *The Work Ethic in Industrial America, 1850-1920*. Chicago: University of Chicago Press, 1978.

Roediger, David R., and Franklin Rosemont, eds. *Haymarket Scrapbook*. Chicago: Charles H. Kerr Publishing Company, 1986.

Roediger, David R., and Philip S. Foner. *Our Own Time: A History of American Labor and the Working Day*. New York: Greenwood Press, 1989.

Rorabaugh, W. J. *The Craft Apprentice: From Franklin to the Machine Age in America*. New York: Oxford University Press, 1986.

Ross, Steven J. *Workers on the Edge: Work, Leisure, and Politics in Industrializing Cincinnati, 1788-1890*. New York: Columbia University Press, 1985.

Smith, Billy G. *The "Lower Sort": Philadelphia's Laboring People, 1750-1800*. Ithaca, NY: Cornell University Press, 1990.

Stiles, T. J. *The First Tycoon: The Epic Life of Cornelius Vanderbilt*. New York: Vintage Books, 2010.

Stowell, David O. *The Great Strikes of 1877*. Urbana: University of Illinois Press, 2007.

Tucker, Barbara M., and Kenneth H. Tucker. *Industrializing Antebellum America: The Rise of Manufacturing Entrepreneurs in the Early Republic*. New York: Palgrave Macmillan, 2008.

Watts, Sarah Lyons. *Order against Chaos: Business Culture and Labor Ideology in America, 1880-1915*. New York: Greenwood Press, 1991.

Wilentz, Sean. *Chants Democratic: New York City and the Rise of the American Working Class, 1788-1850*. New York: Oxford University Press, 2004.

Zieger, Robert. *The CIO, 1930-1955*. Chapel Hill: University of North Carolina Press, 1995.

Law

Frankel, Ellen, and Howard Dickman, eds. *Liberty, Property, and the Foundations of the American Constitution*. Albany: State University of New York Press, 1989.

Horwitz, Morton J. *The Transformation of American Law, 1780-1860*. Cambridge, MA: Harvard University Press, 1977.

Mashaw, Jerry L. *Due Process in the Administrative State*. New Haven: Yale University Press, 1985.

Nelson, William. *Americanization of the Common Law: The Impact of Legal Change on Massachusetts Society, 1760–1830*. Cambridge, MA: Harvard University Press, 1975.

Sklar, Martin. *The Corporate Reconstruction of American Capitalism, 1890–1916: The Market, the Law, and Politics*. New York: Cambridge University Press, 1988.

Sumners, Robert Samuel. *Instrumentalism and American Legal Theory*. Ithaca, NY: Cornell University Press, 1982.

Politics

Galambos, Louis, and Joseph Pratt. *The Rise of the Corporate Commonwealth: U.S. Business and Public Policy in the Twentieth Century*. New York: Basic Books, 1988.

Greene, Julie. *Pure and Simple Politics: The American Federation of Labor and Political Activism, 1881–1917*. New York: Cambridge University Press, 1999.

Hattam, Victoria C. *Labor Visions and State Power*. Princeton, NJ: Princeton University Press, 1993.

Heale, M. J. *The Legitimacy of the Business Corporation in the Law of the United States, 1780–1970*. Charlottesville: University Press of Virginia, 1984.

Heale, M. J. *Twentieth-Century America: Politics and Power in the United States, 1900–2000*. London: Arnold, 2004.

Keller, Morton. *Regulating a New Society: Public Policy and Social Change in America, 1900–1933*. Cambridge, MA: Harvard University Press, 1994.

McCraw, Thomas. *Prophets of Regulation*. Cambridge, MA: Belknap Press of Harvard University Press, 1984.

McCulley, Richard T. *Banks and Politics during the Progressive Era: The Origins of the Federal Reserve System, 1897–1913*. New York: Garland Publishing, Inc., 1992.

Skowronek, Stephen. *Building a New American State: The Expansion of National Administrative Capacities, 1877–1920*. New York: Cambridge University Press, 1982.

Wilson, James Q., ed. *The Politics of Regulation*. New York: Basic Books, 1980.

Social Change

Bellamy, Edward. *Looking Backward: 2000–1887*. Boston: Ticknor and Company, 1888, 77.

Gardner, Todd K. "Population and Population Growth." In *Encyclopedia of American Urban History*. Edited by David Goldfield. Thousand Oaks, CA: Sage Publications, 2007.

Goloboy, Jennifer L., ed. *Industrial Revolution: People and Perspectives*. Santa Barbara: ABC-CLIO, 2008.

Keller, Morton. *Regulating a New Society: Public Policy and Social Change in America, 1900–1933*. Cambridge, MA: Harvard University Press, 1994.

Lissak, Rivka Shpak. *Pluralism and Progressives: Hull House and the New Immigrants 1890–1919*. Chicago: University of Chicago Press, 1989.

Sumner, William Graham. *Earth-Hunger and Other Essays*, ed. Albert Galloway Keller. New Haven, CT: Yale University Press, 1913, 300.

Sumner, William Graham. *Social Darwinism: Selected Essays*, ed. Stow Persons. Englewood Cliff, NJ: Prentice-Hall, 1963, 76.

Sumner, William Graham. *What Social Classes Owe to Each Other*. New York: Harper & Brothers, 1883, 124.

Technology

Buchanan, R. A. *The Power of the Machine: The Impact of Technology from 1700 to the Present*. London: Penguin, 1992.

Chandler, Alfred D. Jr. "The Information Age in Historical Perspective." In *A Nation Transformed by Information: How Information Has Shaped the United States from Colonial Times to the Present*. Edited by Alfred D. Chandler and James W. Cortada. New York: Oxford University Press, 2005.

Cutliffe, S. H., and Reynolds, T. S. *Technology and American History*. Chicago: University of Chicago Press, 1997.

David, Paul. *Technical Choice, Innovation, and Economic Growth*. London: Cambridge University Press, 1975.

Hounshell, David A. *From the American System to Mass Production, 1800–1932*. Baltimore: Johns Hopkins University Press, 1984.

Hunter, Louis C. *A History of Industrial Power in the United States, 1790–1930*. Vol. 1, *Water Power in the Century of the Steam Engine*. 1979.

Hurt, R. Douglas. *American Farm Tools: From Hand-Power to Steam-Power*. Manhattan, Kan.: Sunflower University Press, 1982.

Jenkins, Reese V. *Images and Enterprise: Technology and the American Photographic Industry, 1839 to 1925*. Baltimore: Johns Hopkins University Press, 1975.

Jeremy, David J. *Transatlantic Industrial Revolution: The Diffusion of Textile Technologies between Britain and America, 1790–1830s*. North Andover, MA: MIT Press, 1981.

Karwatka, D. *Technology's Past*. Ann Arbor, MI: Prakken Publications, Inc., 1996.

Kasson, John F. *Civilizing the Machine: Technology and Republican Values in America. 1776–1900*. New York: Grossman Publishers, 1976.

McGrath, Kimberley A. *World of Invention*. Detroit: Gale, 1998.

Millard, A. J. *Edison and the Business of Innovation.* Baltimore: Johns Hopkins University Press, 1990.

Noble, David F. *America by Design: Science, Technology, and the Rise of Corporate Capitalism.* New York: Knopf, 1977.

Reich, Leonard S. *The Making of American Industrial Research: Science and Business at G.E. and Bell, 1876–1926.* New York: Cambridge University Press, 1985.

Segal, Howard. *Technological Utopianism in American Culture.* Chicago: University of Chicago Press, 1985.

Smith, Merritt R. *Harpers Ferry Armory and the New Technology.* Ithaca, NY: Cornell University Press, 1977.

Stapleton, Darwin H. *The Transfer of Early Industrial Technologies to America.* Philadelphia: American Philosophical Society, 1987.

Transportation

Ambrose, Stephen E. *Nothing Like It in the World: The Men Who Built the Transcontinental Railroad, 1863–1869.* New York: Simon and Schuster, 2000.

Gordon, Sarah H. *Passage to Union: How the Railroads Transformed American Life, 1829–1929.* Chicago: Ivan R. Dee, 1996.

Greenberg, Dolores. *Financiers and Railroads, 1869–1889: A Study of Morton, Bliss & Company.* Newark: University of Delaware Press; London: Associated University Presses, 1980.

Haites, Erik F., James Mak, and Gary M. Walton. *Western River Transportation: The Era of Early Internal Development, 1810–1860.* Baltimore: Johns Hopkins University Press, 1975.

Shaw, Ronald E. *Canals for a Nation: The Canal Era in the United States, 1790–1860.* Lexington, KY: University Press of Kentucky, 1990.

Thompson, Mark L. *Steamboats and Sailors of the Great Lakes.* Detroit: Wayne State University Press, 1991.

Williams, John Hoyt. *A Great and Shining Road: The Epic Story of the Transcontinental Railroad.* New York: Times Books, 1988.

INDEX

Page numbers in **boldface** reflect main entries. An italicized *f* following a page number indicates a figure.

ABOUT THE AUTHORS

James S. Olson is Distinguished Professor of History at Sam Houston State University in Huntsville, Texas. A Pulitzer Prize nominated author, Professor Olson has published over thirty books, including Greenwood's *Historical Dictionary of the 1970s, Historical Dictionary of the 1960s,* and *Historical Dictionary of the 1950s.*

Shannon L. Kenny is a veteran writer and educator whose published works include ABC-CLIO's *Gold: A Cultural Encyclopedia.* Based in Santa Barbara, California, Kenny is a passionate advocate for the study of history and is the proprietor of an editorial and writing services agency specializing in history, lifestyle, and travel.